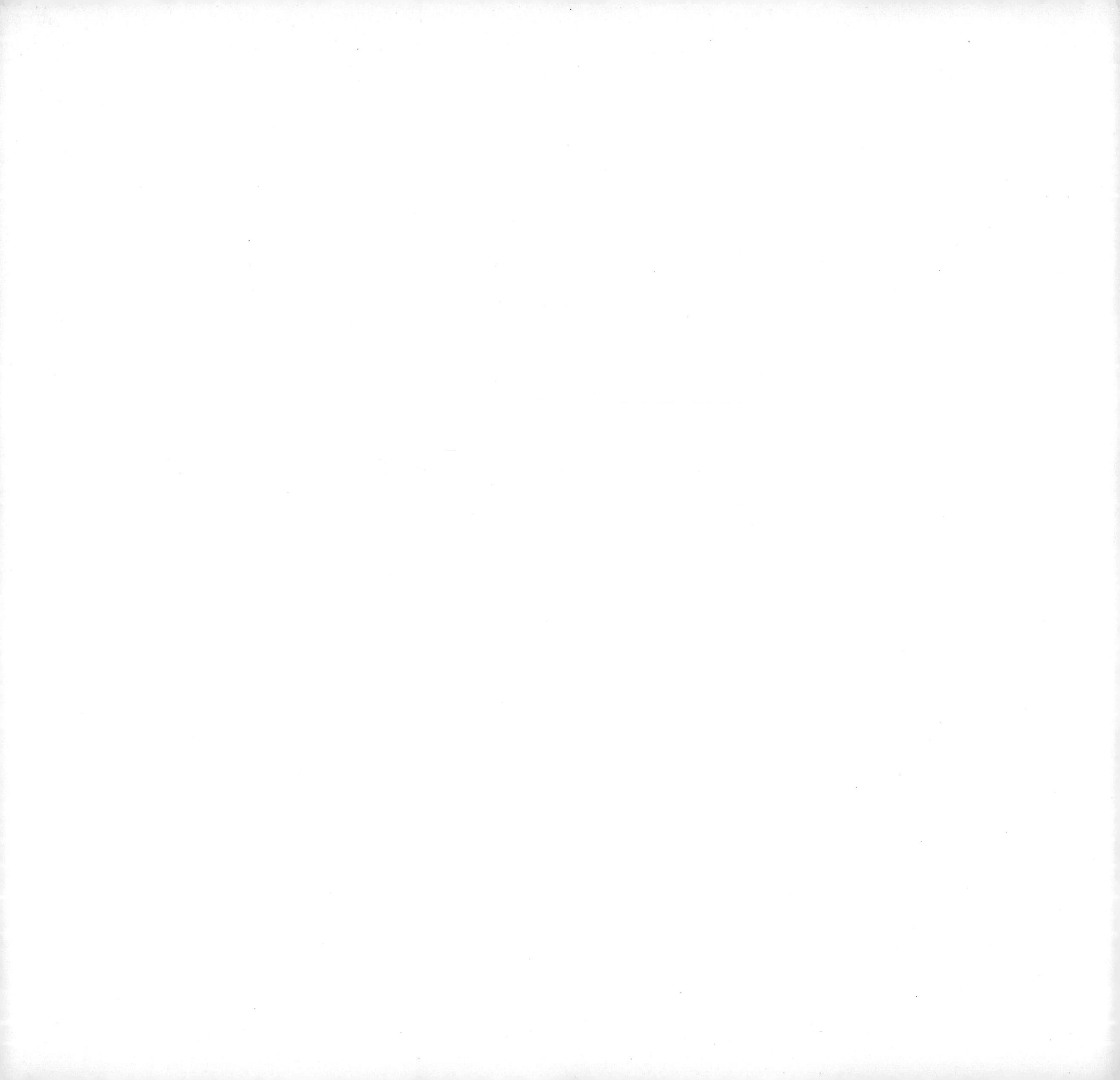

GLORIOUS BERKSHIRE

COLIN ROBERTS

HALSGROVE

First published in Great Britain in 2016

British Library Cataloguing-in-Publication Data
A CIP record for this title is available from the British Library

ISBN 978 0 85704 298 9

HALSGROVE
Halsgrove House,
Ryelands Business Park,
Bagley Road, Wellington, Somerset TA21 9PZ
Tel: 01823 653777 Fax: 01823 216796
email: sales@halsgrove.com

Part of the Halsgrove group of companies
Information on all Halsgrove titles is available at:
www.halsgrove.com

Printed in China by Everbest Printing Investment Ltd

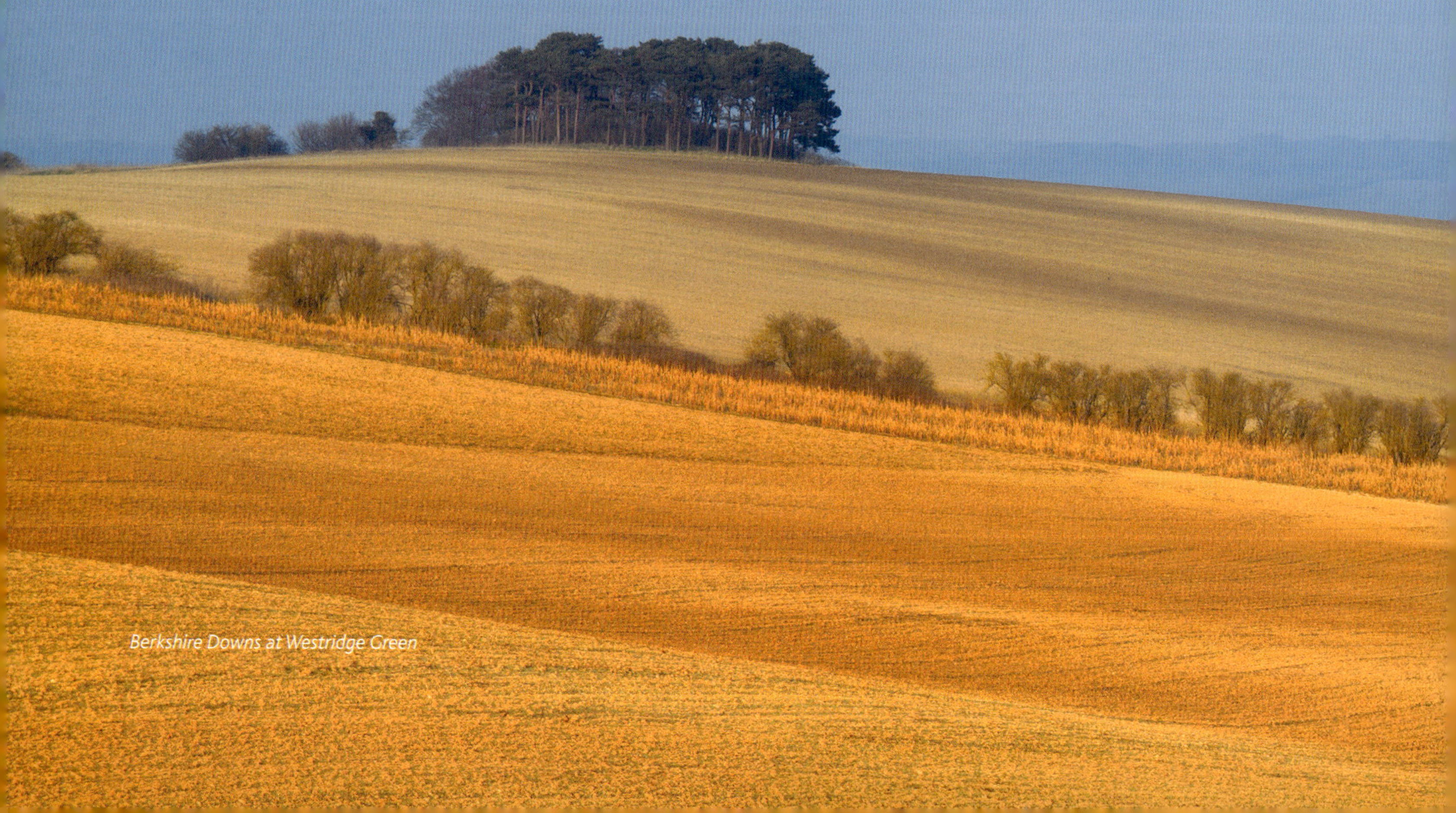

Berkshire Downs at Westridge Green

CONTENTS

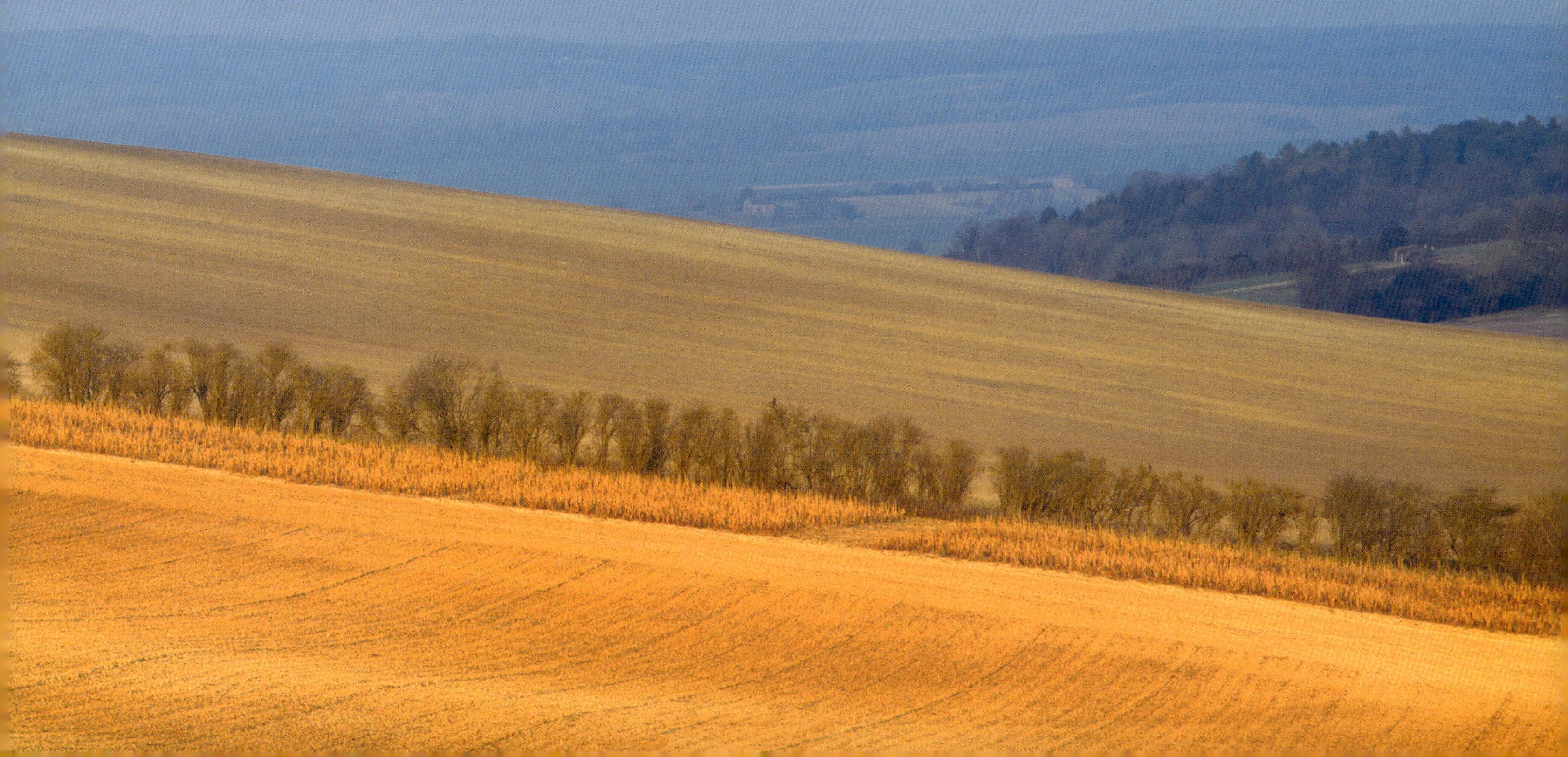

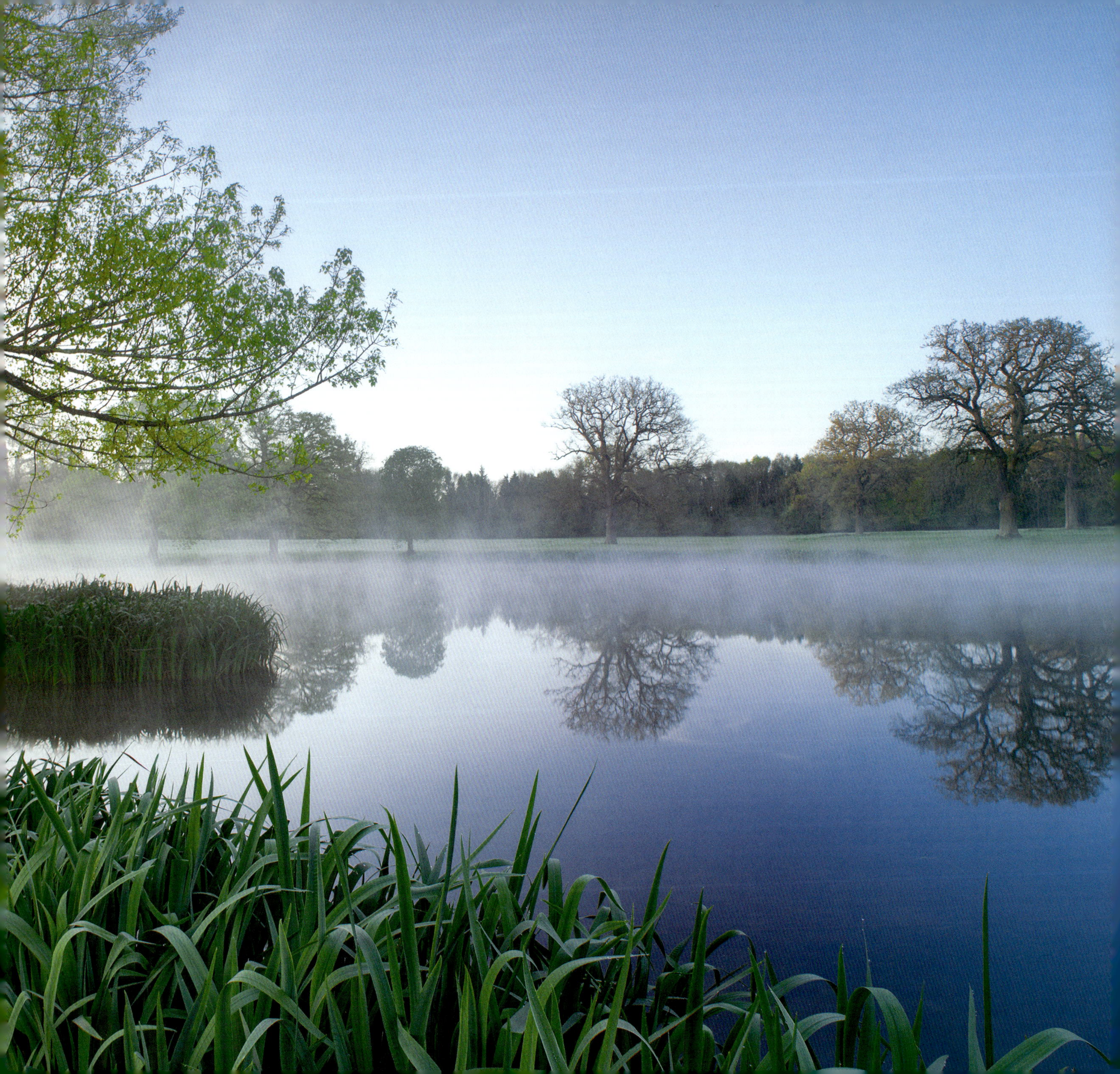

INTRODUCTION

Near Bucklebury, in central Berkshire, a small lane branches away from the highway and descends into a pocket of peaceful woodland – a wilderness which has probably remained unchanged for centuries. After a short distance the lane emerges from the trees, revealing a view which looks north across a patchwork of fields and copses to the Pang Valley. The route, known locally as the 'Quiet Lane', is just one of many enchanting places covered in this book; others include isolated trees, remote ponds and meadows of wild flowers. Typically, these little-known treasures lie off the beaten track, but together they form an essential part of rural Berkshire, and so make up around half of the subject matter in the book.

Alongside these images are others more familiar, like the beautiful reed-lined lake on the nature reserve at Englemere, and the romantic ruin of Wilder's Folly on the hillside above Sulhamstead. Also included are a number of historic churches which stand in picturesque scenery. And then there are the iconic landmarks: the outline of Windsor Castle seen from the Great Park, and the view of Temple Island reflected in the Thames at sunset. Finally, there are a handful of locations which lie just over the border, but which are included as part of the extended landscape. These include the downland vistas surrounding The Ridgeway, and the fascinating plantings of trees at Dorney Lake.

Apart from day-to-day changes in the weather, it is the seasons which guide my work. Following this cycle the book is divided into four chapters, allocating each image to the season which it portrays.

Exploring the Berkshire countryside and working in its landscape has been particularly rewarding. The pages that follow represent my visual highlights and I hope they will inspire others to enjoy the scenery of this historic county.

The pond at Shottesbrooke Park

SPRING

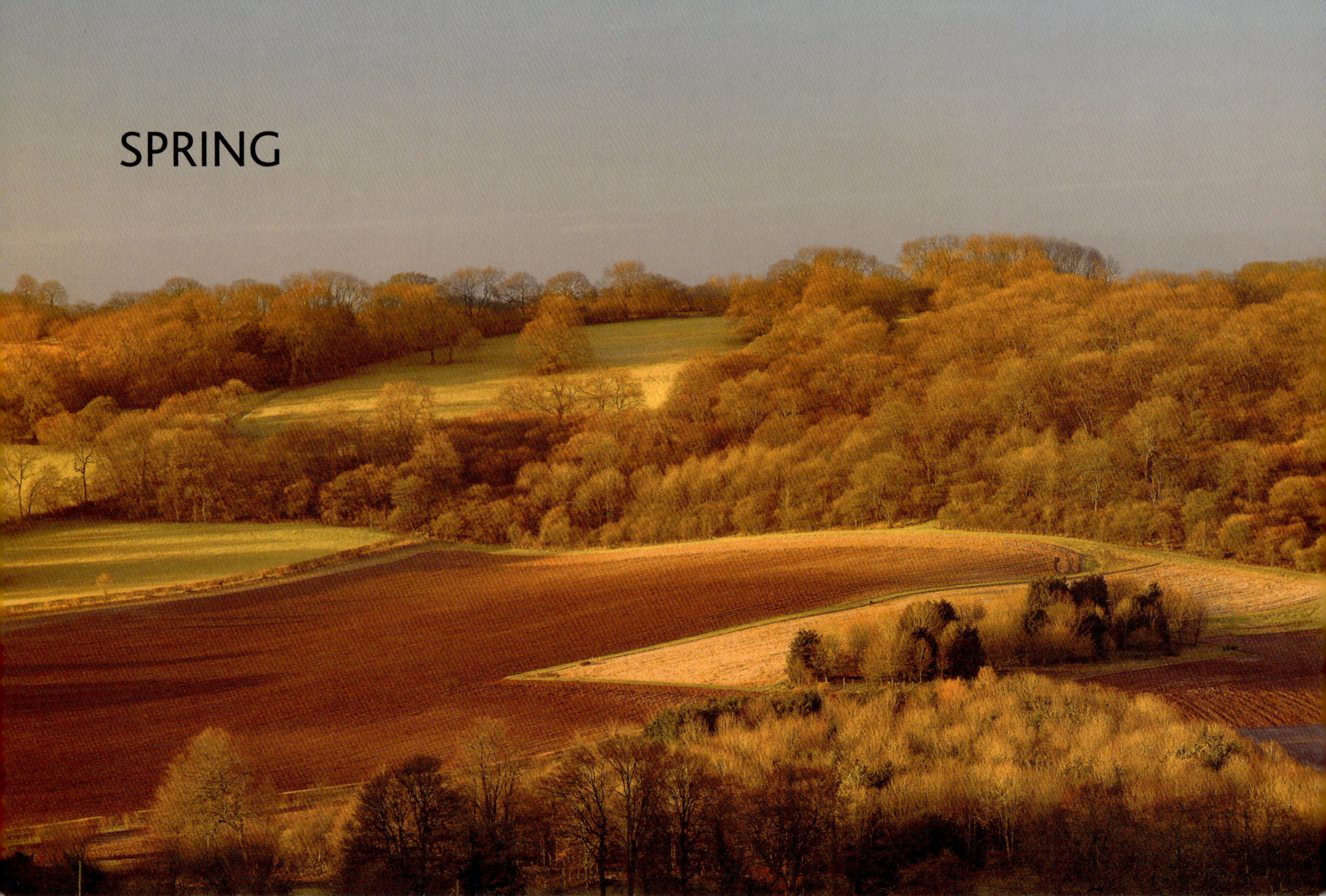

Summer Hill near Combe
It would be easy to assume that the great chalk ridge which cuts across Berkshire's south-west corner marks the end of the county, but this is not so. Hidden beyond the hills of Inkpen and Walbury is one of the county's quietest and most beautiful places – a wide basin of land surrounding the hamlet of Combe.

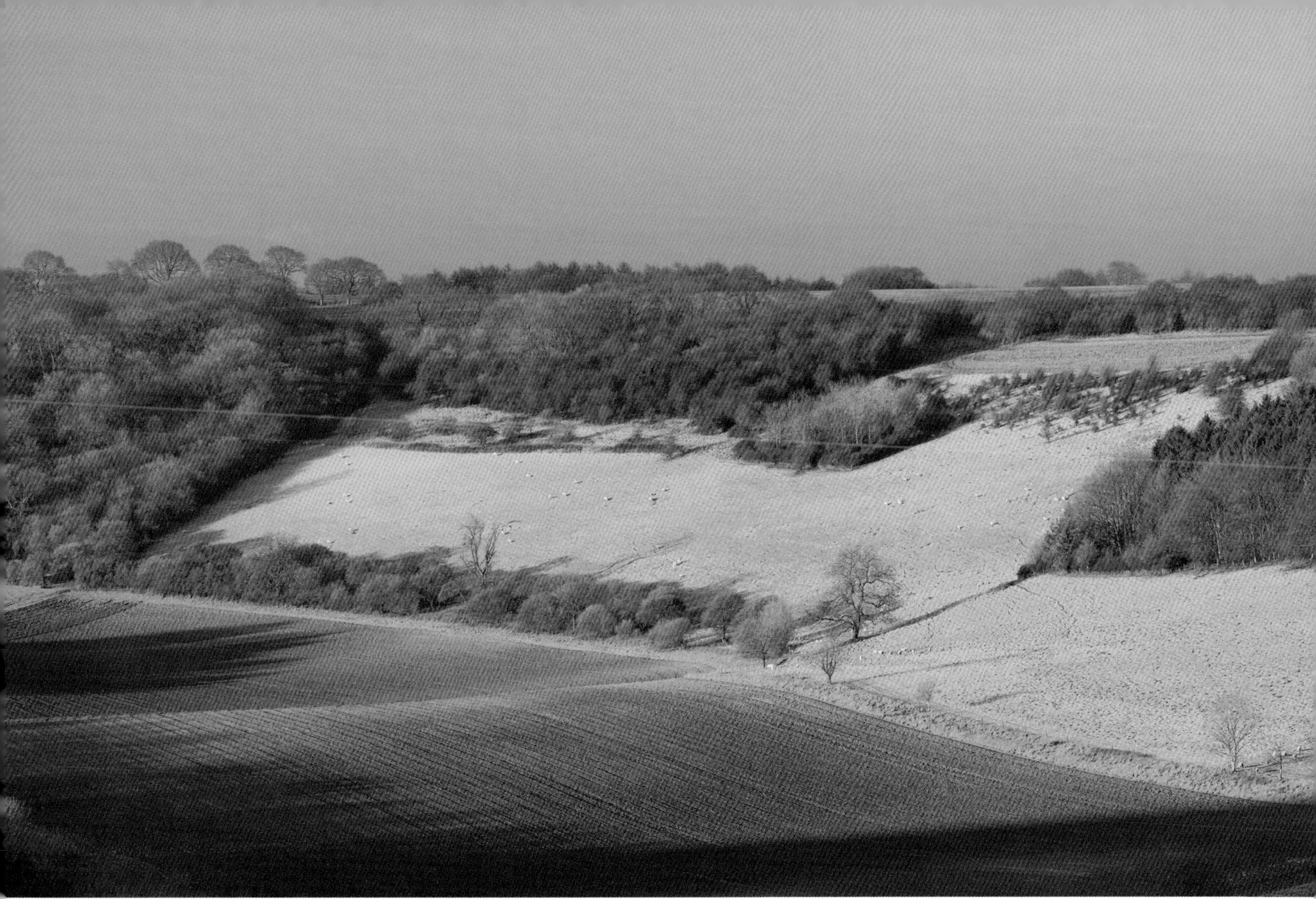

One of Berkshire's finest views – the landscape above Combe

This image shows the view looking south-west from the Wayfarer's Walk, across to the slopes of Summer Hill with its mix of fields, native woods and wild grassland. The russet tones in the trees and the warm-tinted morning light give the scene an autumnal look, but in technical terms these were the early days of spring.

Oak Trees in Windsor Great Park
Grand oaks are a symbolic feature of the Great Park at Windsor – these two veterans lie on the edge of the cavalry exercise ground near Queen Anne's Gate. In a scene which could easily pass for winter, the only real evidence of spring are the new season's leaves just beginning to appear on the taller tree.

It's said that the park has the largest collection of ancient oaks in Western Europe, with the oldest measuring over 30 feet in girth and being perhaps 500 years old.

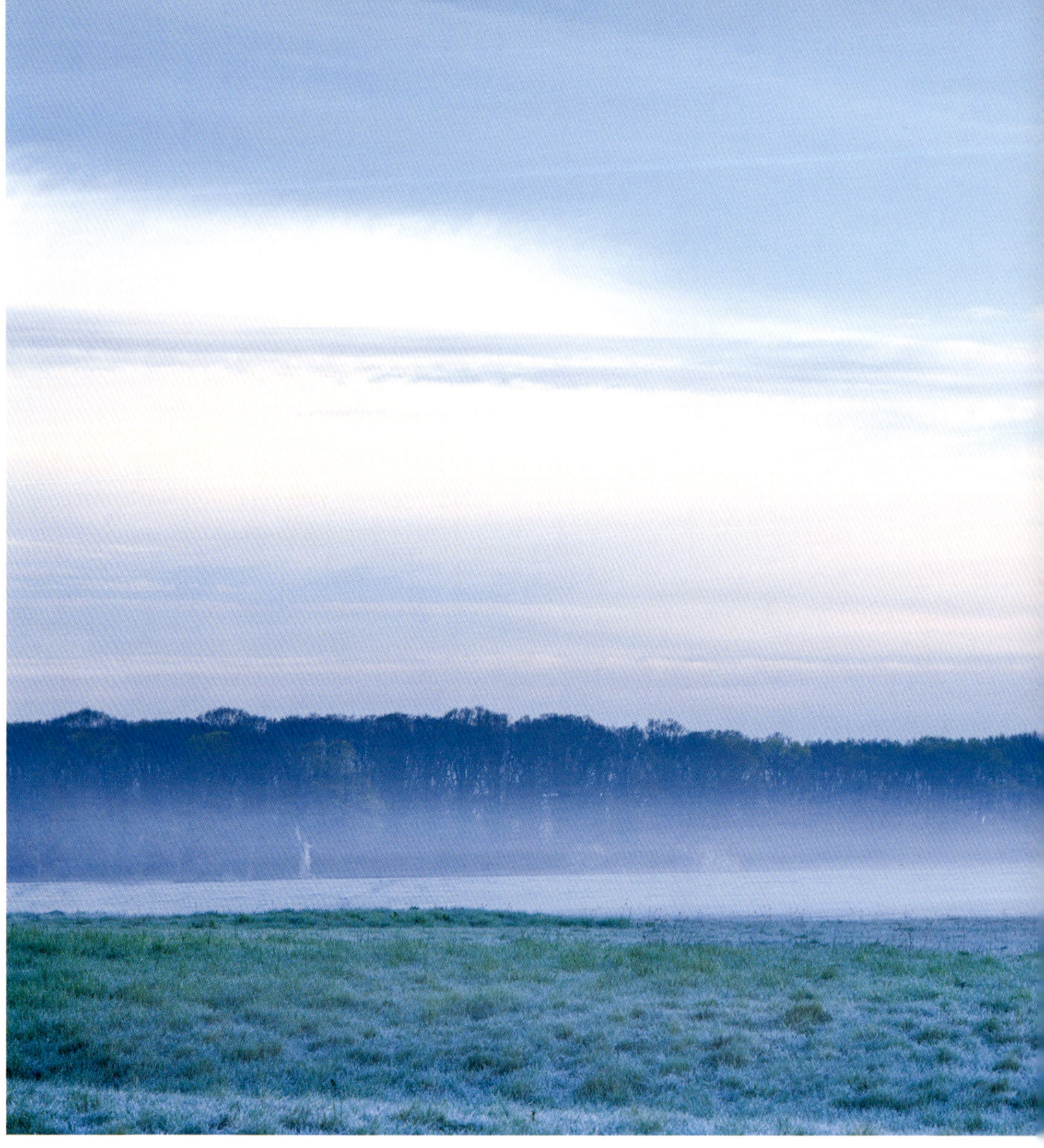

Two of the many wonderful old oaks at Windsor

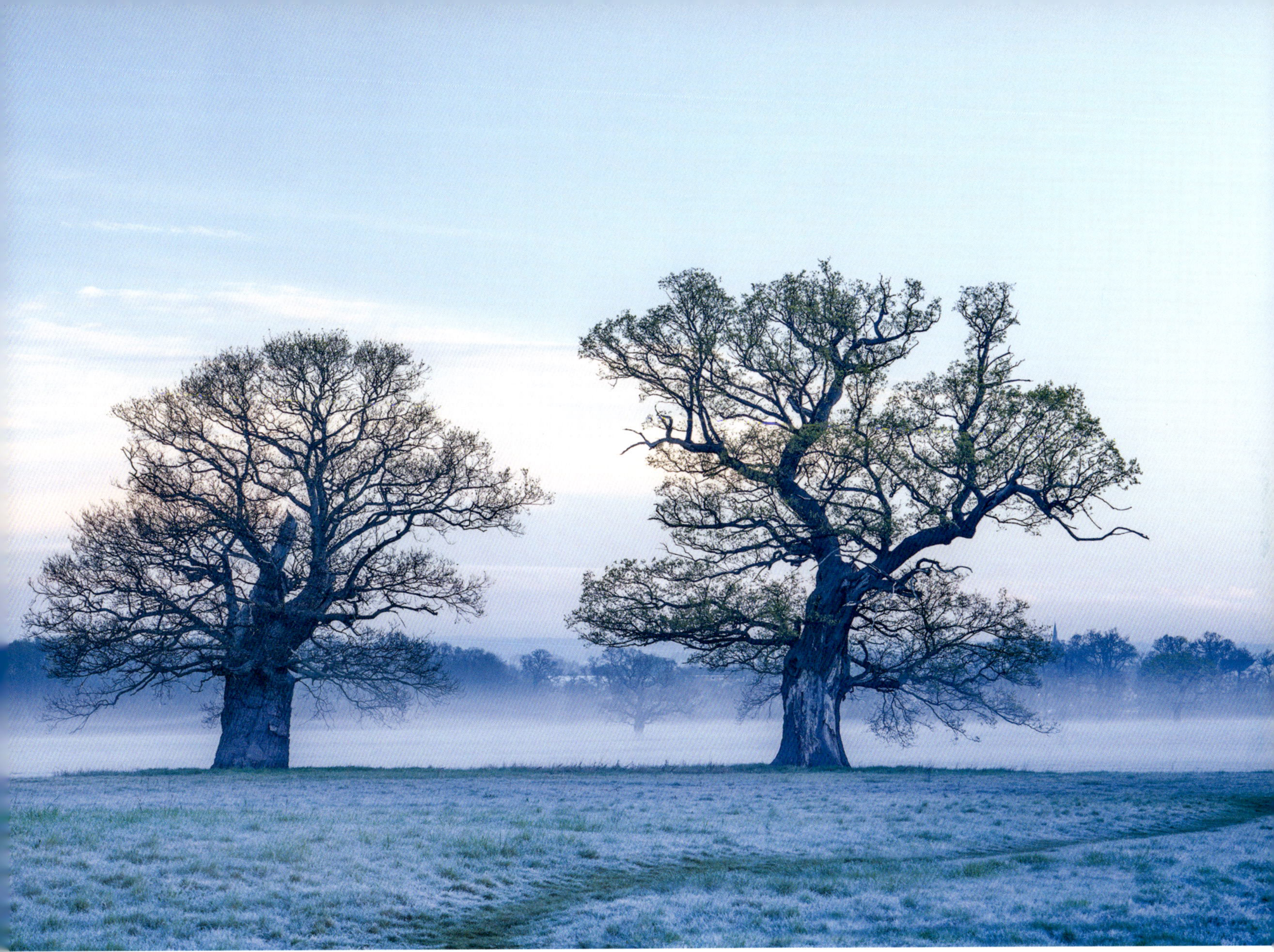

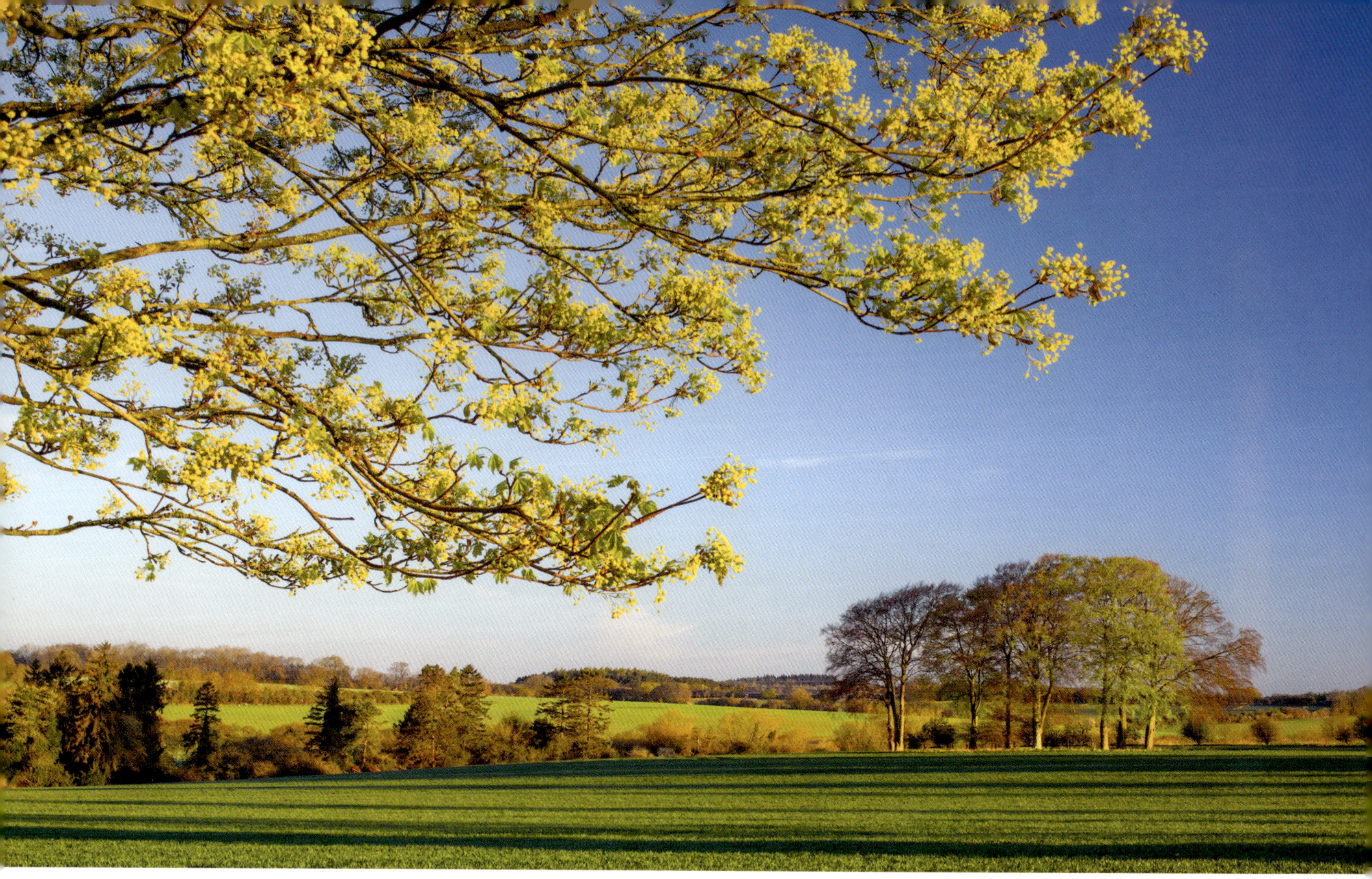

A show of spring leaves over the landscape at Standen

Standen near Hungerford

Located south-west of Hungerford and at the very western edge of Berkshire, the settlement of Standen consists of just a few buildings. It's a crossing point of two footpaths, and when I explored the area in late April the hedgerows were dotted with spring flowers. But the most prolific features of the landscape are three neat clumps of beech trees which mushroom up from the surrounding fields.

Planted by previous generations – perhaps as wildlife havens, shade for livestock, or simply as focal points – the mature trees now add interest and character to the landscape. This image was taken from under the boughs of a large maple and shows one of the beech clumps in the distance.

Aldworth Church

I first visited St Mary's at Aldworth to see the renowned yew tree which stands (with the aid of wooden supports) in the churchyard. Considered to be over 1000 years old it is one of the oldest in Berkshire, and despite being brought down by a gale in 1976 it's still partly alive, with a bowed and hollow shell composed of beautifully knotted wood.

The flint-built church, which celebrated its 700-year anniversary in 2015, has an attractive tower and blends well with the downland scenery. Interestingly, the interior is dominated by the 'Aldworth Giants', nine stone effigies of the de la Beche family which date from the early part of the fourteenth century.

This view was taken from the lane which leads to The Ridgeway and shows the north side of the church on a clear spring morning.

St Mary's church making a focal point in the spring landscape

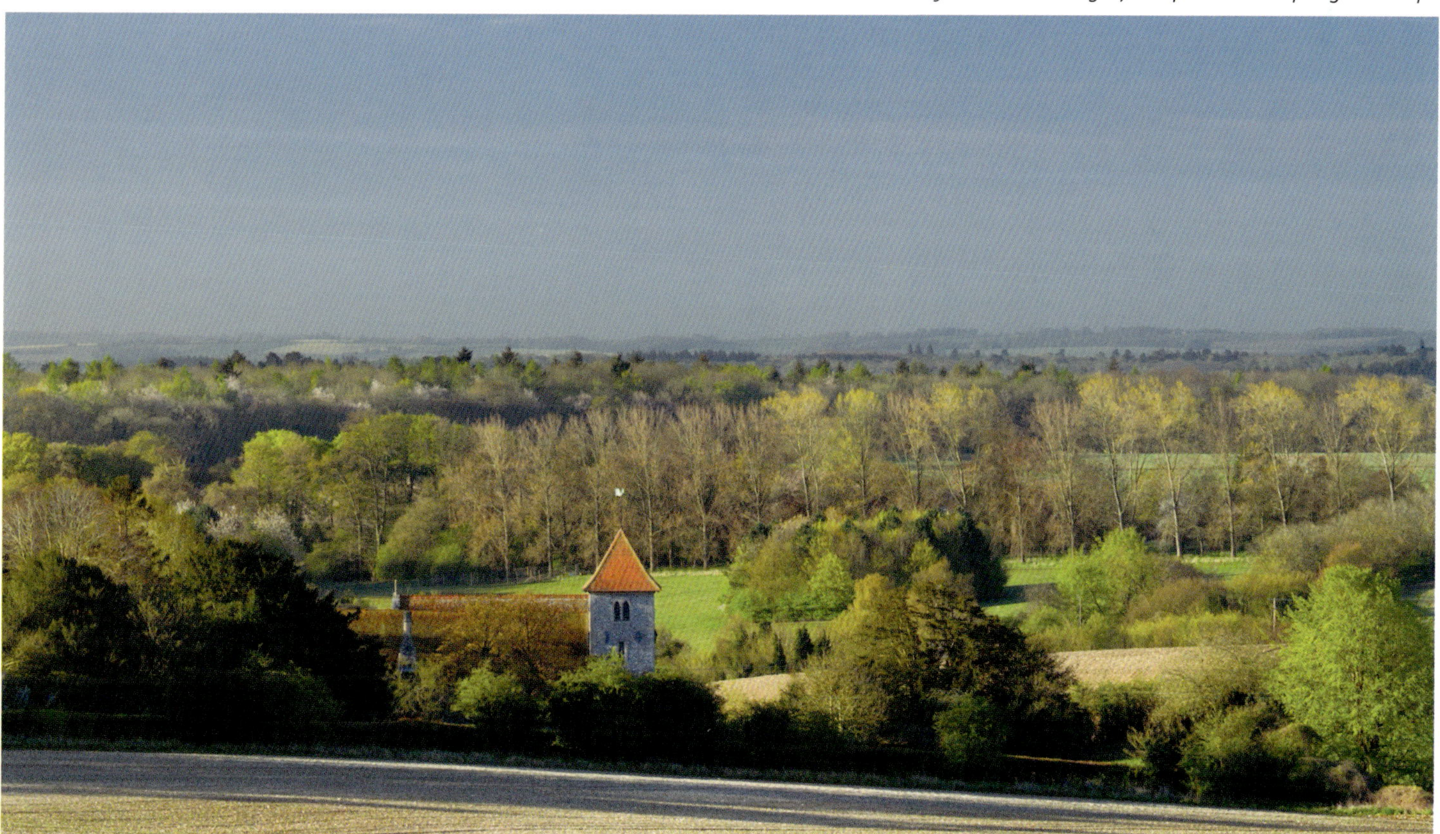

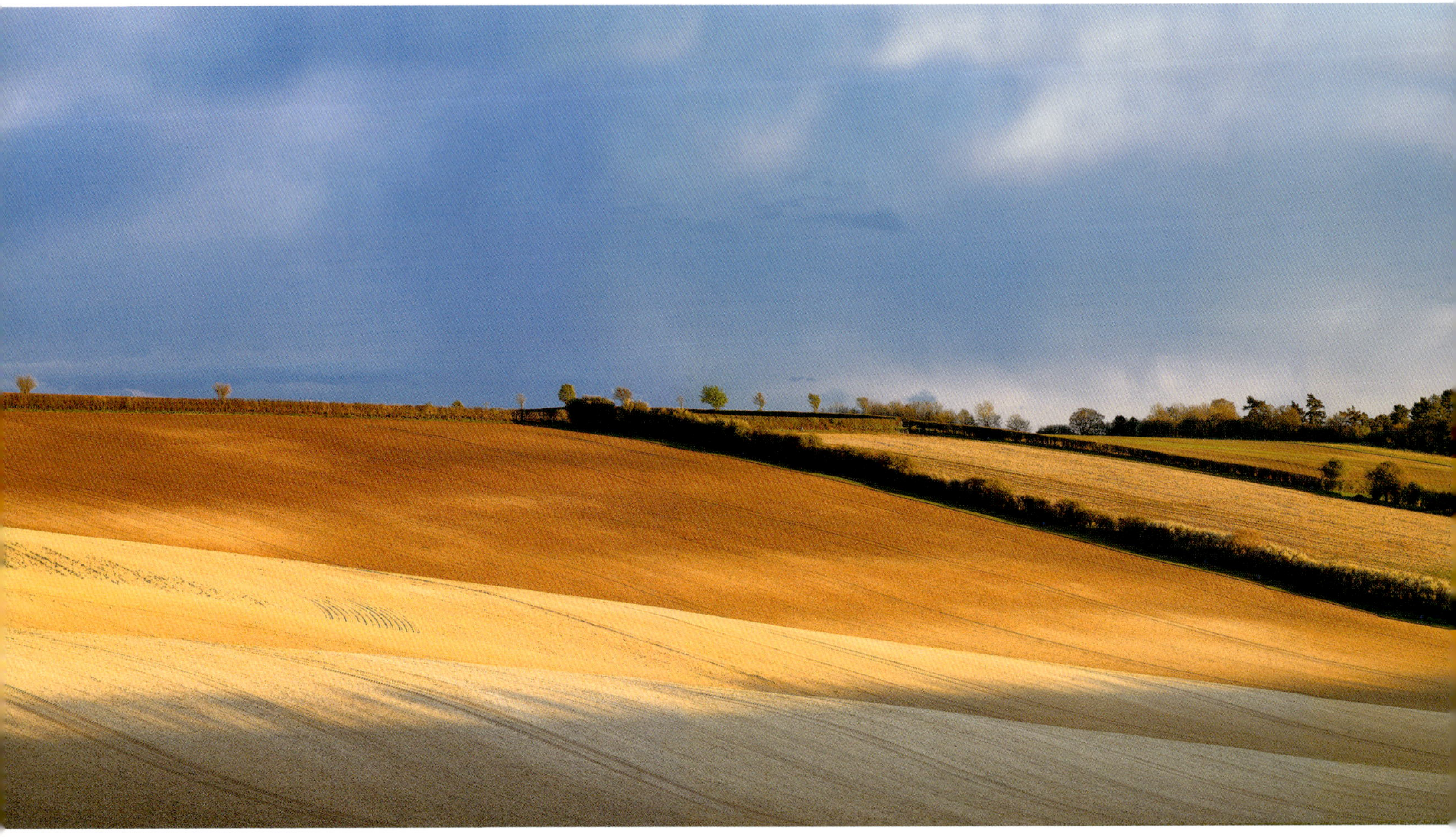

Starveall at Sunset

Located 1-mile north of Aldworth at the end of a narrow lane is the tiny settlement of Starveall. It consists of just a handful of dwellings in an isolated downland setting with stunning views to the west. The unusual name describes an area of inferior land and occurs elsewhere in Berkshire (notably at Starveall Farm near West Ilsley), and in a number of places across England.

But regardless of its agricultural value, the landscape here – in visual terms at least – is some of the finest in the county. Indeed, it's perhaps not surprising that the route from Aldworth to Starveall (and onwards to The Ridgeway), is part of a 5-mile stretch which was recently named as one of Britain's best walks.

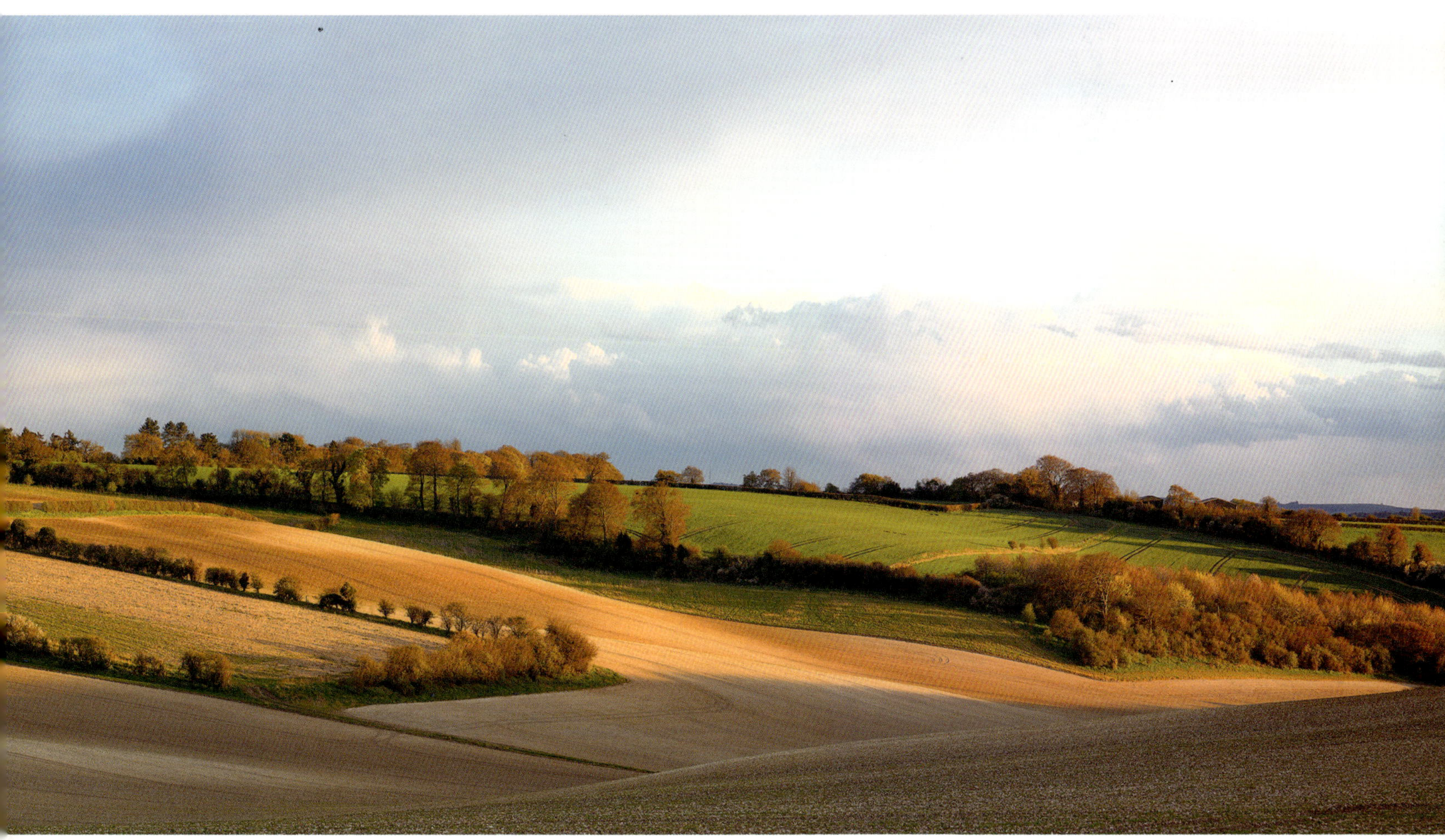

Raking light on the downs at Starveall

Visitors passing this way in early summer will see a meadow filled with ox-eye daisies which adjoins Starveall Cottage; the flowers fill the foreground while rolling fields stretch away beyond. The image on this page was taken on an April evening and shows the side-lit view from the footpath which heads west; the amber-tinted light seemed the perfect ingredient for bringing out the russet tones in the bare fields.

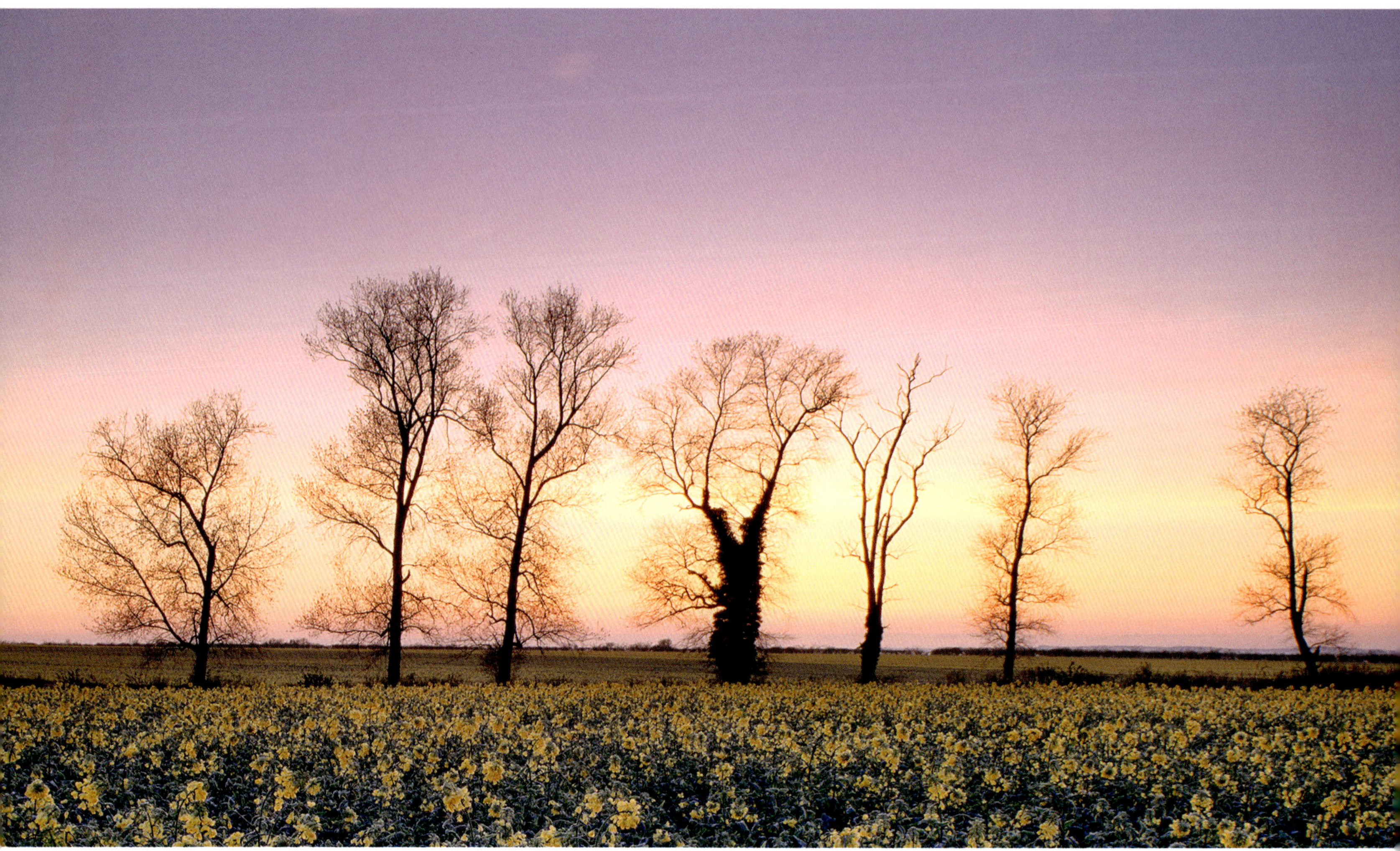

Spring sunrise in the Pang Valley

The Pang Valley

The River Pang flows for some 15 miles through West Berkshire, following a crescent-shaped course which resembles one giant meander of a much larger river. From its source on the downs near Compton, it heads due south for 5 miles before turning abruptly east near Bucklebury. It then flows on through Stanford Dingley and Bradfield before swinging north as it approaches Tidmarsh. It finally joins the Thames at Pangbourne, having passed through some of the county's most attractive countryside.

A field of flowering rapeseed was the setting for this image taken in the luminous light shortly before sunrise.

Goddard's Green near Mortimer

A stream known as Lockram Brook rises on Wokefield Common and flows east towards Goddard's Green, passing through a delightful tree-lined landscape along the way. It runs under Lockram Lane and then drains into Millbarn Pond, a small reservoir above a dam; no mill survives. Oaks dominate the surrounding area, and among them are two fine specimens that stand mid-field above the brook and alongside a footpath. The larger of the two has a broad full crown and a low sweeping bough which, observant walkers will notice, frames the view to the south.

This photograph was taken from the edge of the lane, and shows the trees in a moment of slanting sunlight.

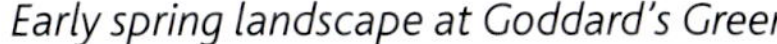

Early spring landscape at Goddard's Green

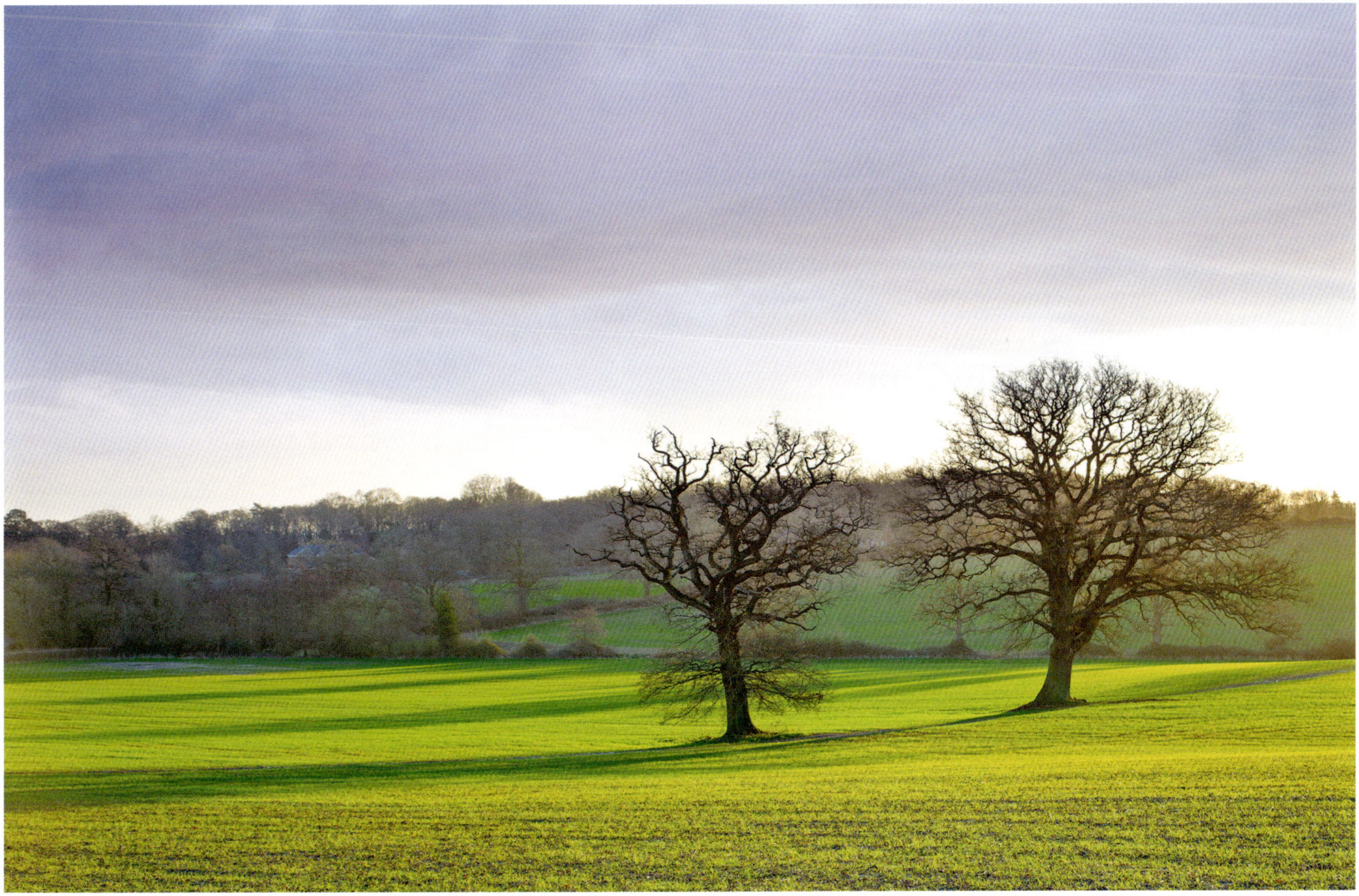

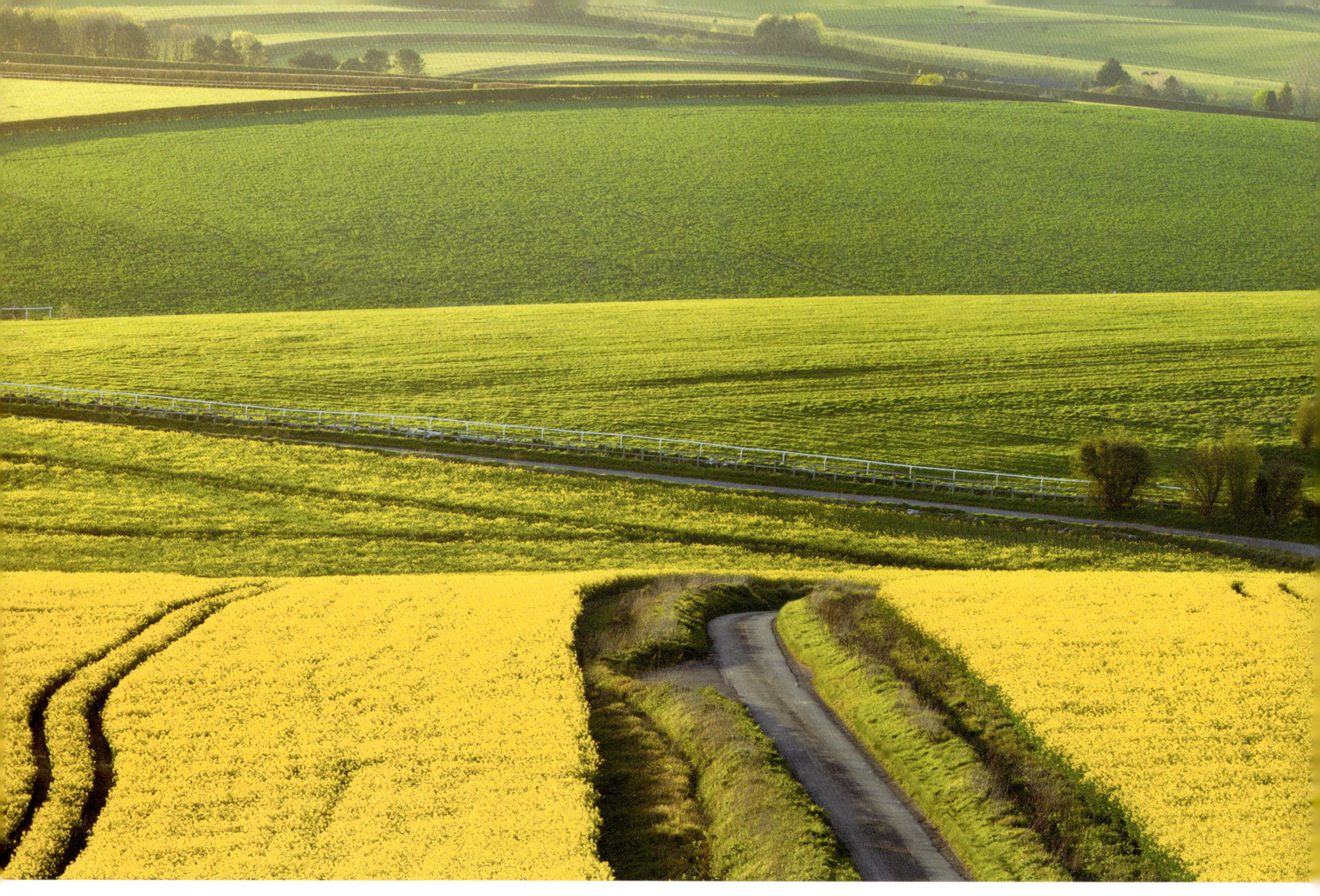

Woolley Down

As a bold newcomer, rapeseed drew much attention when it first began to appear in England over thirty years ago; nowadays it's become so familiar that it seldom merits more than a passing glance. As a landscape photographer I rarely see it as a potential subject, although now and again it can become the key element in a composition – like it was in this scene which shows the beautifully folded landscape along the southern side of Woolley Down.

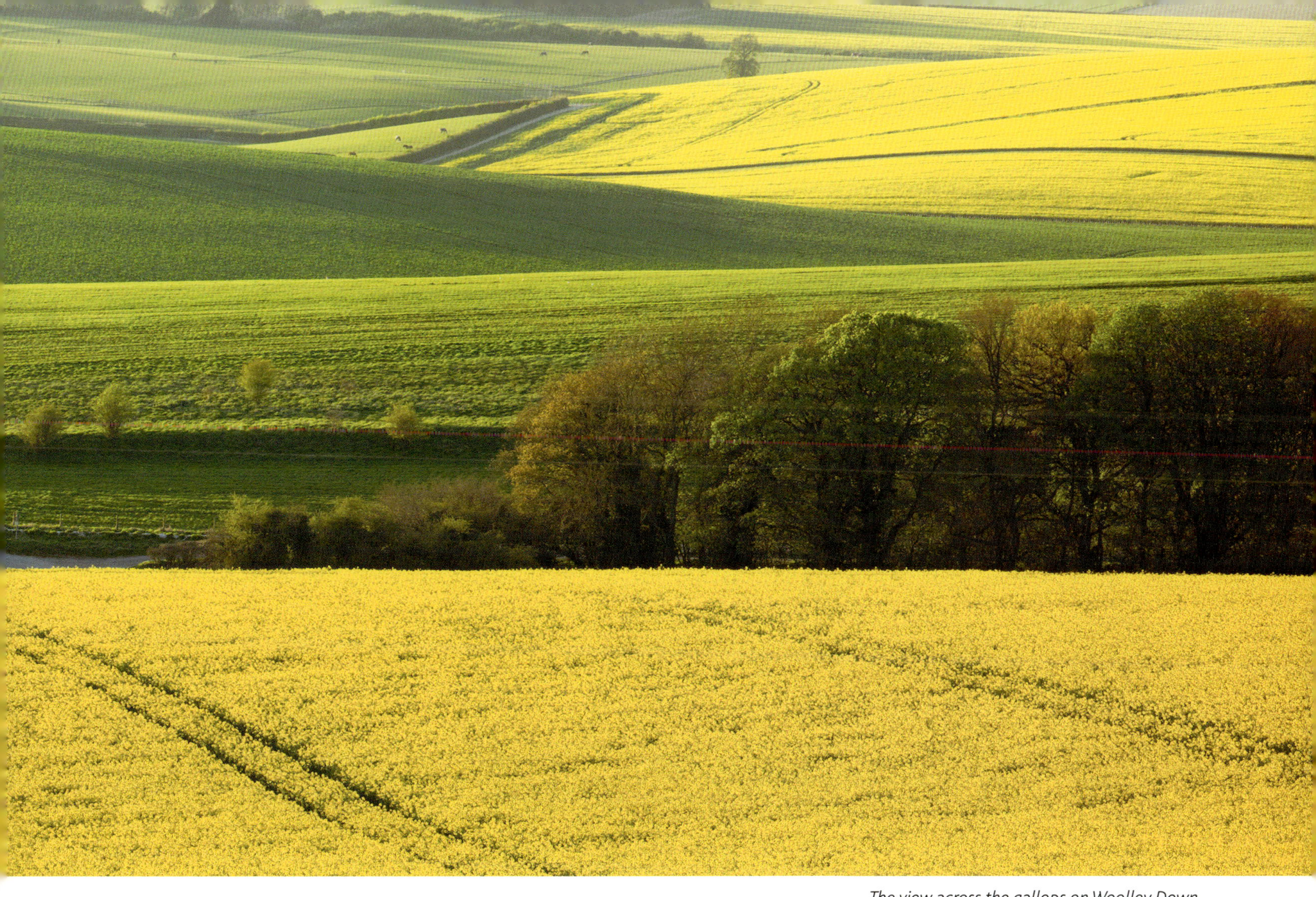

The view across the gallops on Woolley Down

The lane draws the eye into the image and the layered landscape beyond helps to convey a feeling of depth – but without the sweep of yellow across the foreground and again at the top right, the view would have been much less dramatic.

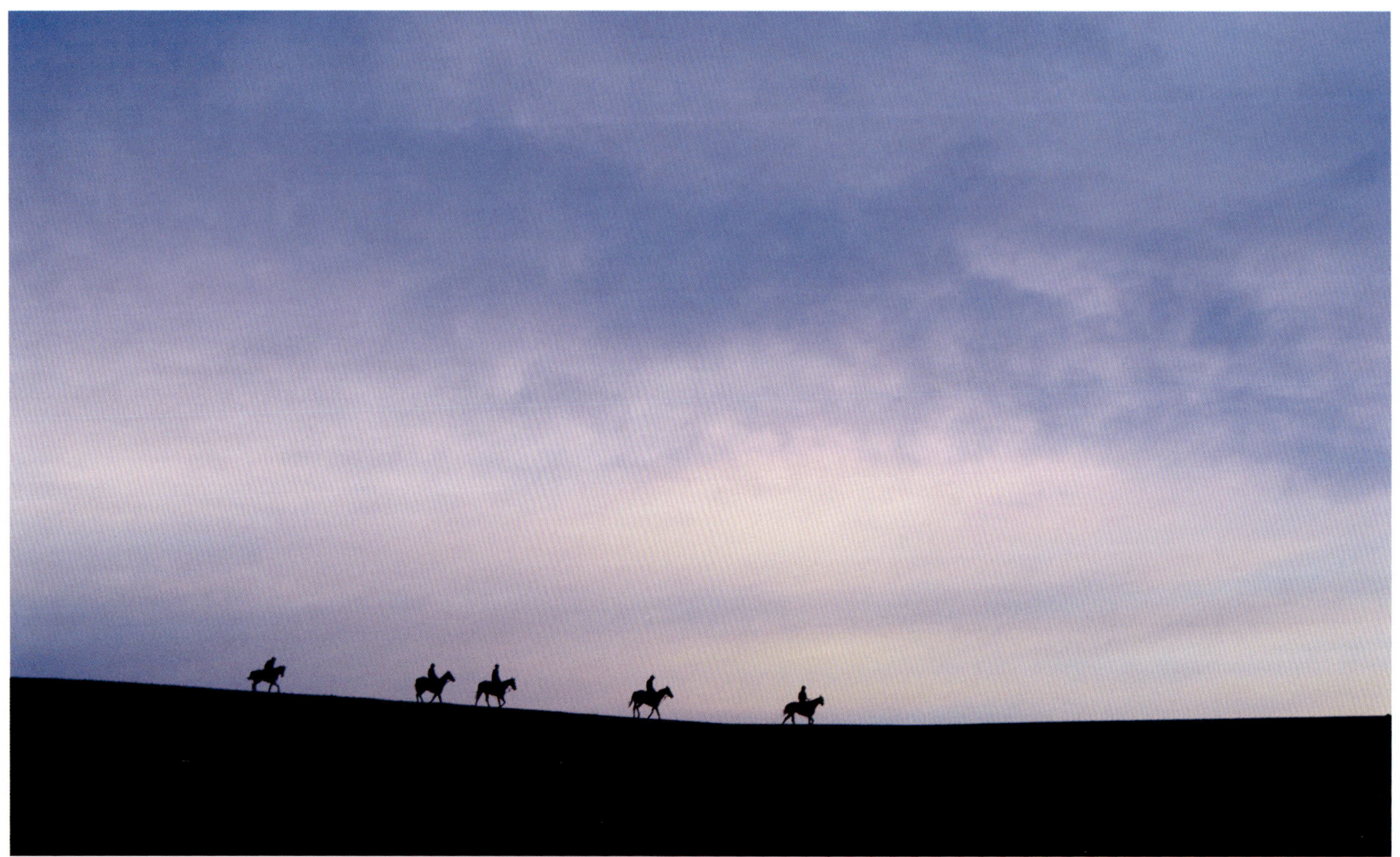

A morning outing for the horses on Sparsholt Down

The Valley of the Racehorse

Lambourn's association with horse racing can be traced back to the early eighteenth century when races were first held on Bailey Hill Down. This marked the start of a long tradition of race horse training in the area – something which is reflected in the surrounding landscape with gallops extending over the downs in all directions. As a result, this stretch of rolling chalk country has now become known as 'The Valley of the Racehorse'.

But far from being exclusive, it seems that there's a happy harmony on the downs between walkers and riders, with by-ways and gallops running side by side in many places. The bonus for walkers is some stunning glimpses of the horses, especially when they're seen on the skyline.

Horses on Pit Down above Seven Barrows on a blustery day in March

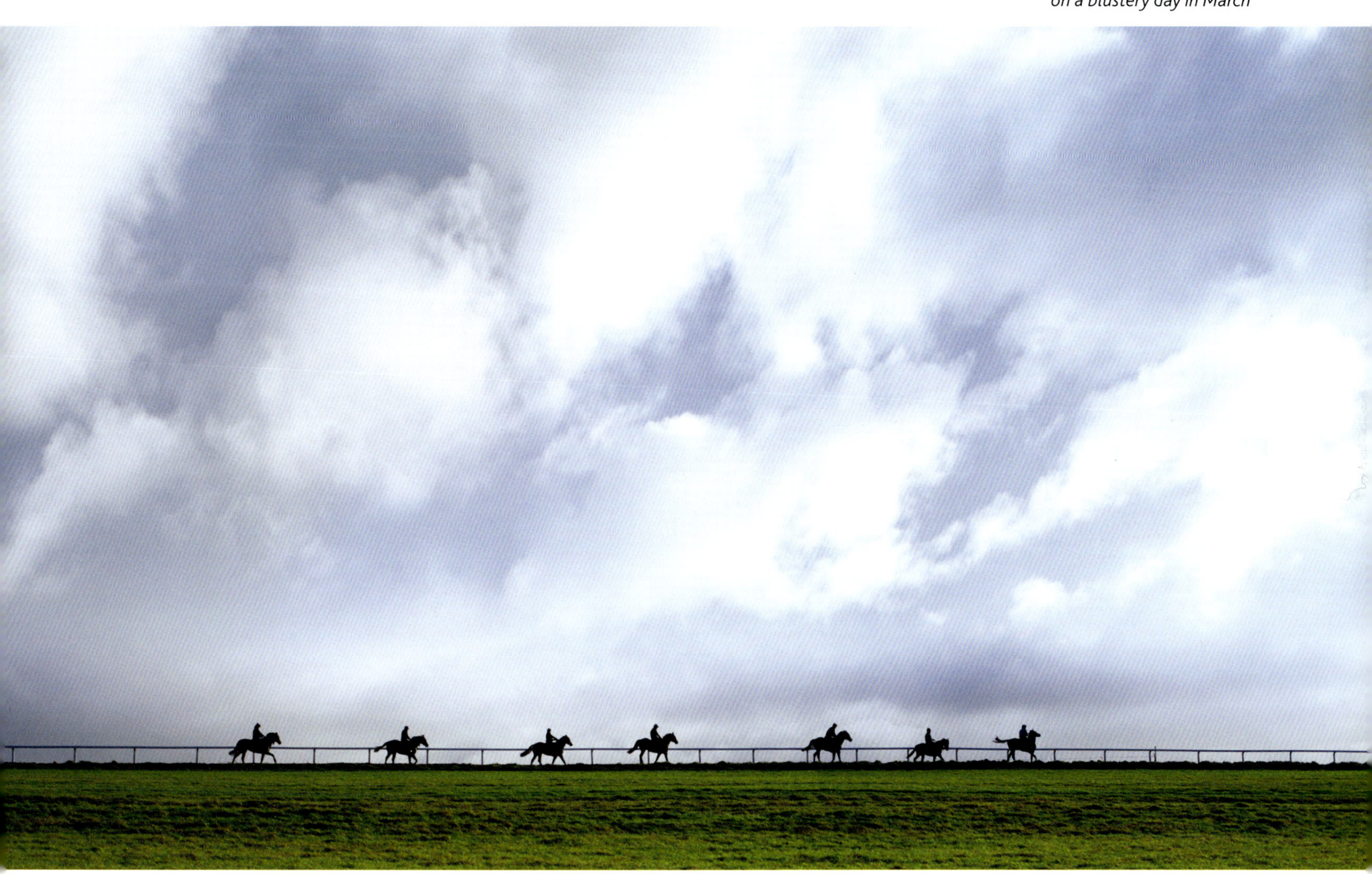

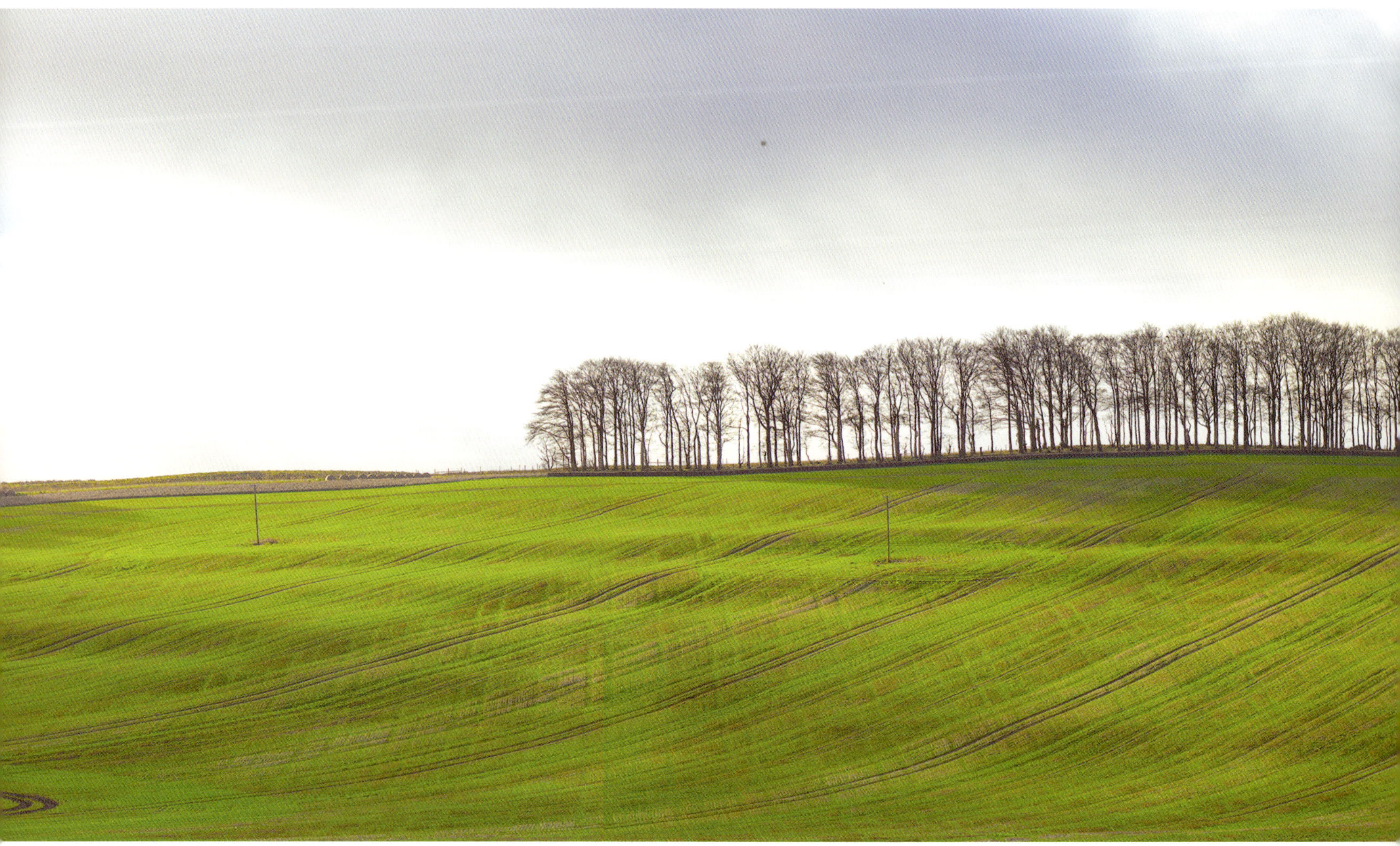

Hackpen Hill
Originally part of Berkshire, this tree-topped landscape now lies just over the border in Oxfordshire, following boundary changes made in 1974. The location is just north of The Ridgeway on the northern edge of Hackpen Hill, not far from the deep hollow known as the Devil's Punchbowl.

The line of beech trees – well over 200 in all – can be seen from a great distance to the north; this view is taken from the lane which

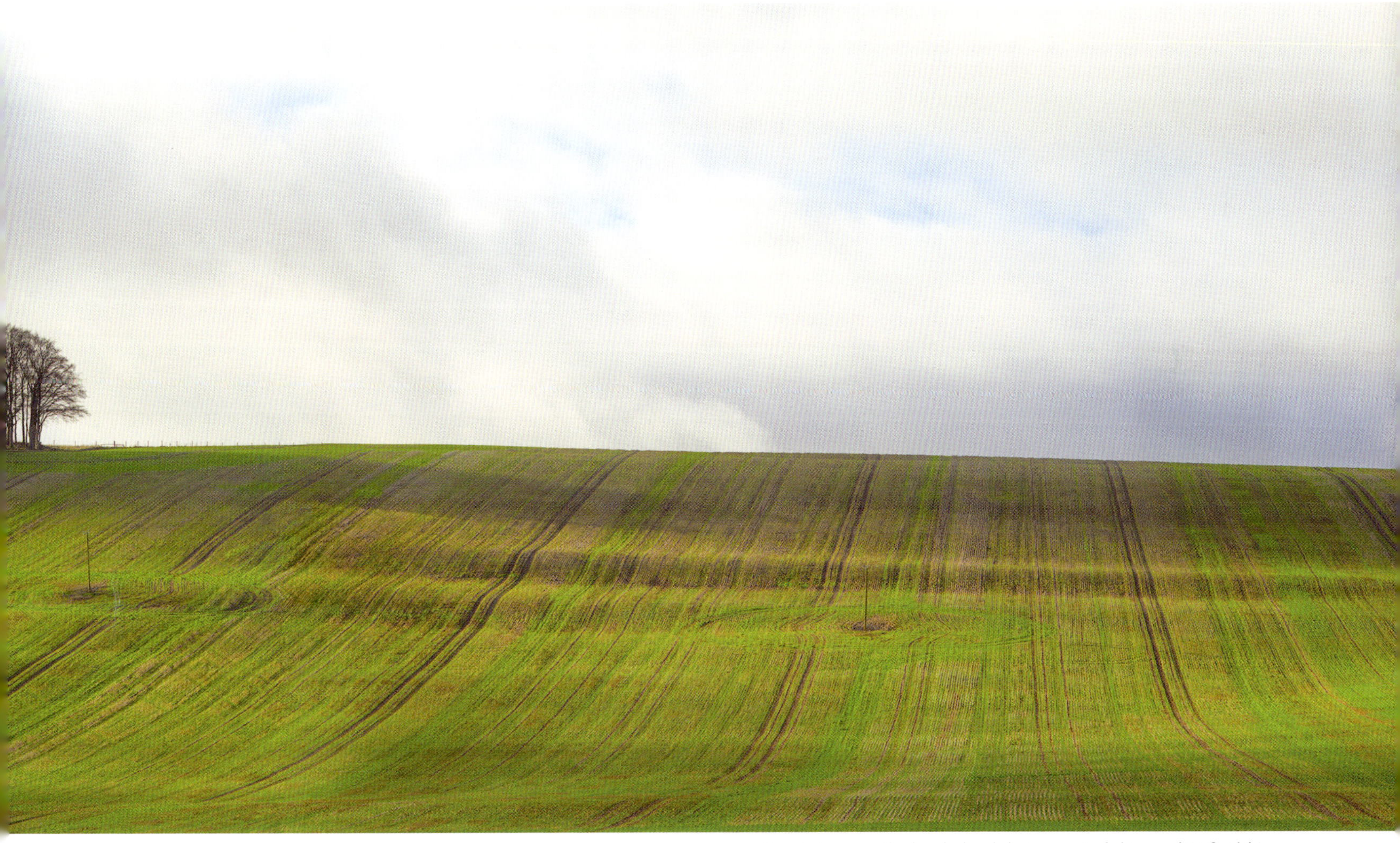

Beech trees on the borderlands between Berkshire and Oxfordshire

leads to Letcombe Bassett. They make a prominent feature on the broad horizon and look most impressive in winter when their skeletal outlines can be seen in detail.

Isolated stands of beech are scattered right across this part of the downs – some grow in tightly rounded plantations which blend particularly well with the rolling landscape.

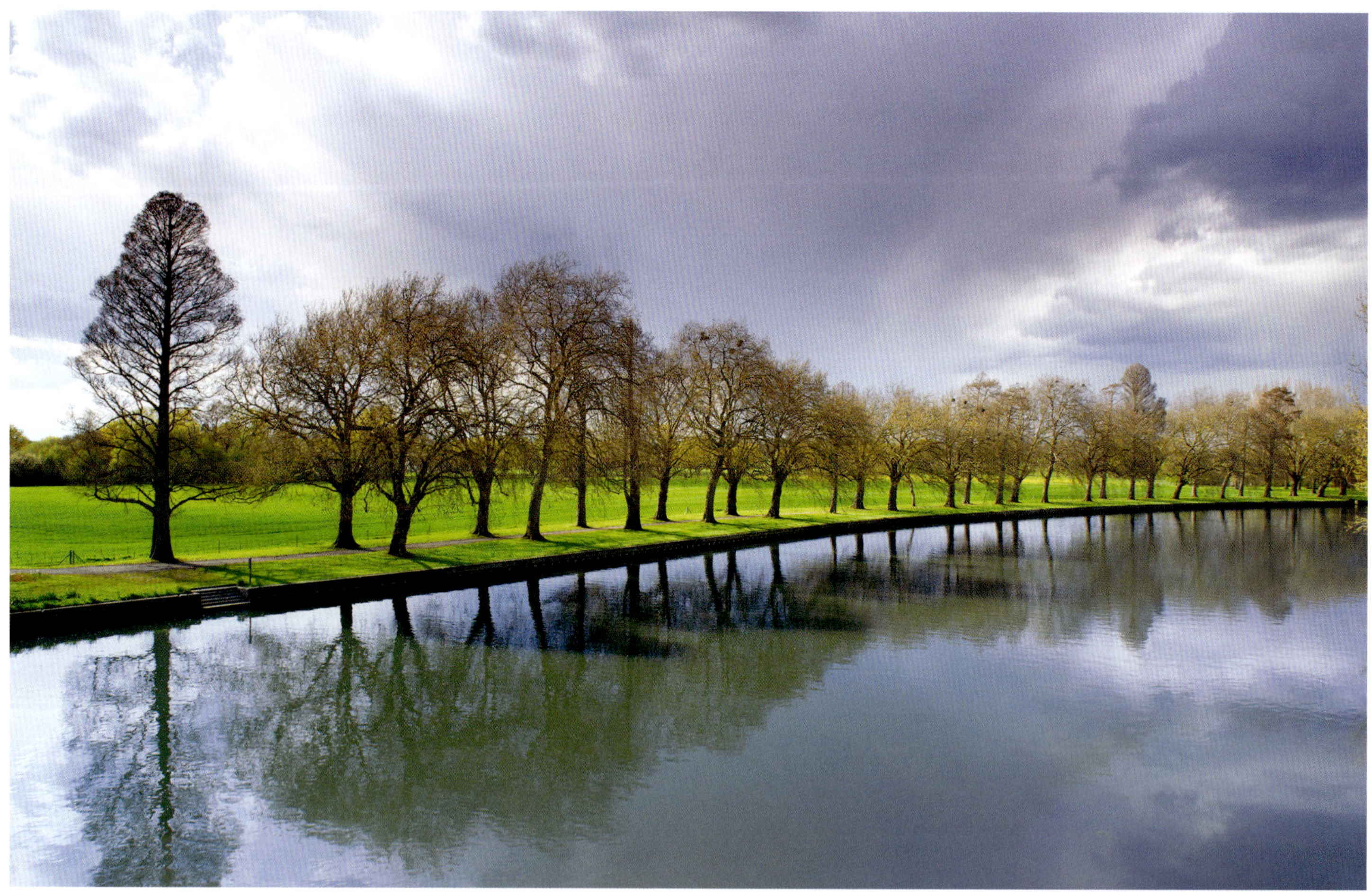

Looking to Windsor's Home Park from Albert Bridge

Albert Bridge

This tree-lined stretch of the Thames can be seen from Albert Bridge which crosses the river between Windsor and Datchet. The view goes unseen by most drivers who use the bridge owing to the high walls on either side; however, several small viewing bays have been built into the structure, allowing pedestrians to enjoy an elevated view down to the avenue of plane trees which stand within Windsor's Home Park.

The red-brick bridge was built in 1927 to replace a cast iron one which had stood on the site since 1850.

Streatley to Moulsford

The historic village of Streatley lies along the west side of the Thames, backed by a steep wooded hillside, looking out across the river towards Goring in Oxfordshire. The two villages are connected by a bridge, opened in 1923 and unusual in that it consists of two sections built on either side of an island. It also marks the only point where The Thames Path and The Ridgeway meet.

Heading north from here, The Thames Path follows the western bank towards Moulsford, along a picturesque stretch of the river lined with thickets of bulrush, alder and willow. It's a place for any season, but perhaps looks best at sunrise on a crisp spring morning.

Sunrise on the Thames north of Streatley

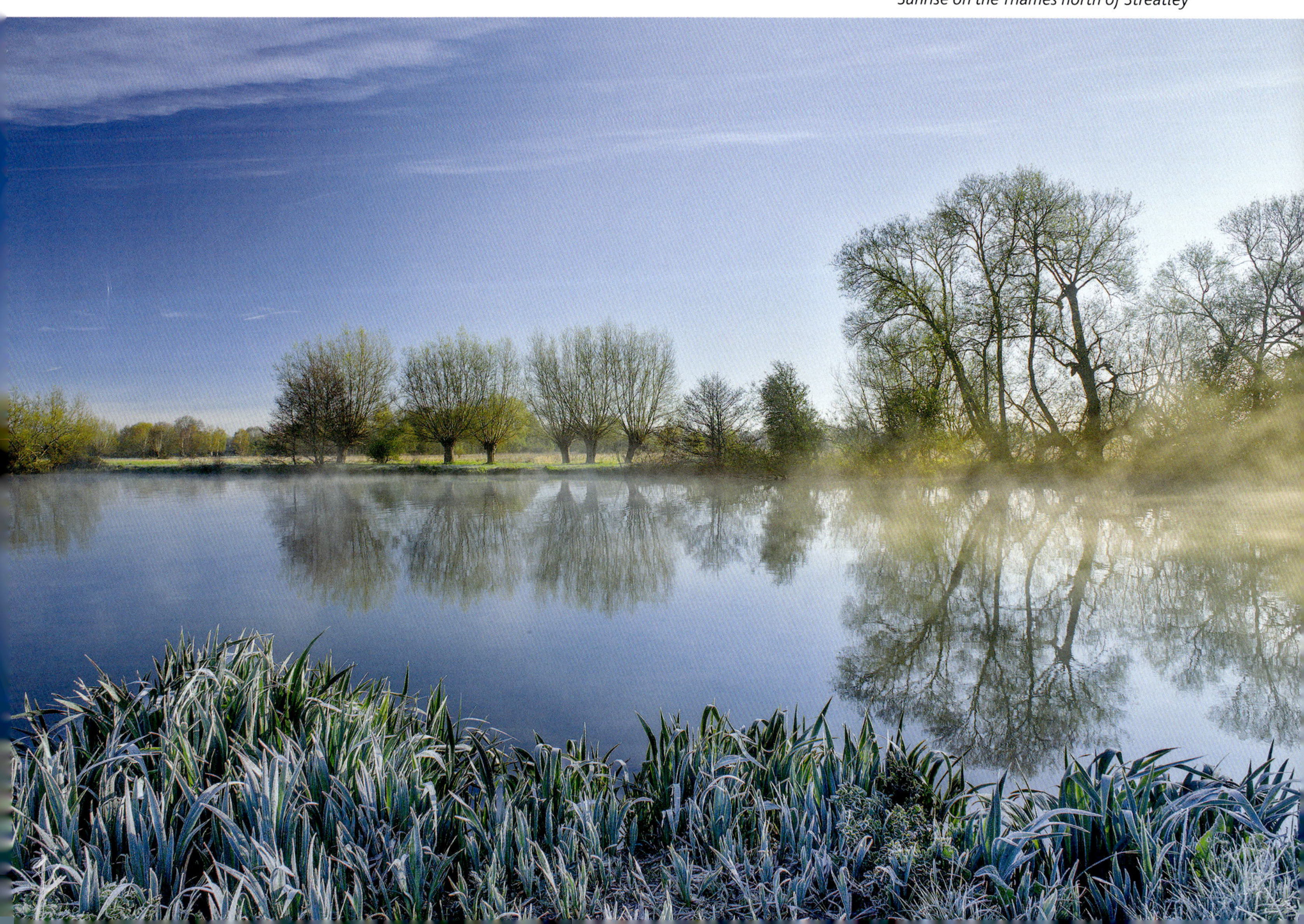

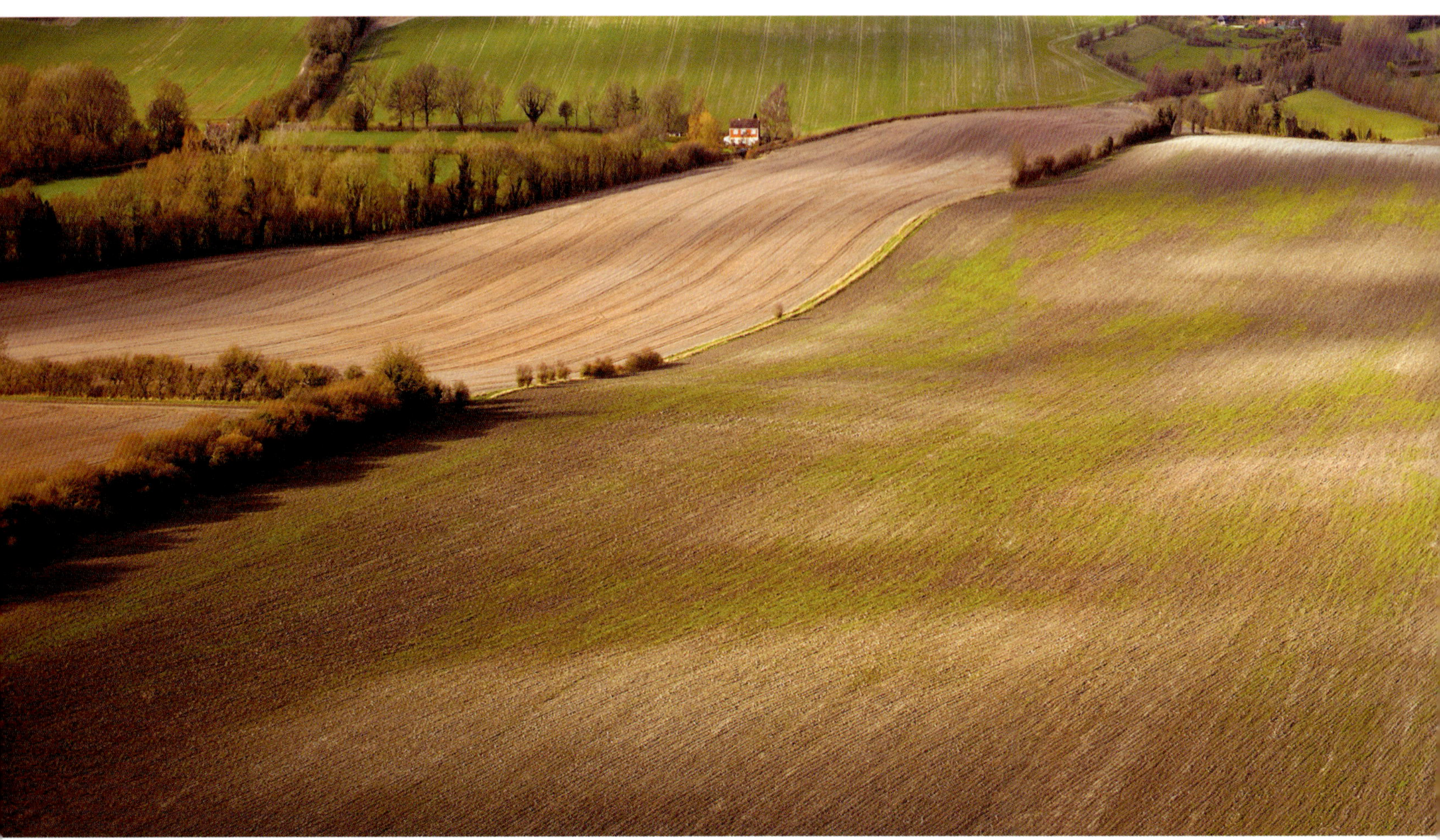

Landscape below Inkpen Hill

The tight circle of trees which stands on the landscape below Inkpen Hill makes a prominent feature, especially when the surrounding fields are ploughed and empty – this particular view can be seen from the footpath which crosses the ominously-named Gallows Down. The image has an air of spring about it, but on this day there was a bitter north wind blowing directly up the slope from the fields below.

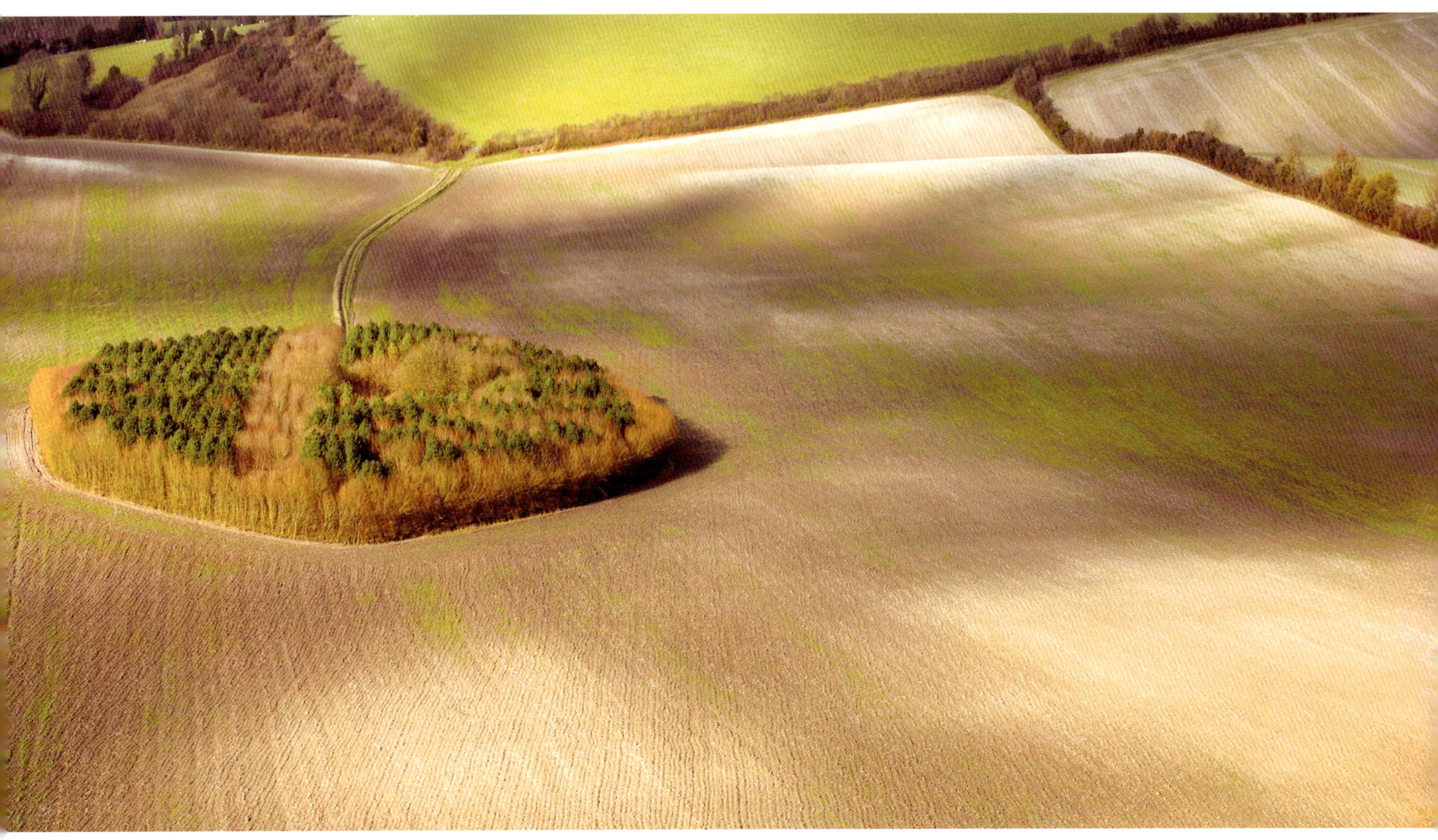

The splendid vista seen from the northern slope of Inkpen Hill

Walkers who wander a little higher up the hill from this spot will be surprised to find a small pool which is lined with rushes. It's known as Wigmoreash Pond but was historically called the 'Murderer's Pool', having been the place where the victims of the gibbet murderers were found.

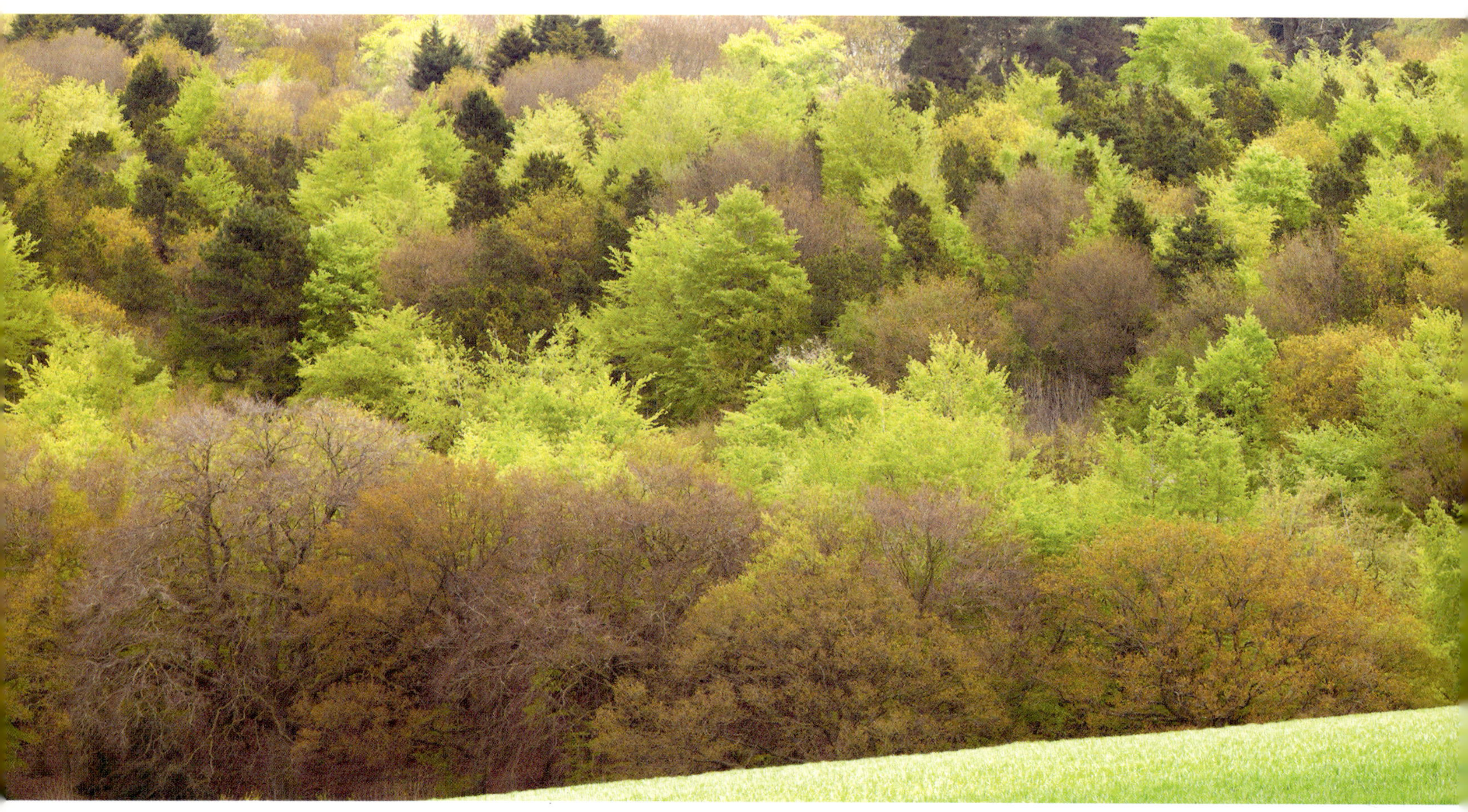

Letcombe Wood near Streatley
Berkshire is among the most wooded counties in England, and forestry surveys show that tree cover has been increasing for the last fifty years or so. The great forests of Windsor and Swinley account for much of the total, but there is also plenty of woodland in West Berkshire where the landscape is dotted with dozens of copses.

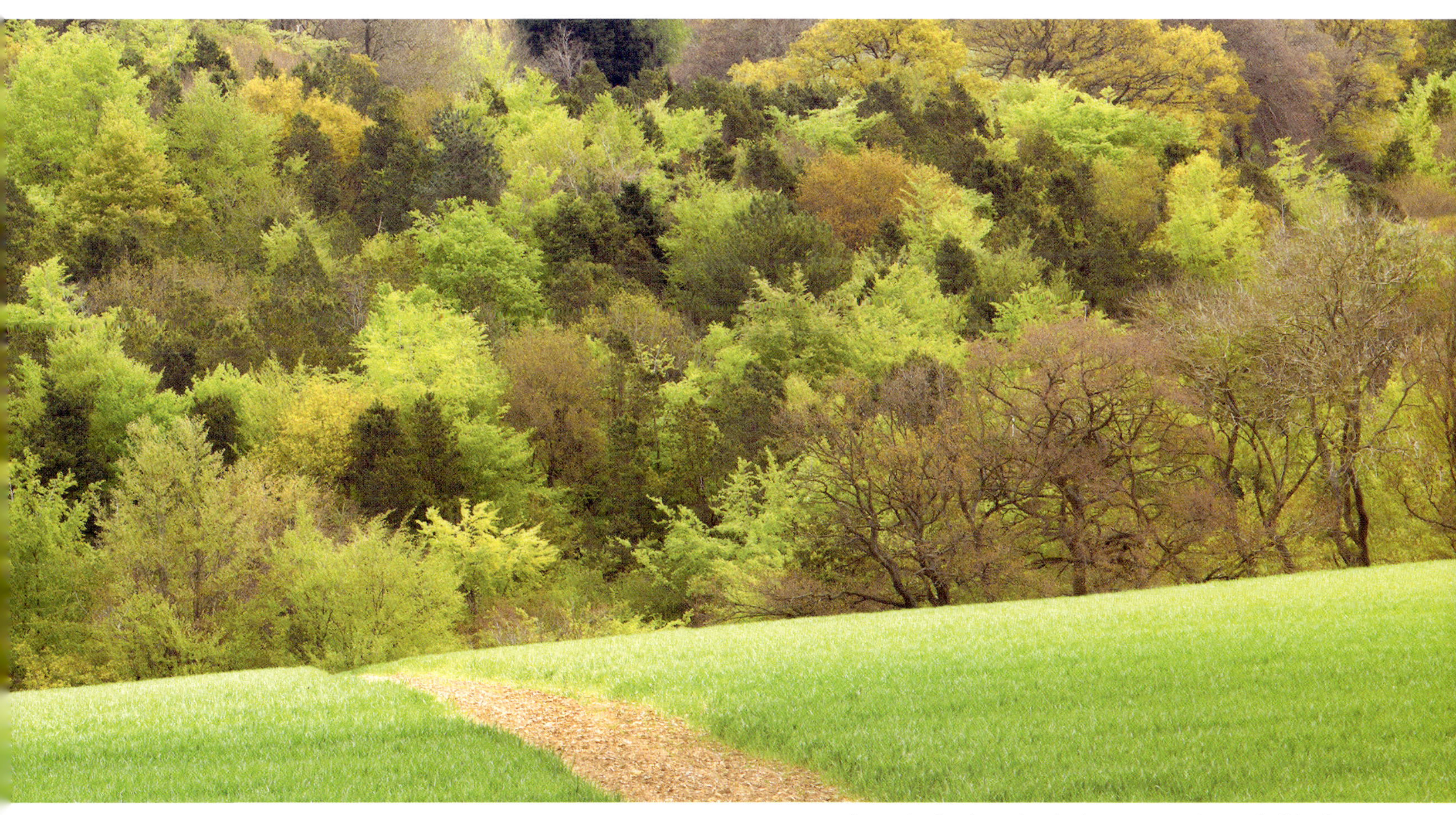

A mosaic of spring colour in the treetops at Letcombe Wood

One of the quietest of these is Letcombe Wood, located a mile west of Streatley – just below Lardon Chase. It extends for barely half a mile from end to end (and is only named on large-scale maps), but consists of a pleasant mix of broadleaves and conifers which line the slopes of a steep valley. There are no footpaths directly through the wood, but a path which approaches from the west gives a fine view across the leafy canopy – a mosaic of greens which look splendid in spring.

Landscape near Ashampstead

The fine beech tree shown here lies alongside a footpath near Ashampstead. The path leads up from the Aldworth road and can be followed eastwards along the side of Hartridge Lye Wood, beyond which it leads to Bowler's Copse where it crosses a section of the ancient earthwork known as Grim's Ditch.

The tree is one of three which stand in a line at the top of the slope – this view is looking south-east on a day of low cloud and lingering mist in early April.

The silhouette of a beech tree in the mist

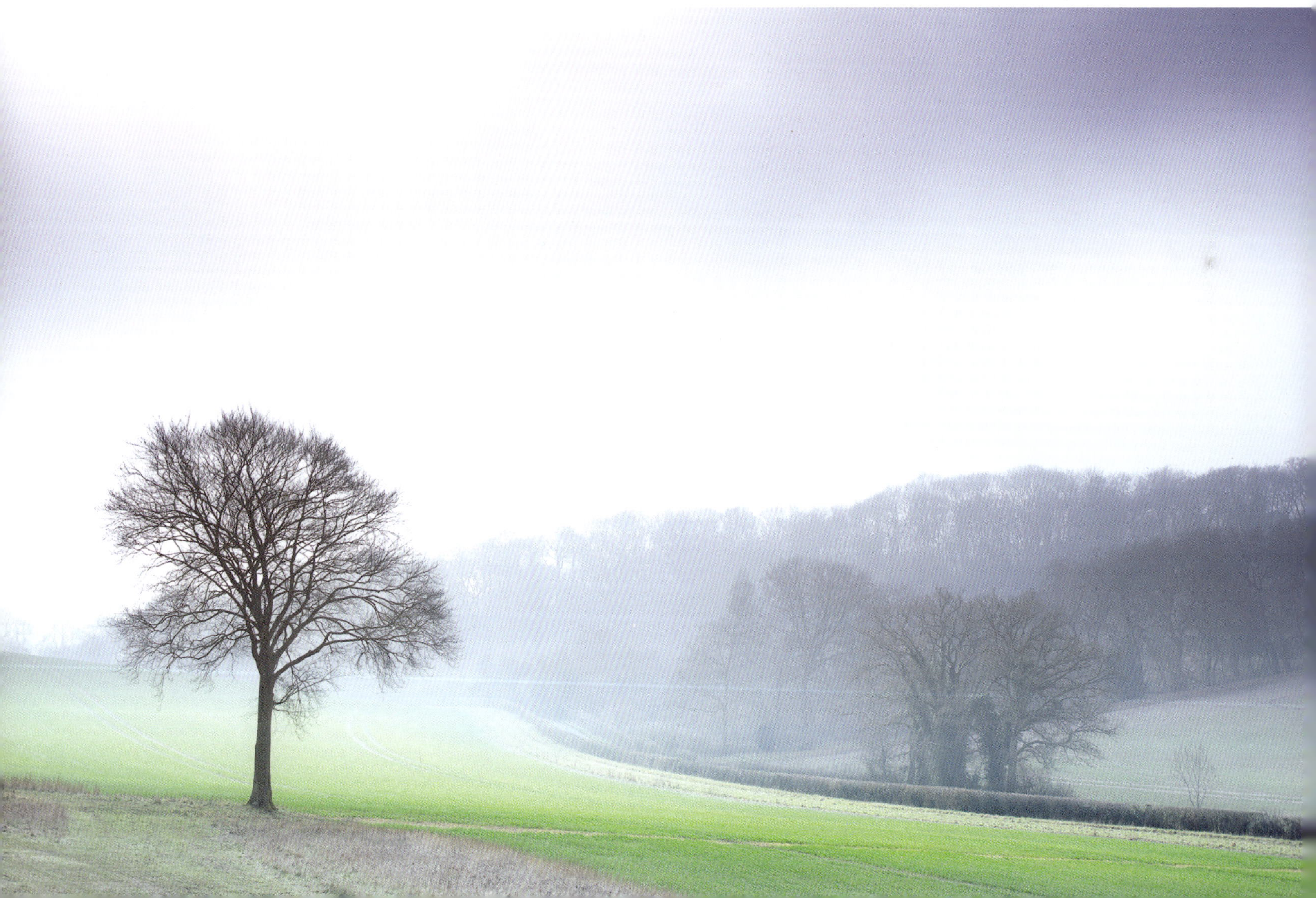

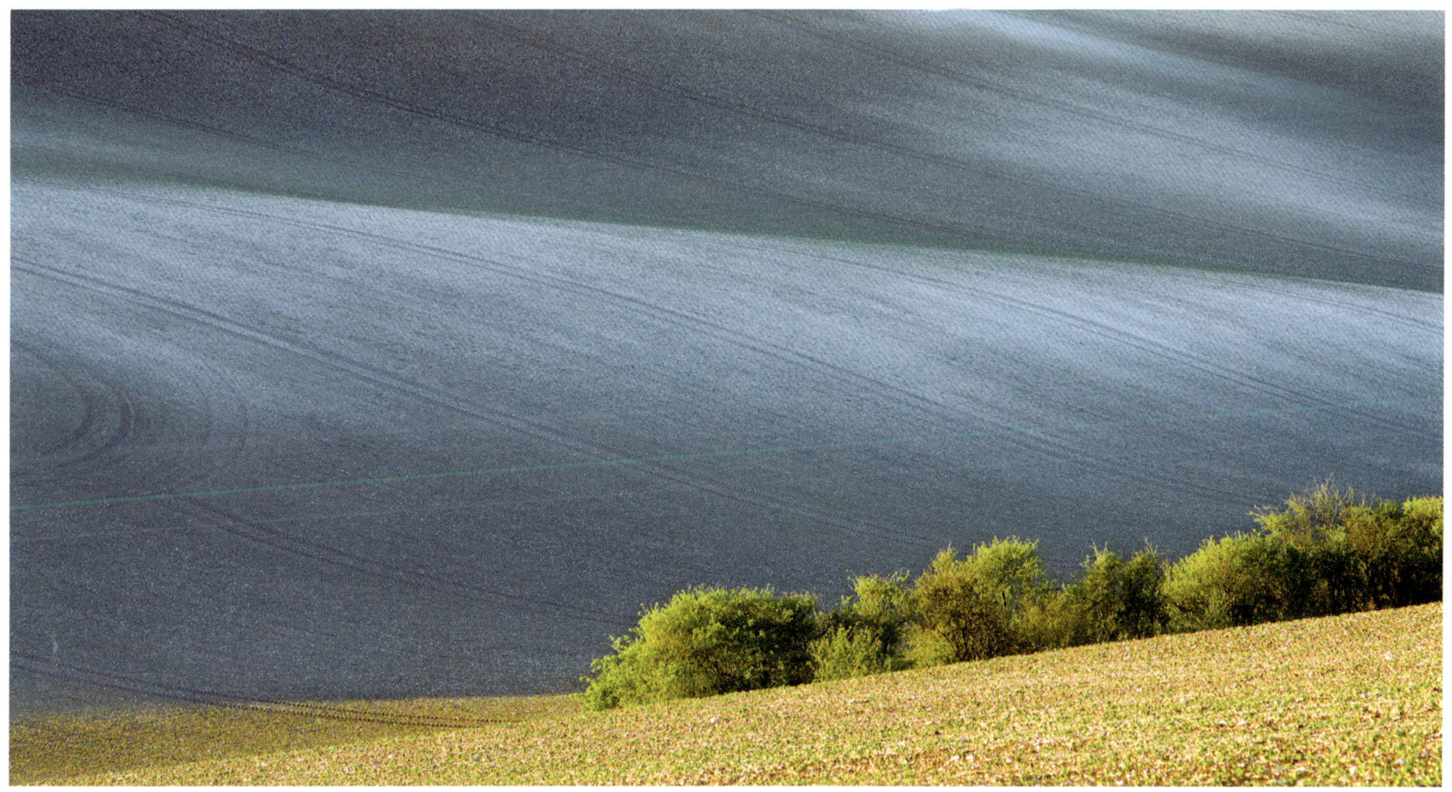

Frost on the bare fields at Starveall

Starveall at Sunrise

An interesting side of landscape photography is revisiting locations to see them in a new light. A change of weather, season or simply the passage of time can prompt a fresh approach – which is why I've continued to make occasional visits to some of my favourite locations for over twenty years.

I first visited Starveall in early April and captured a panoramic view of the landscape just before sunset (pages 12-13). I returned at sunrise on a frosty morning in May when the fields were still bare but the trees and bushes were coming into leaf. On this occasion I opted for a very different composition by using a telephoto lens to isolate a small section of the landscape. The image is slightly abstract – the foreground is warm and sun-lit while the background, still in shadow, remains frosted.

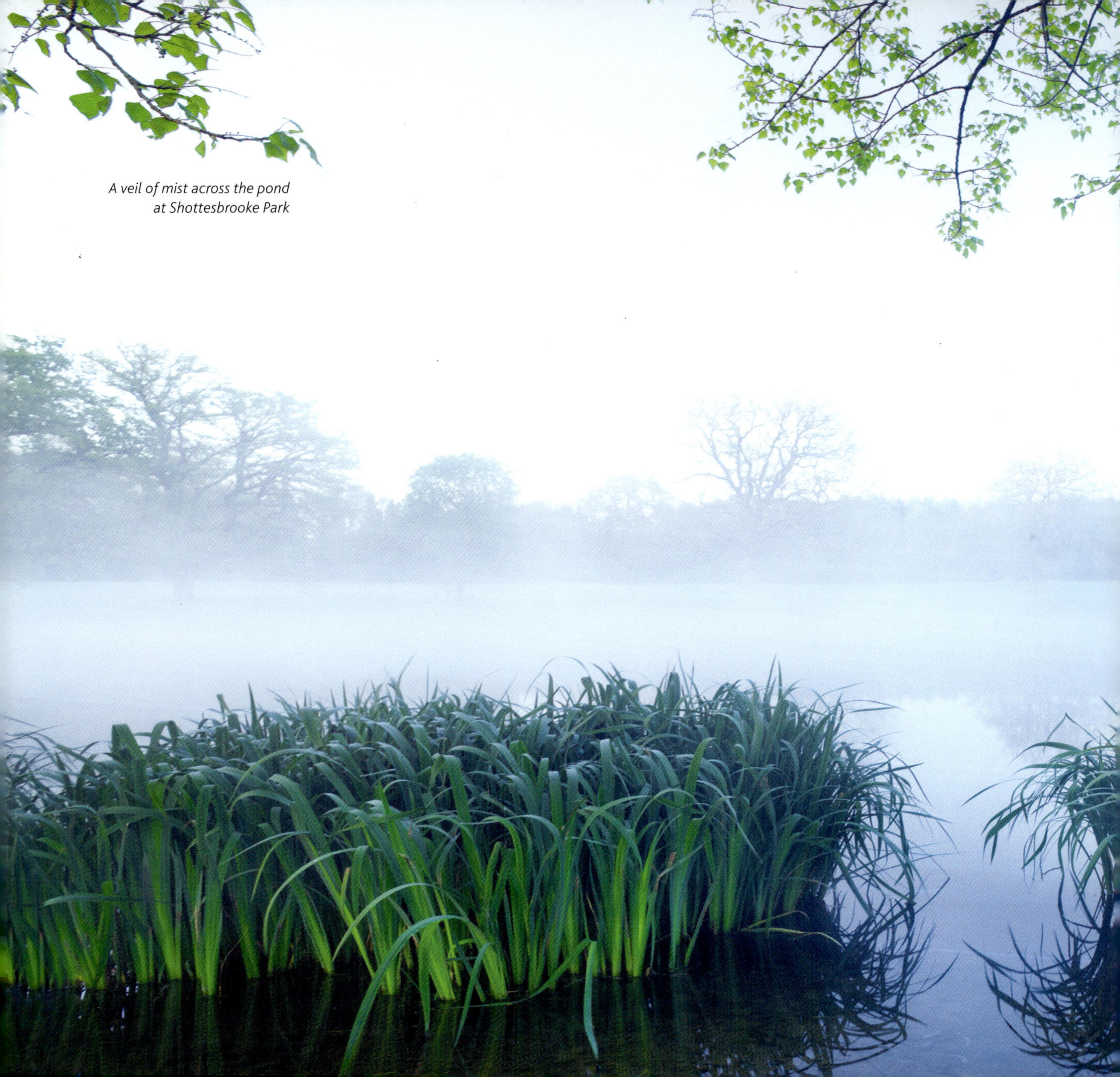

A veil of mist across the pond at Shottesbrooke Park

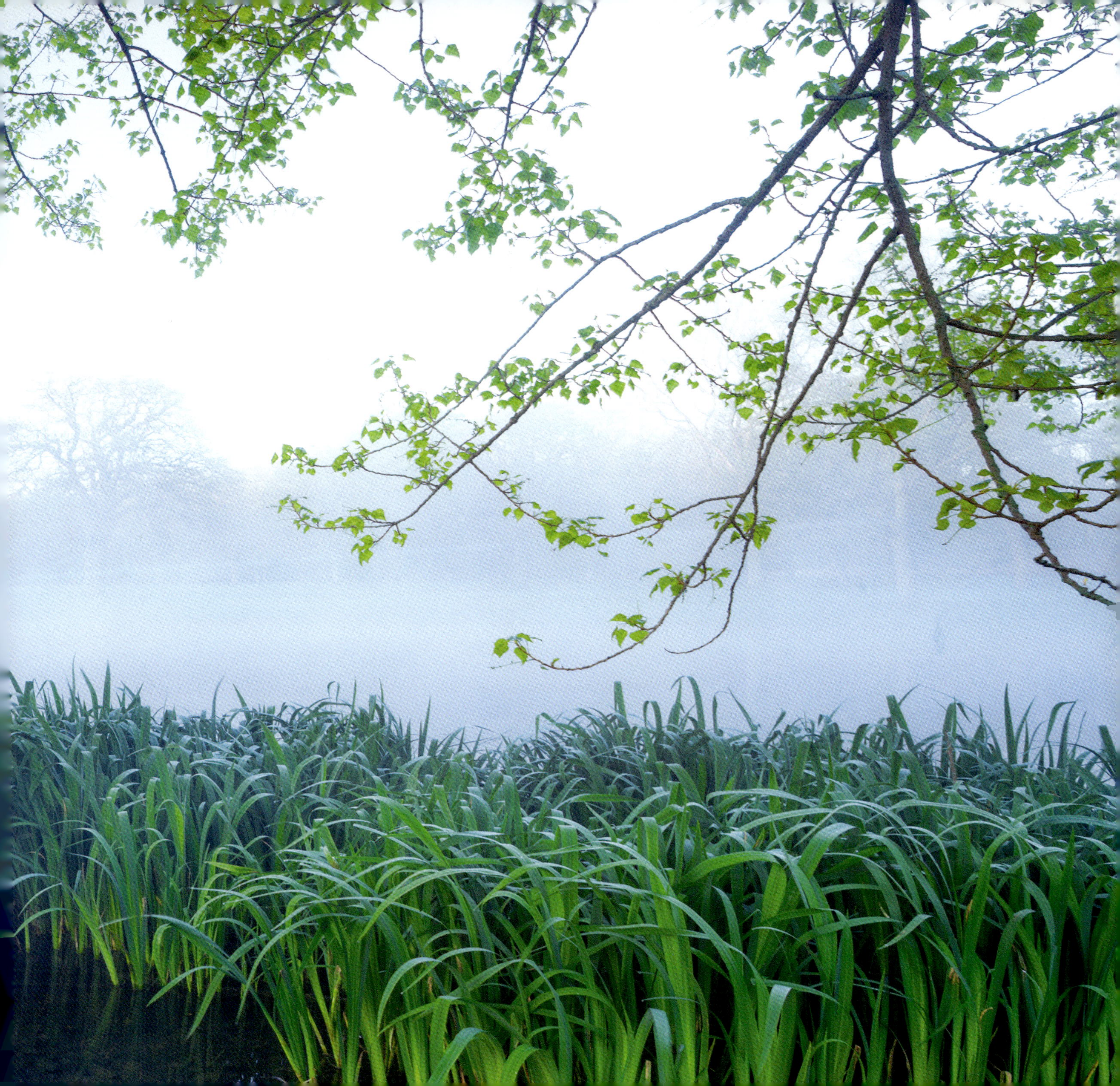

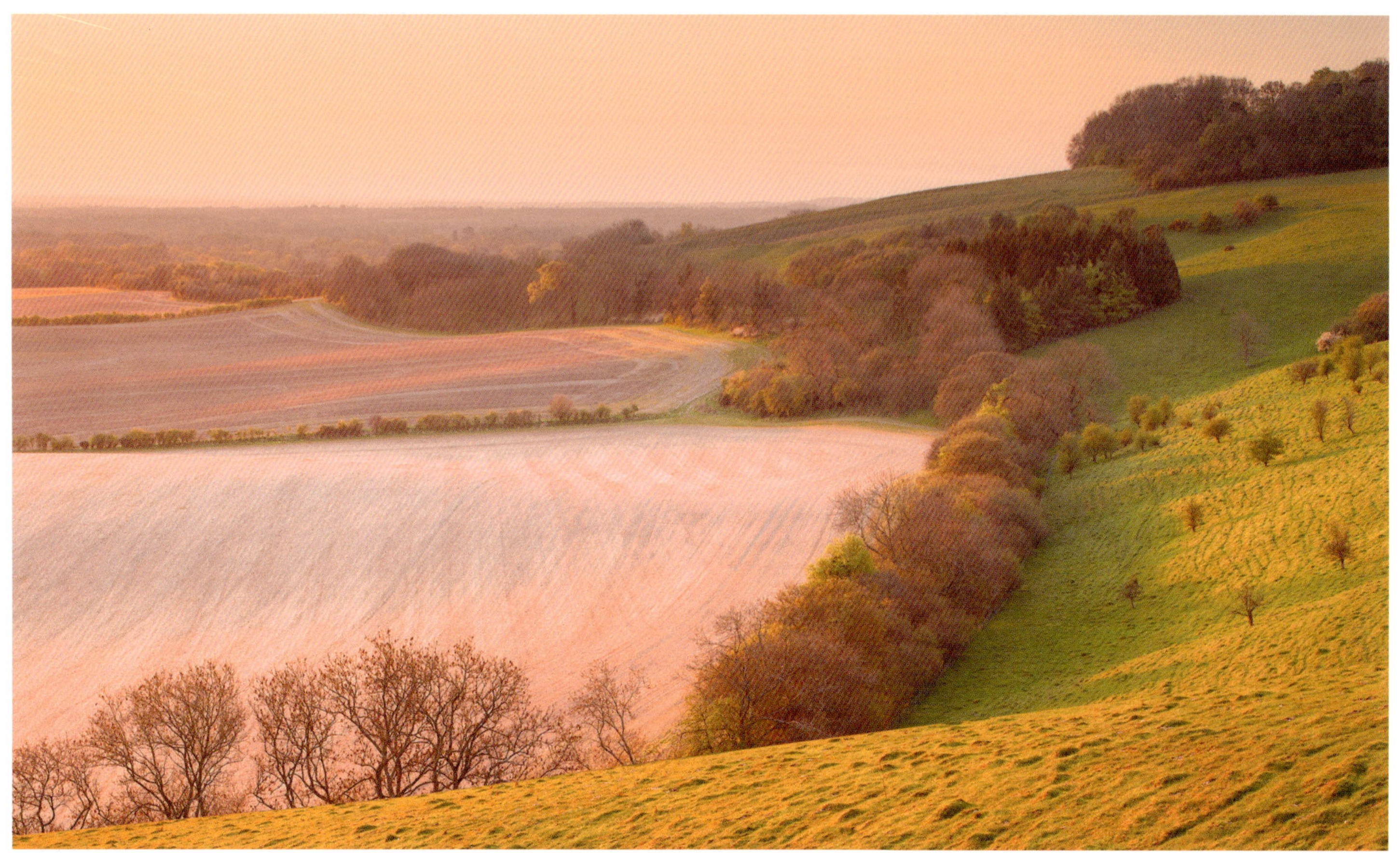

Red kite territory on West Woodhay Down

Sunrise over West Woodhay Down

This image shows the view looking due east across the rough chalk grassland of West Woodhay Down. Lined with ash, and scattered with a few wind-blown hawthorns, the sweeping landscape is an ideal place to enjoy a sunrise. And like many parts of rural Berkshire, the down has once again become a haunt for red kites, which are often seen wheeling and turning in the skies above.

These impressive birds were wiped out in England in the nineteenth century, but have staged a comeback following re-introductions in the last twenty-five years – the programmes have been so successful that the RSPB is no longer able to survey the numbers on an annual basis.

Deer in Windsor Great Park

Historically, the land in Windsor Great Park was shared by both red and fallow deer, but this came to an end after the war when both species were removed. However, over thirty years later the reds made a return – the current herd originated in February 1979 when two stags and 40 hinds were introduced from Balmoral. The red population is now maintained at around 600 animals which roam freely among the ancient trees.

This image shows a small group picking their way across the Long Walk in the stretching shadows of horse chestnut and London plane trees.

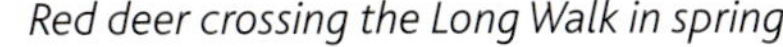

Red deer crossing the Long Walk in spring

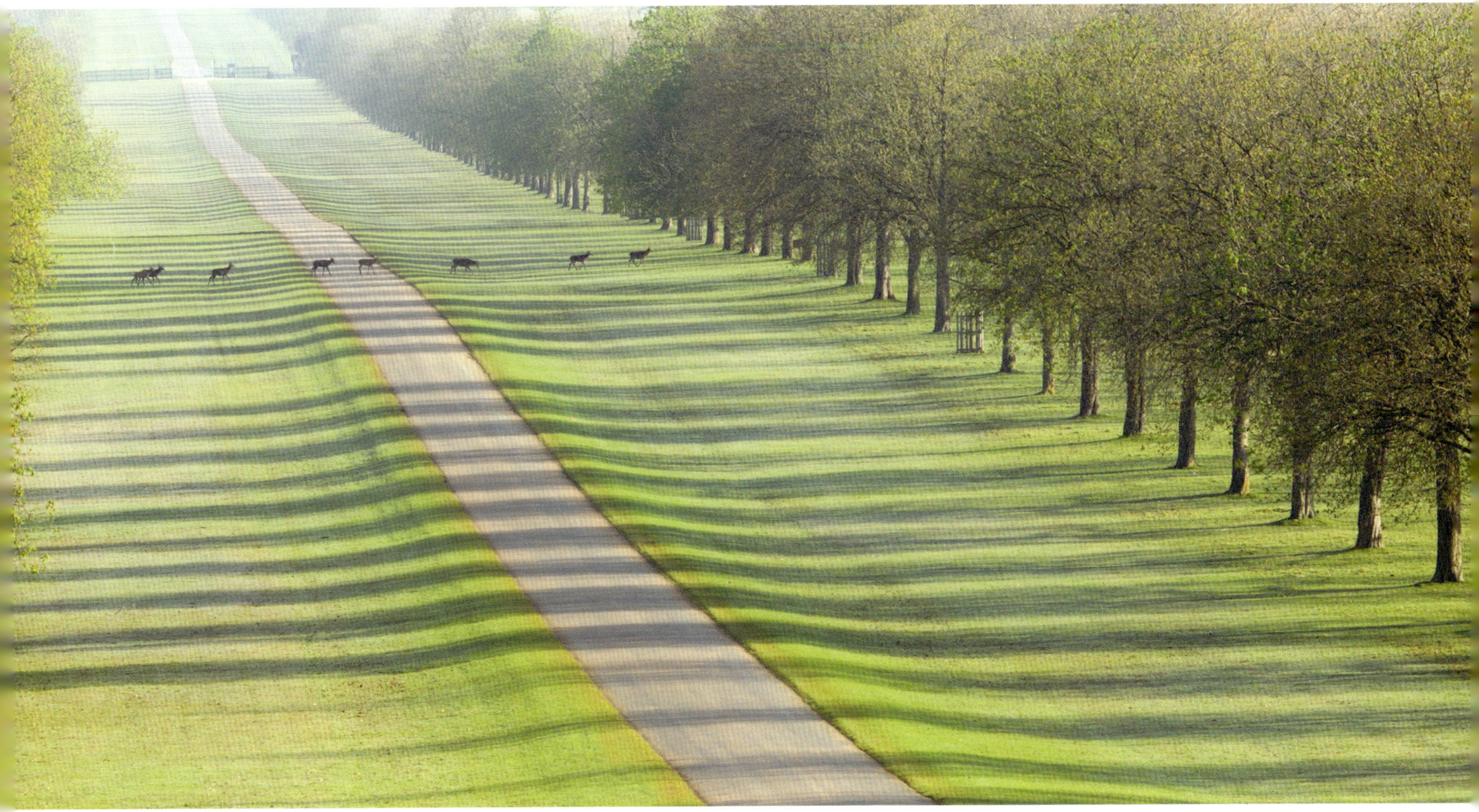

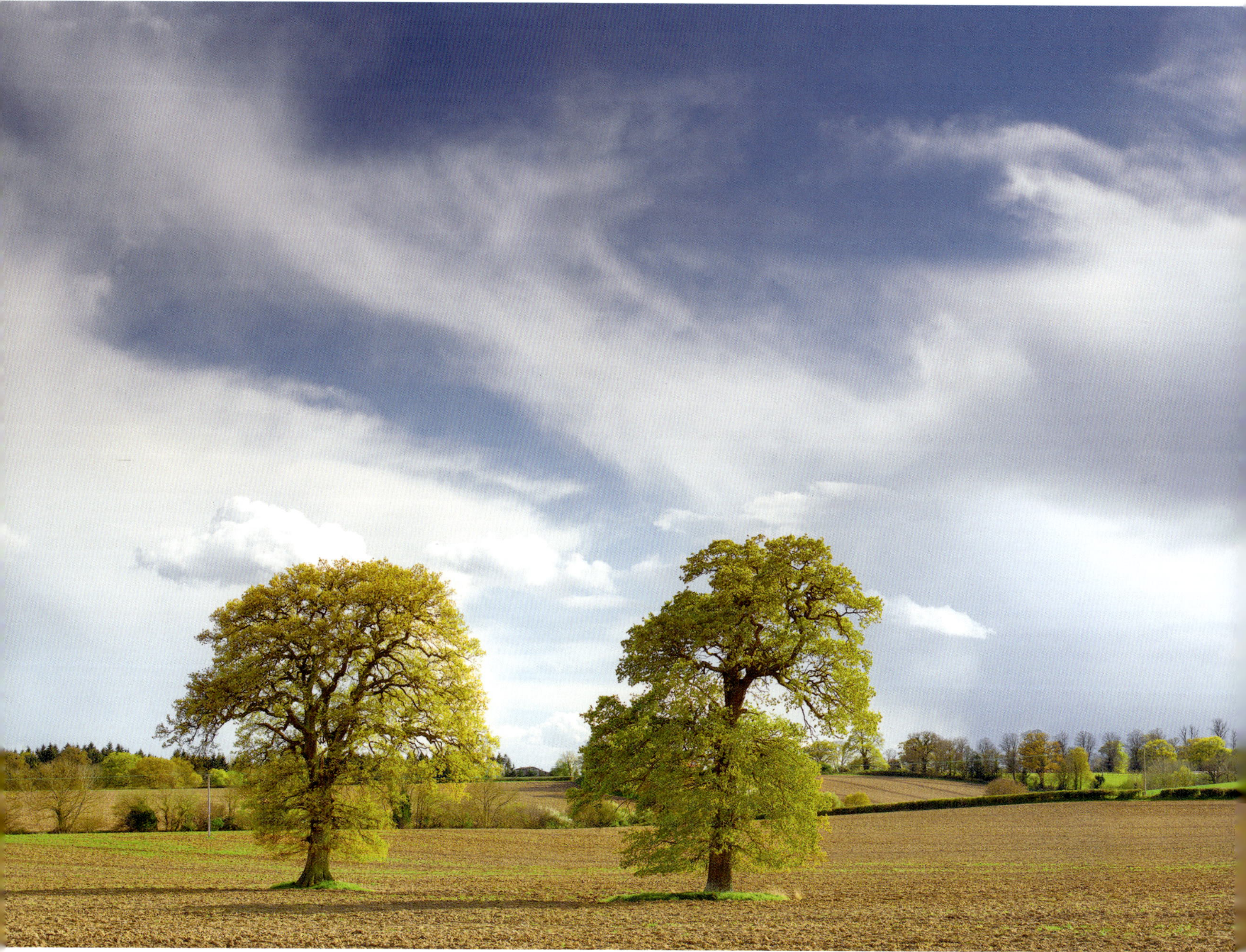

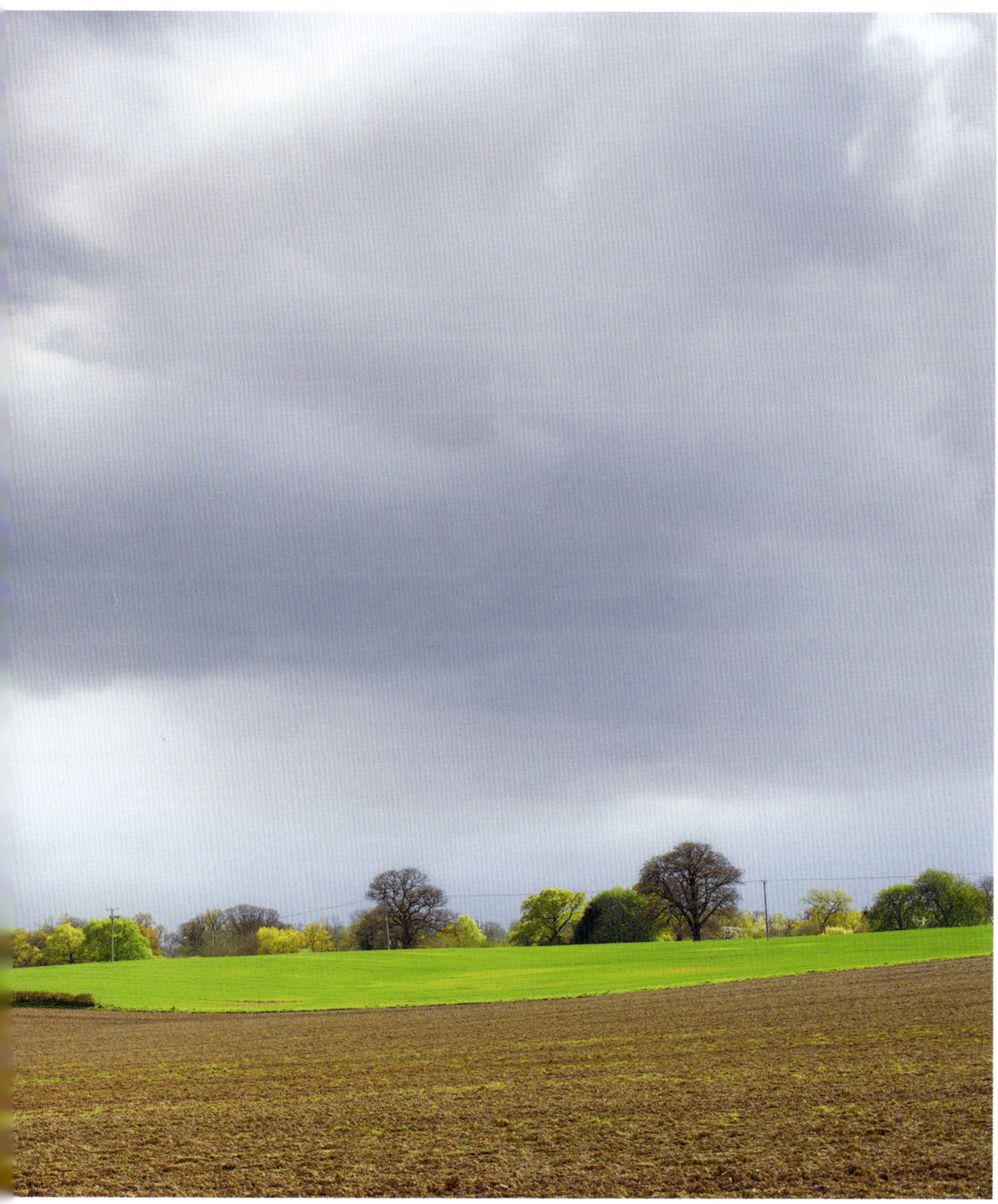

Wokefield Park near Mortimer

On the corner of the lane at Wokefield Park is a small stile which marks the start of a footpath to Mortimer. The route follows the edge of a large field – a fine open space, and a splendid westerly view for those who live in the local cottages. The focal point of this stretch of landscape is a group of three oaks which stand in the centre of the field in a north-south line.

I first visited the place in the wet January of 2016; the field had only recently been ploughed and the whole area was saturated by the persistent rains. Three months later the scene was very different – spring had come, the ground had dried and the oaks looked pristine in their fresh foliage. It was a day of April showers, although none of these had actually reached Wokefield Park when I captured this view showing the two largest of the three oaks.

April sky over the landscape at Wokefield Park

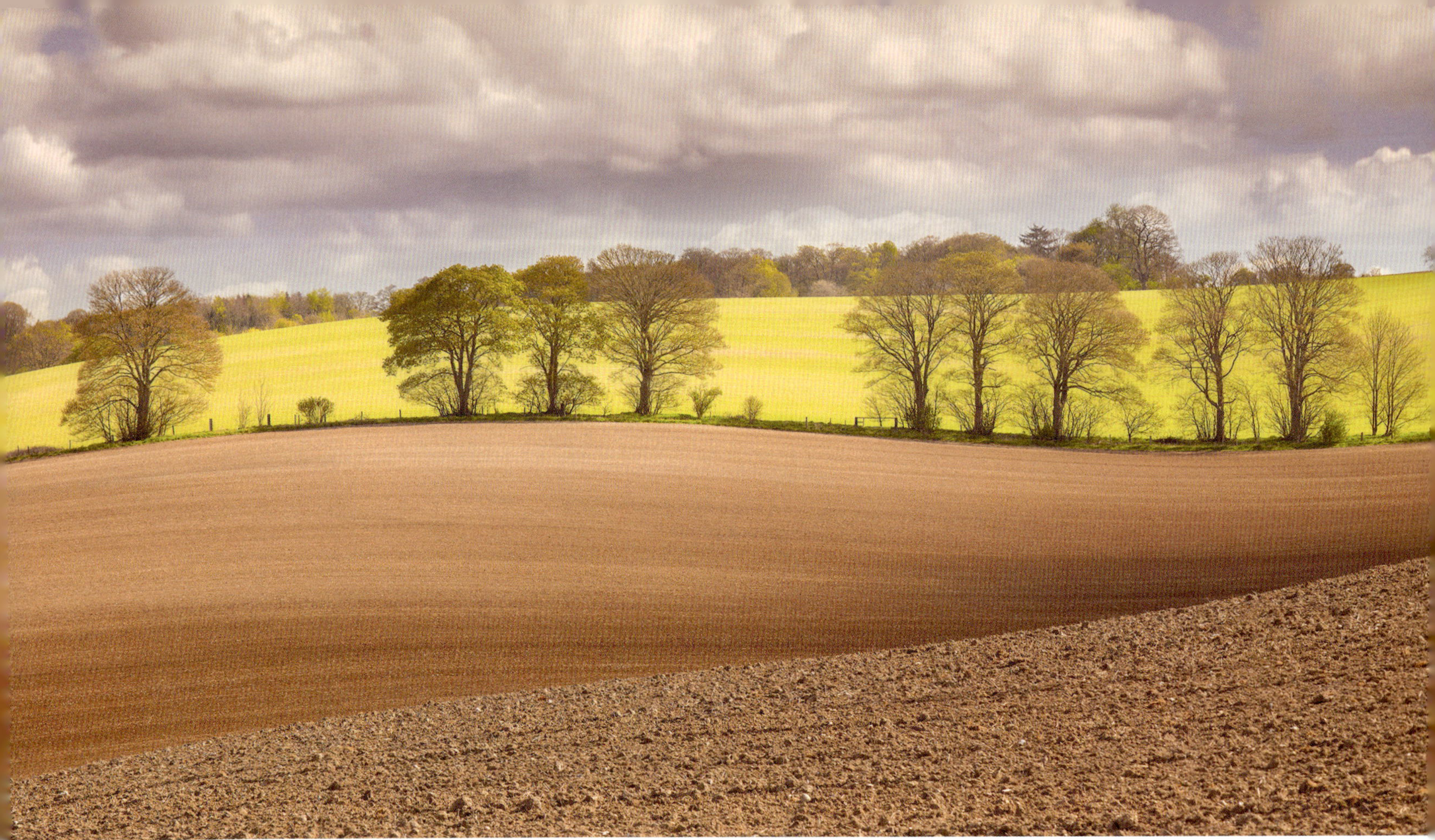

Sycamores in the rolling landscape near Chaddleworth

Landscape near Chaddleworth

The historic village of Chaddleworth lies on the Berkshire Downs between Brightwalton and Great Shefford; it was recorded in the Domesday Book and has a church which dates from the late twelfth century.

The surrounding landscape consists mostly of open farmland, although there is a lovely stretch of parkland adjoining Chaddleworth House, and a sizeable copse known as Spray Wood to the north-east.

This graceful line of trees can be glimpsed from the lane which turns north-west out of the village. The route takes two sharp bends before dropping down the hillside above Manor Farm – the trees come into view part-way down, beyond a pleasantly rolling field which was newly ploughed when this photograph was taken.

World's End

This solitary oak tree stands to the west of the curiously-named hamlet of World's End near Beedon. It had just come into leaf when this photograph was taken, and its pale new foliage was tinted yellow by the late evening sunlight.

The scene is mellow and pastoral, but also a little unusual because the heaps of golden straw in the foreground suggest the season is late summer rather than early spring. However, the crop is not what it seems – it turns out that this is a species of miscanthus, commonly called 'elephant grass', which can reach 10ft in height and is now being grown as a biomass crop; it is left standing in the field over winter and harvested in early spring.

An unusual spring harvest at World's End

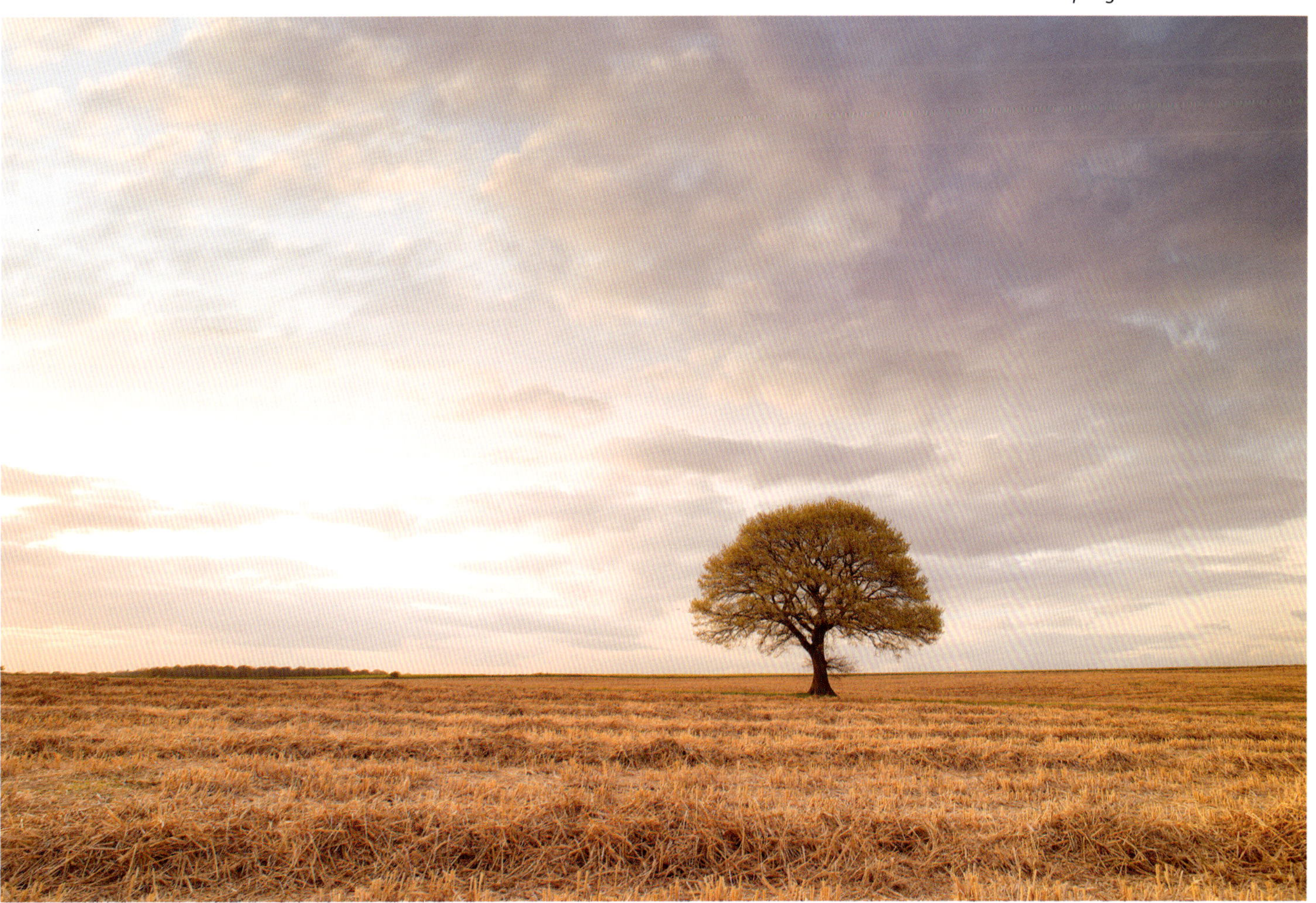

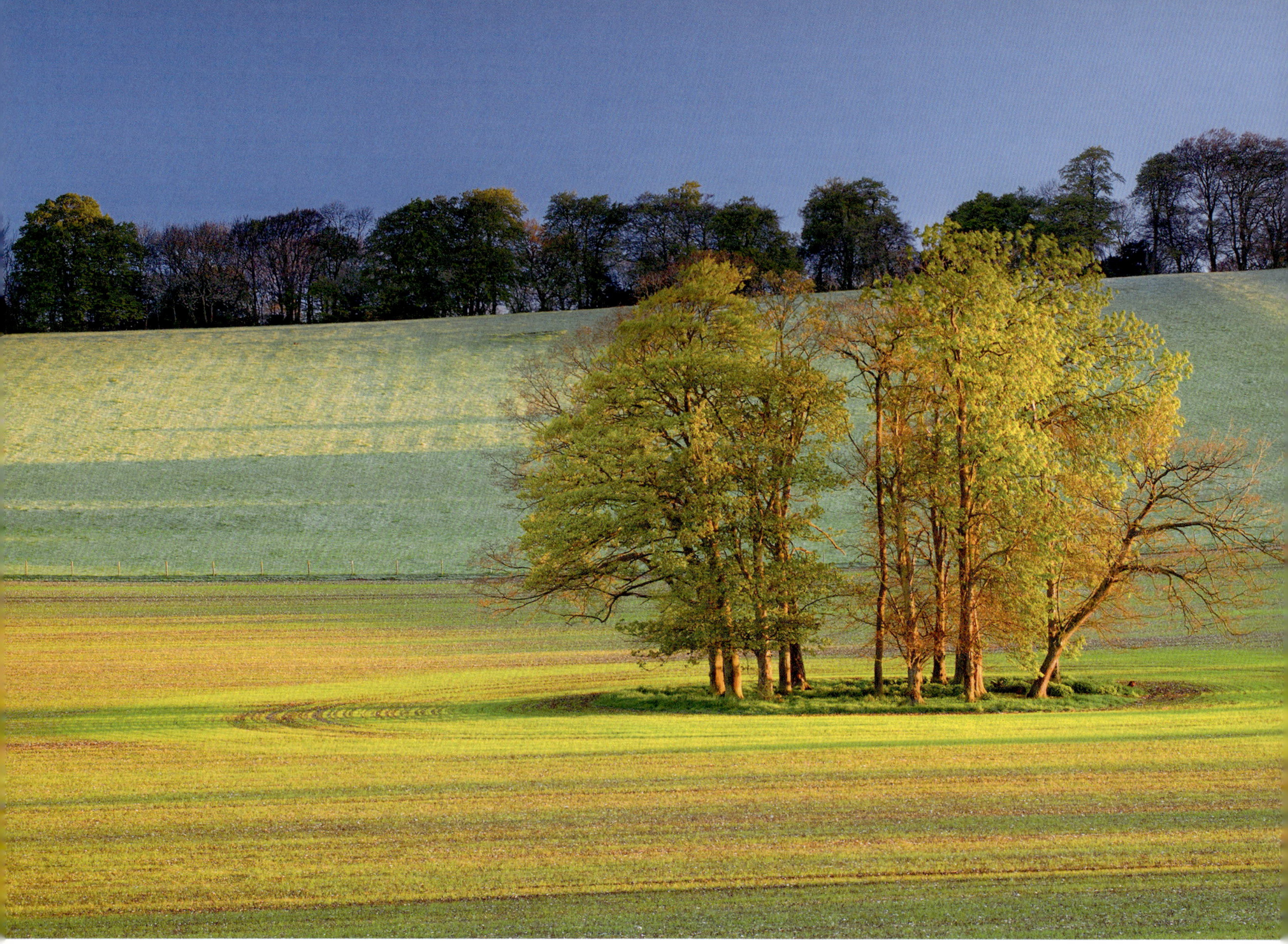

Thurle Down

On a westerly route The Ridgeway enters Berkshire at Streatley, and within a mile it reaches the dry valley below Thurle Down. This quiet area is a beautiful place to walk, overlooking wide undulating fields dotted with islands of trees. Where the by-way leaves the lane a signpost points to Overton Hill, 41 miles away at the western end of the trail.

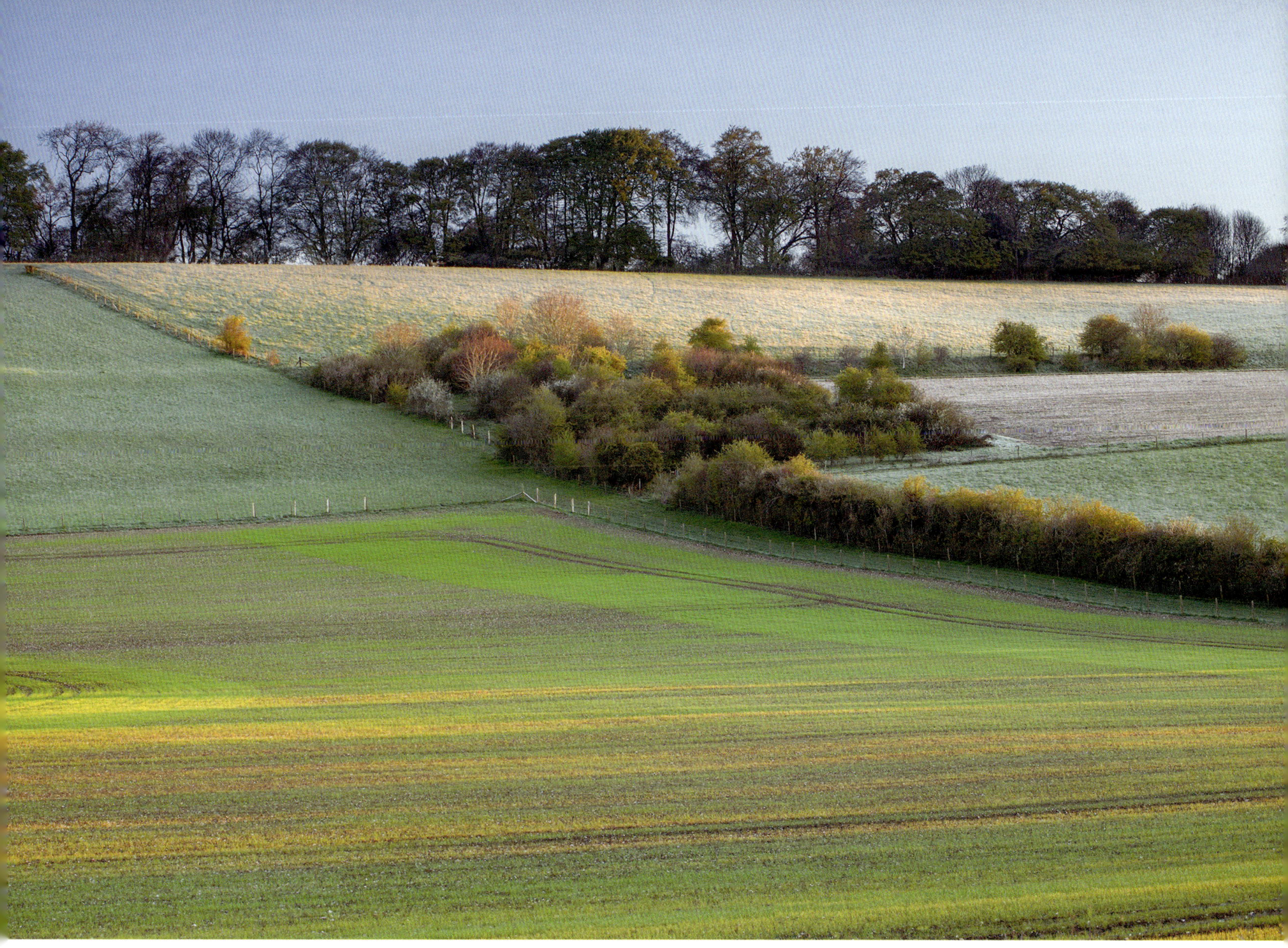

Daybreak at Thurle Down

Ascending Thurle Down, the route is lined with trees which, when in leaf, tend to screen the views except for a few gaps here and there. But higher up the trees give way to grassy banks (brimming with knapweed in summer) and wide views open up to the south. The track eventually reaches a highpoint near Warren Farm and then leads on to the downs of Roden and Blewbury.

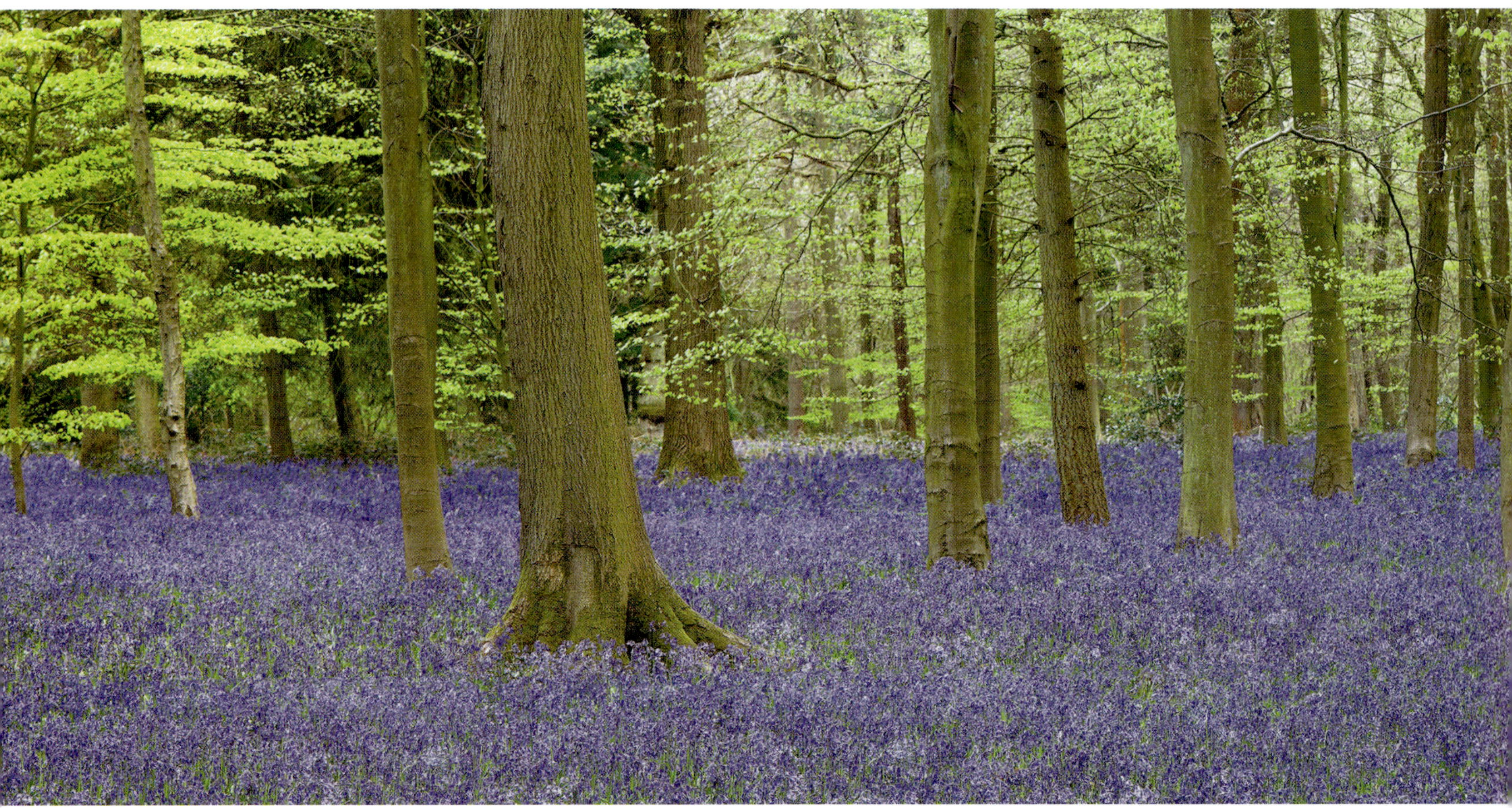

Springtime in Portobello Wood

Portobello Wood near Aldworth

This carpet of bluebells can be seen in Portobello Wood, one of the many quiet copses between Ashampstead and Aldworth. The area is a hot-bed for these flowers, as anyone who's travelled this way in late April will know. Some of the best displays are alongside Grim's Ditch which passes through the area from east to west.

The use of the name 'Portobello' at this location is intriguing, given that the word originates from 'Puerto Bello' meaning 'Beautiful Port'. Of course, the name is usually associated with the busy street market in London, or the coastal suburb of Edinburgh – but exactly how it came to be used in this quiet corner of Berkshire remains a mystery.

Cowslips at Pinkneys Green

The show of cowslips on the common at Pinkneys Green is probably the most extensive in Berkshire, covering many acres of flat grassland with the occasional oak tree towering above. The deep yellow flower heads hang on stalks about 6 inches high and last from April to May; the display is then followed by ox-eye daisies and a host of other wild flowers which crowd the long grasses throughout the summer.

The site is cared for by the National Trust as one of a number of local landscapes known as the Maidenhead and Cookham Commons. The land here has almost certainly never been ploughed but instead has been maintained as natural grassland with occasional grazing over the centuries. The Trust now cuts the meadow for hay in late summer, a practice which encourages the distribution of seed for the following year.

Cowslips are the first of many wild flowers on the common at Pinkneys Green

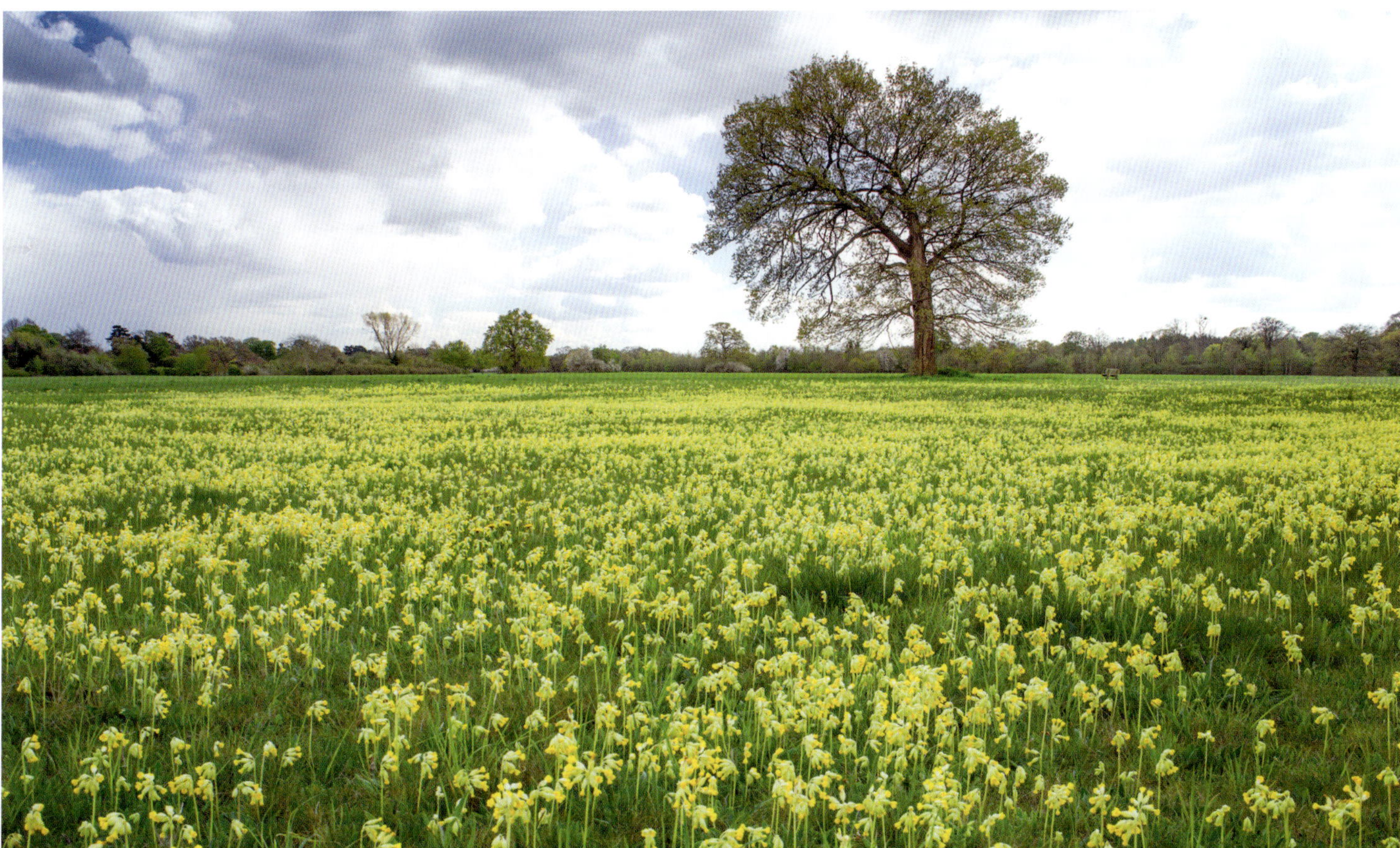

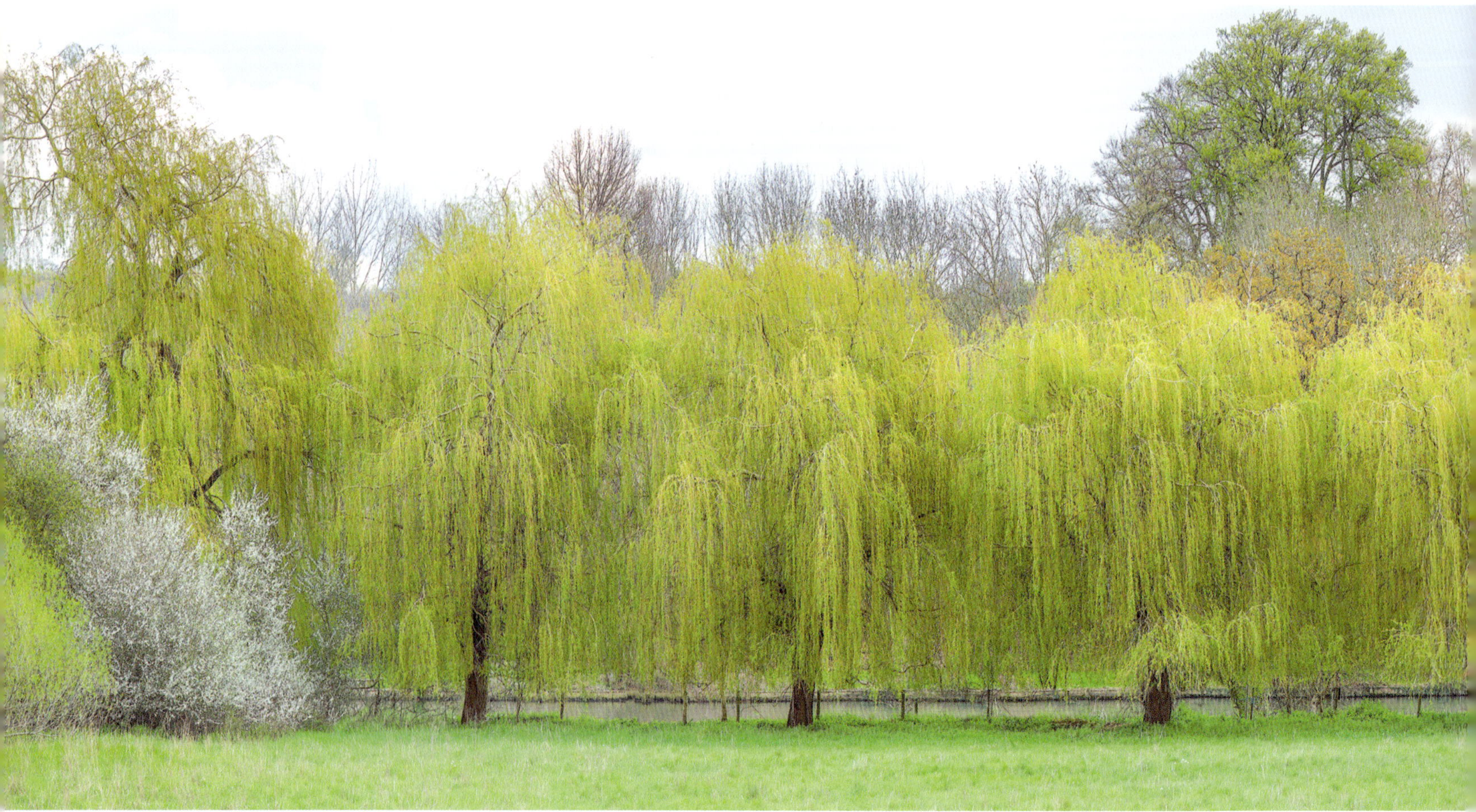

Willows at Pangbourne

This line of weeping willows can be seen from the road which approaches Pangbourne from the west. They could easily be overlooked in any other season, but on this morning in late April they seemed to make a luxuriant spectacle, framed by blackthorn blossom to the left and a fresh-leaved beech tree to the right. The river is just visible in the background but the angle of view makes it look quite narrow – it is in fact around 100 yards across at this point. The calm conditions were ideal for this photograph, keeping the pendulous stems motionless in the soft light of early morning. The trees are part of a larger group of willows which run alongside the Thames towards the village.

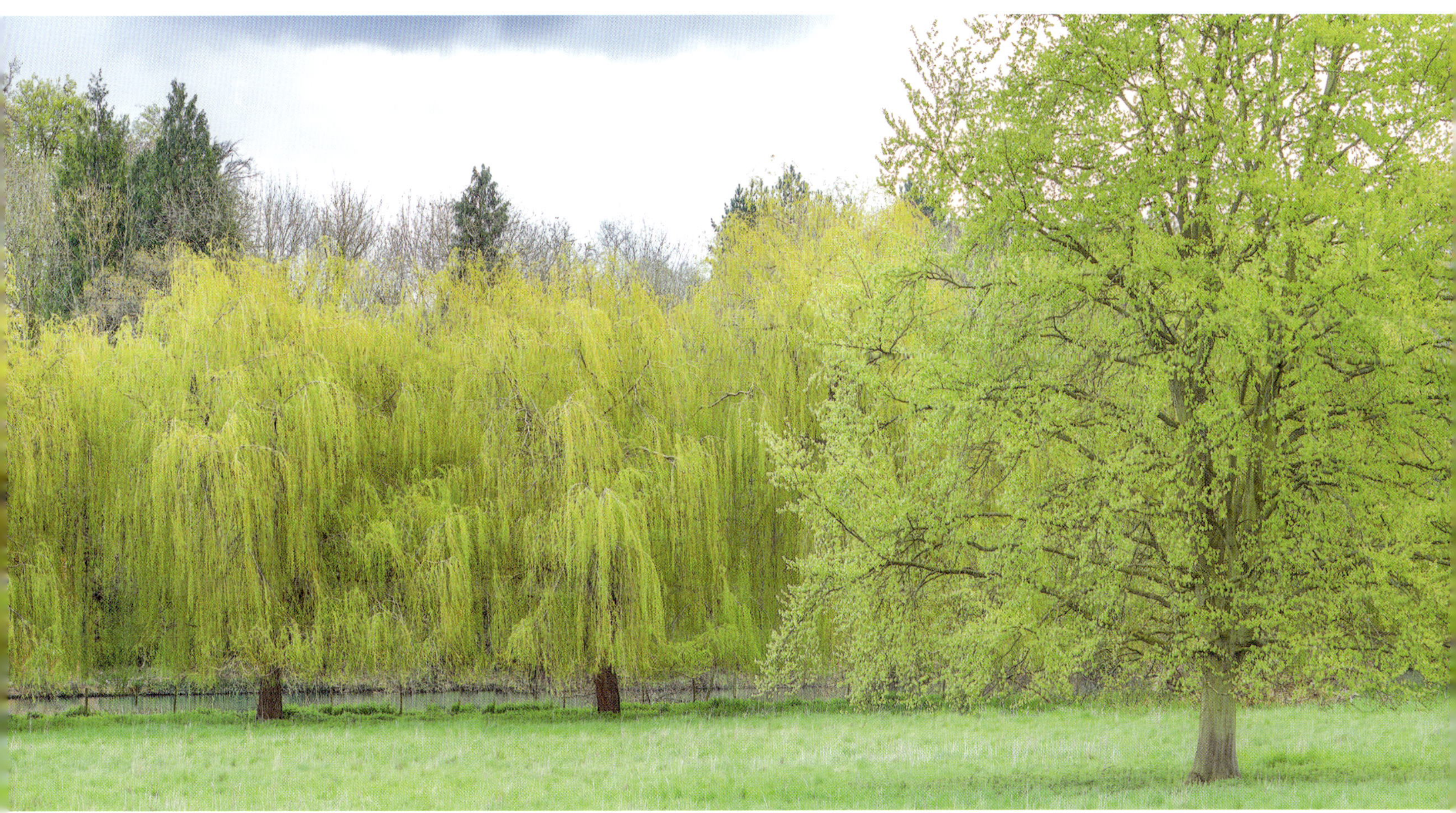

Weeping willows in a meadow by the Thames

It was only after taking this photograph that I learned of the area's association with Kenneth Grahame, author of ***The Wind in the Willows***, who retired to Church Cottage in Pangbourne in 1924. The local scenery is also believed to have been the inspiration for E. H. Shepherd's illustrations used in the book.

Spring Landscape at Boxford

Trees make an engaging subject when they're back-lit, especially in spring when the light filters through their translucent new foliage. These poplars near Boxford were just coming into leaf when I photographed them in early May – an elevated viewpoint made it possible to include their lengthening shadows in the foreground. Late afternoon sunlight and wonderfully clear air helped to render the sharp outlines of the vertical trunks – a close look reveals that some of the trees are more advanced, with leaves that are greener and darker than the rest.

Poplar trees coming into leaf at Boxford

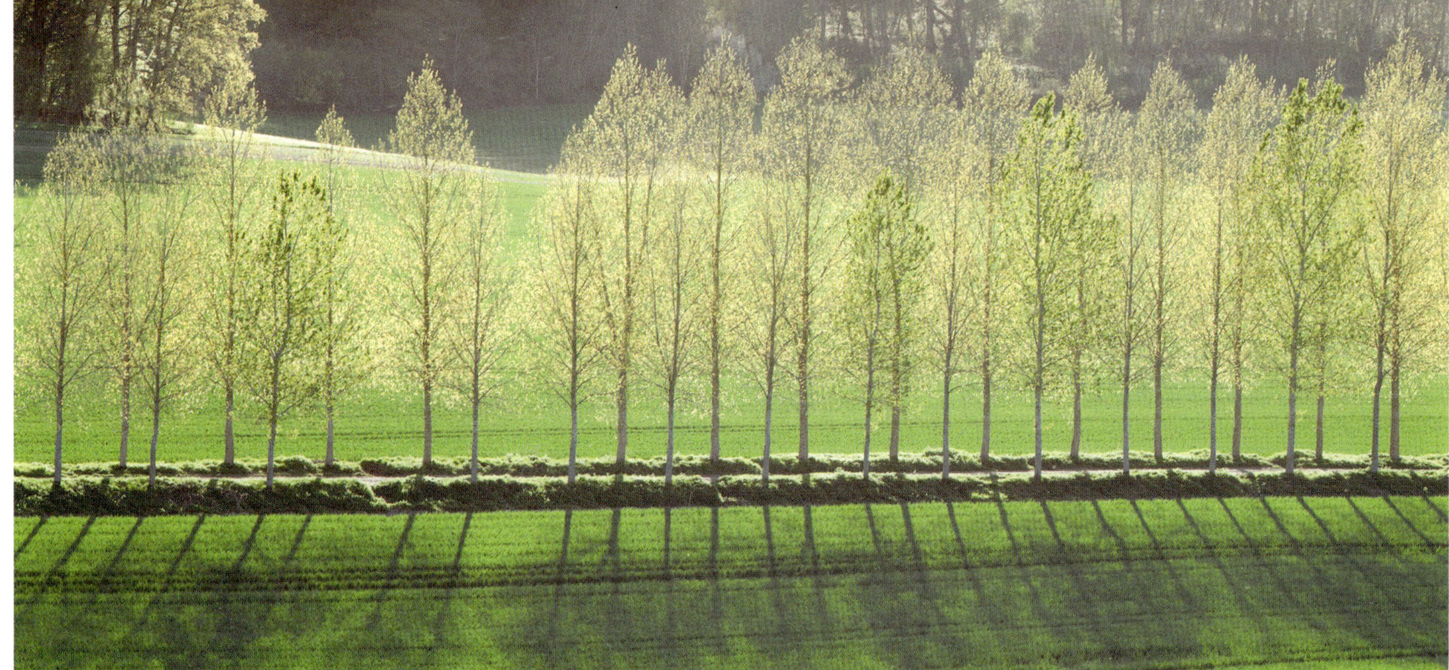

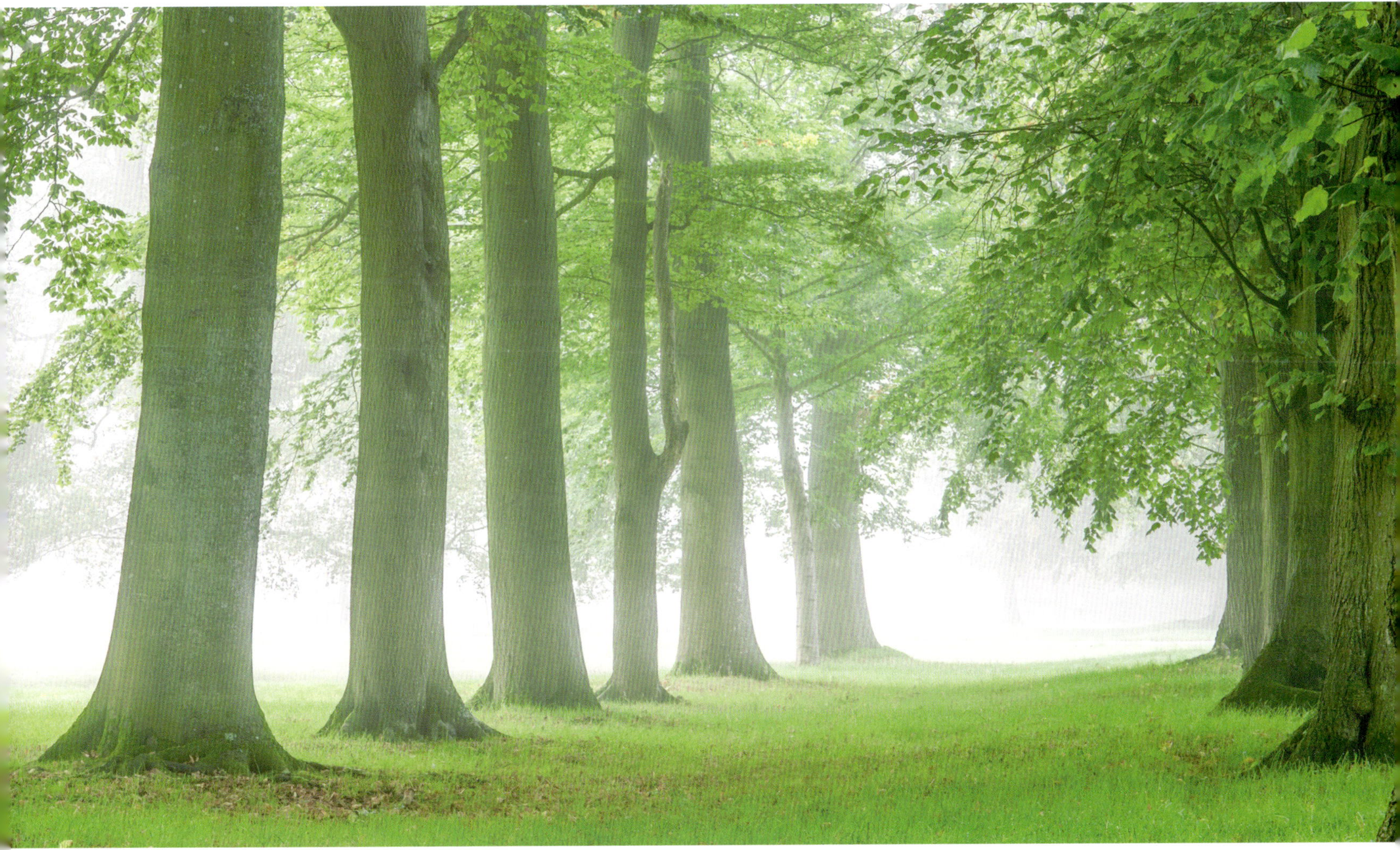

Spring foliage on the east side of the avenue at Hamstead Park

Tree-lined Avenue at Hamstead Park

The avenue which leads into Hamstead Park is bordered by lime trees for part of its length, ending at the brow of a small hill where the main house comes into view. This kind of tree-lined approach is not uncommon on large estates, but what makes this one slightly unusual is that a second row of trees have been planted on either side, creating a double line. Interestingly, the second row is made up of beech rather than lime, adding an extra dimension to this woody spectacle.

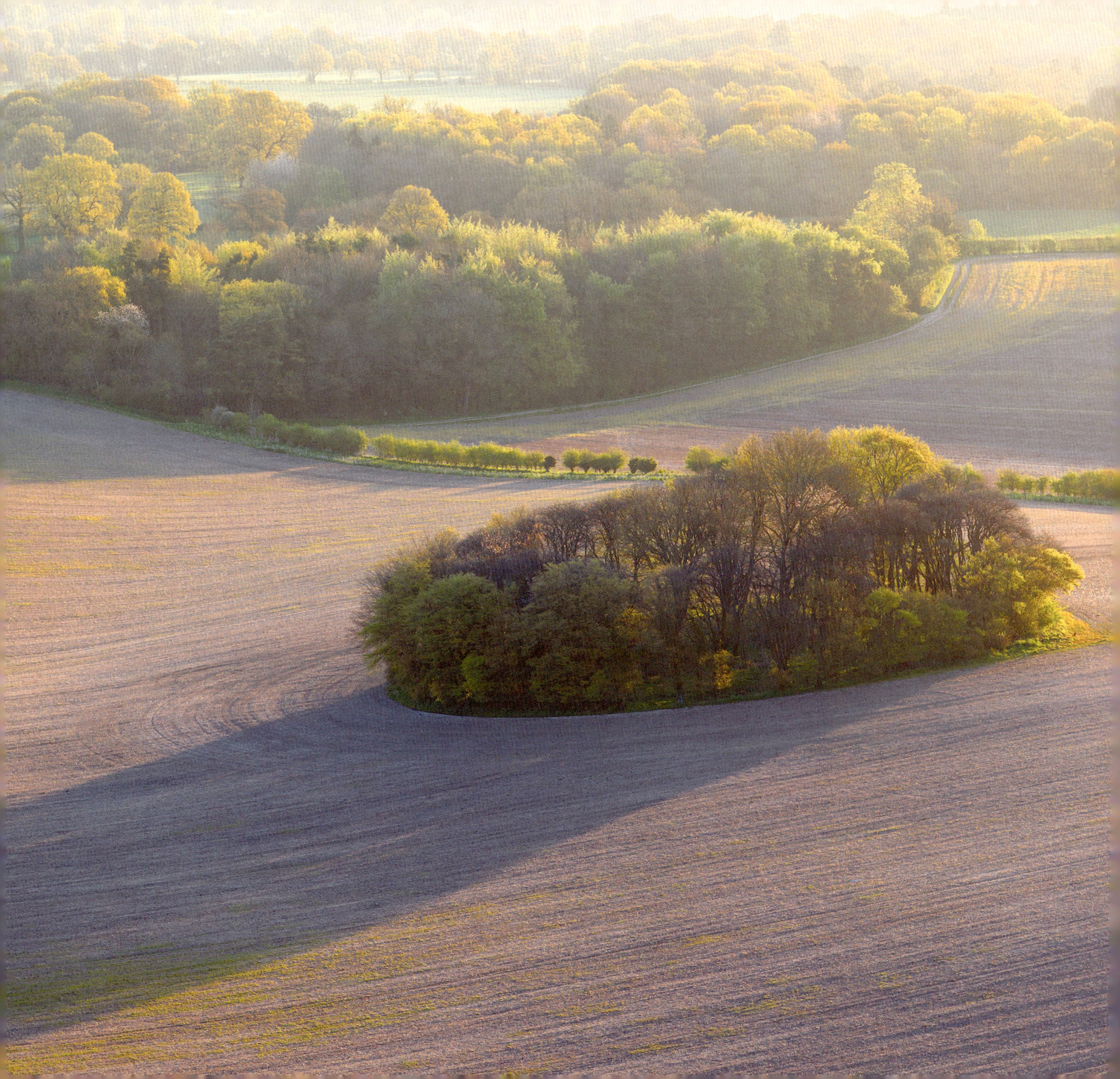

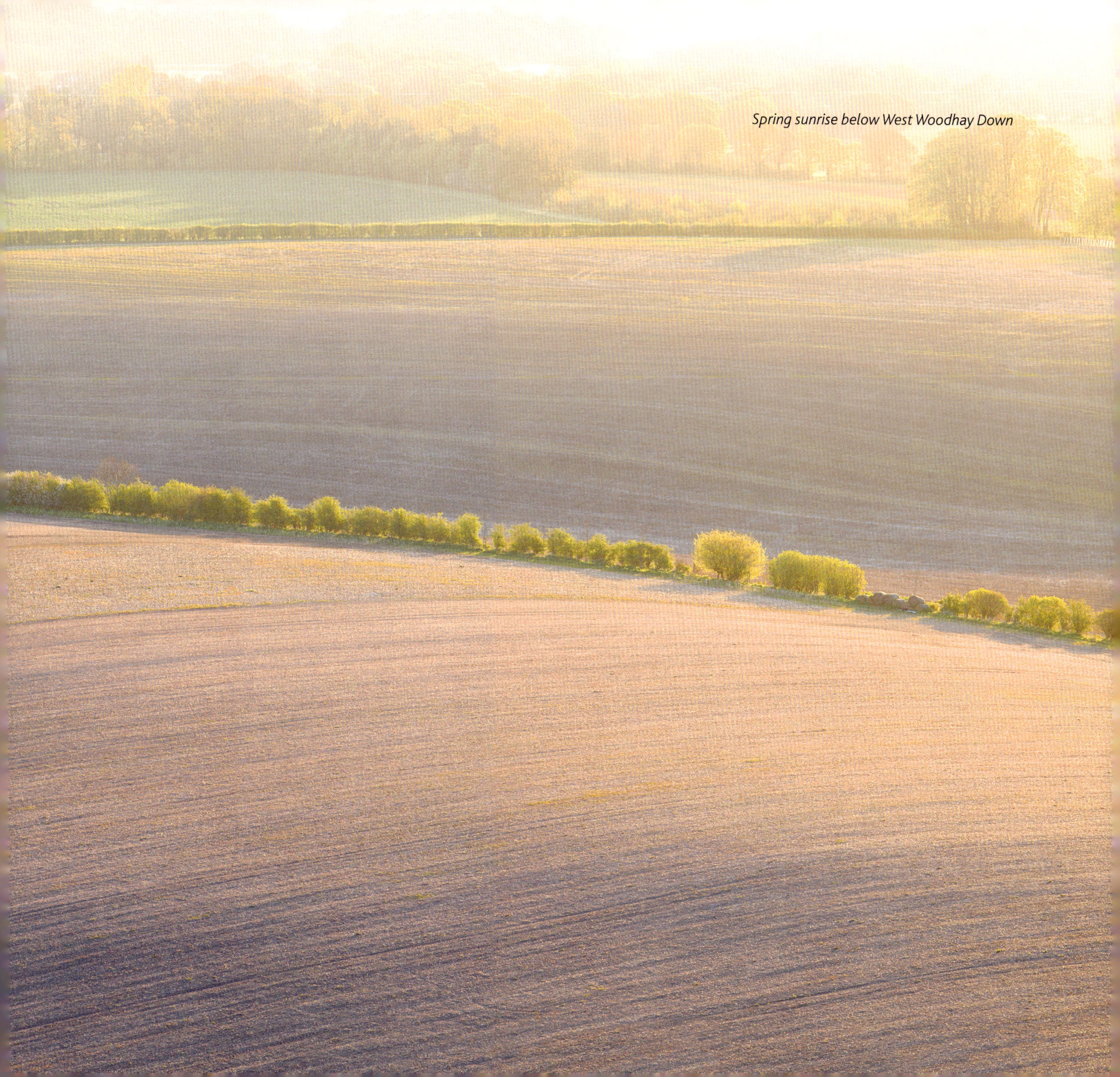

Spring sunrise below West Woodhay Down

SUMMER

Poppy Crops
Oriental poppies have been commercially grown in many parts of England in recent years, and Berkshire is no exception. This field at Haw Farm near Hampstead Norreys, bordered by the footpath to Ashampstead, was in full flower when I came across it on a June morning. Without an obvious focal point, the tram-lines running through the field became an important part of the composition, adding a sense of depth to the endless mass of flowers.

Grown for their seed, these alien plants draw mixed opinions from country-lovers, but it has to be said that they make an eye-catching feature in the midsummer landscape.

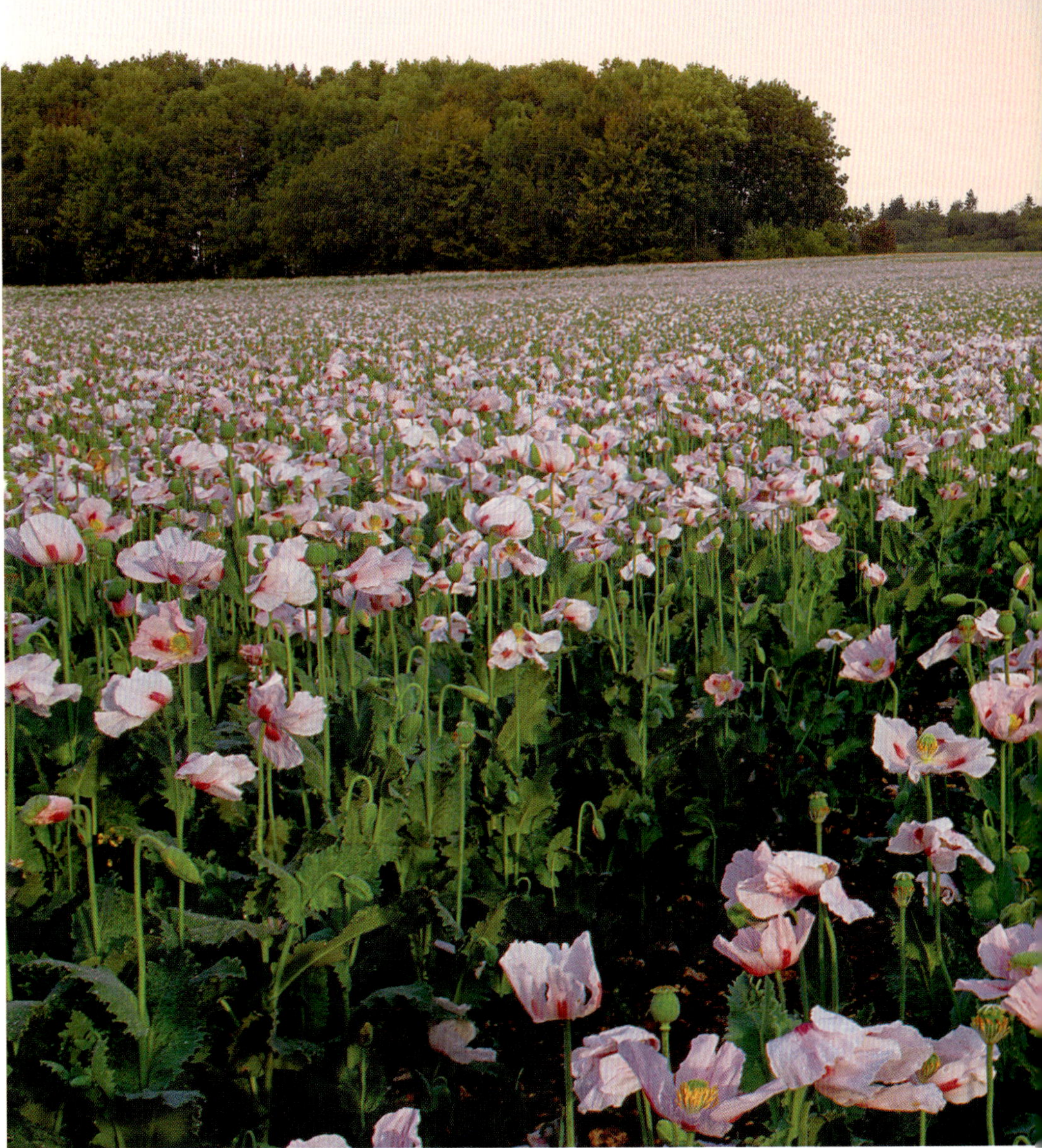

A sea of alien poppies near Hampstead Norreys

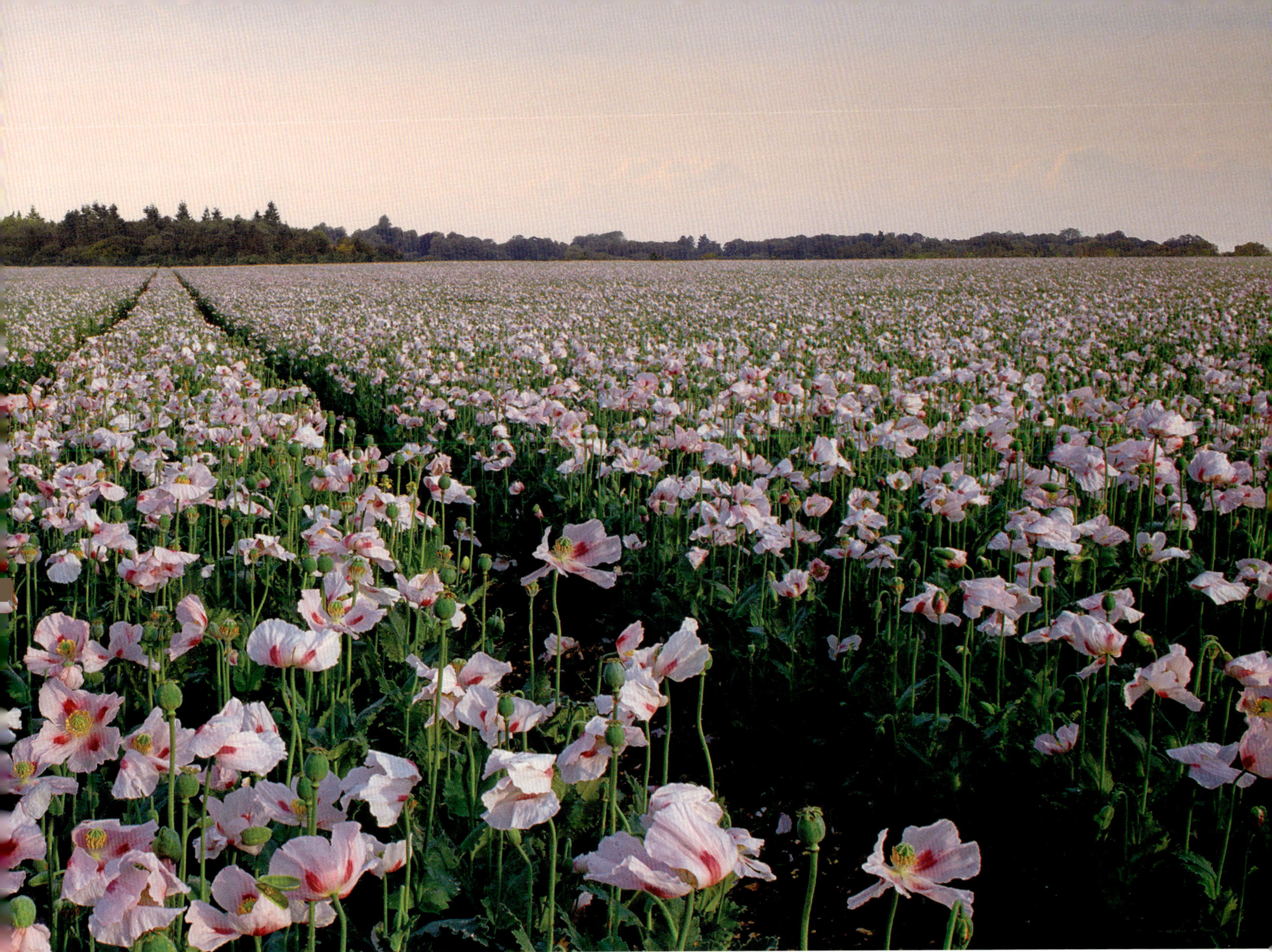

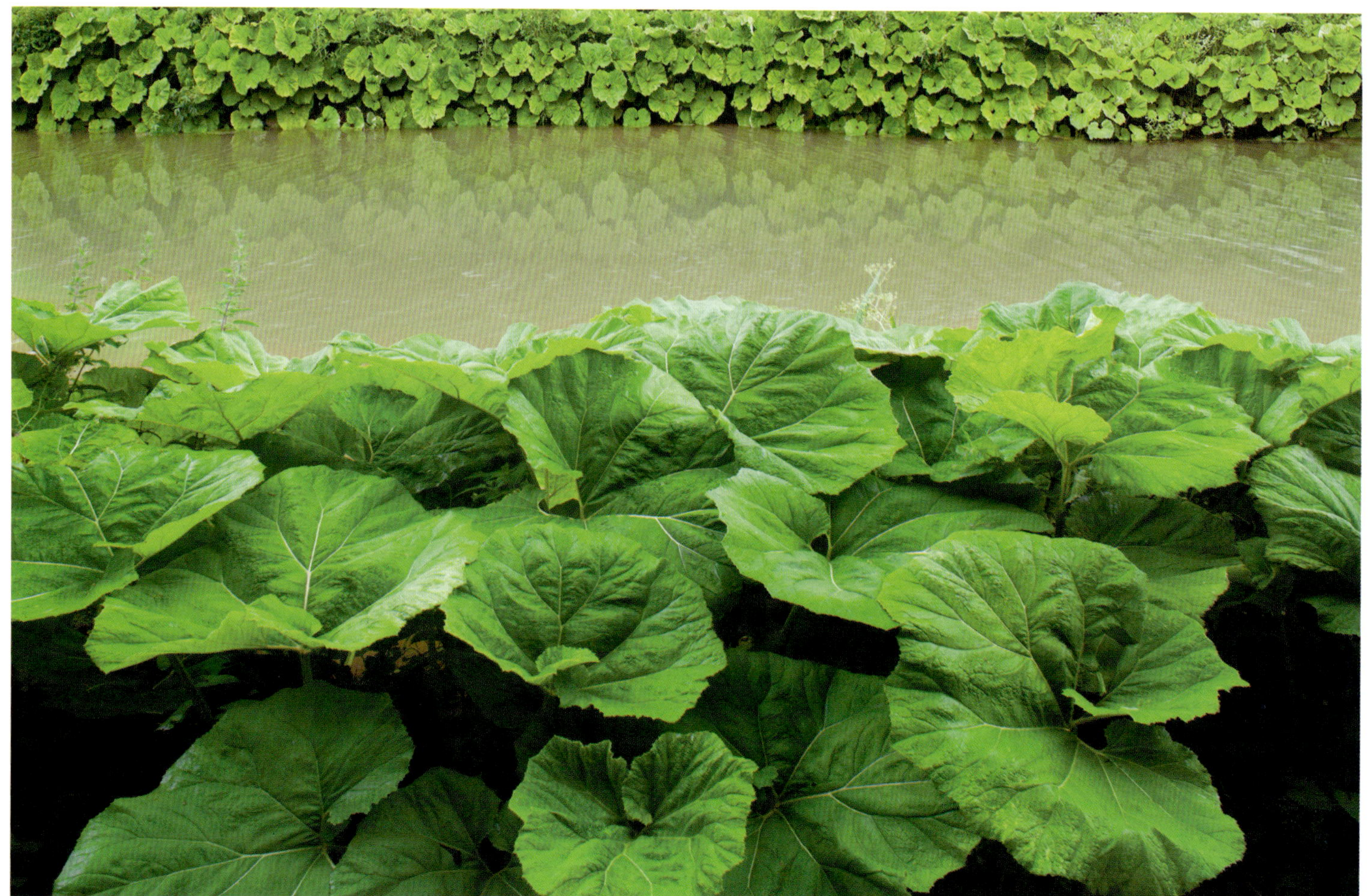

Banks of butterbur leaves near Hungerford

Butterbur on the Kennet and Avon Canal

By late June the banks of the Kennet and Avon Canal are thick with lush vegetation – some stretches are dominated by common reeds and cow parsley, while in other parts the giant-leaved butterbur takes over, cloaking the watersides with a dense green canopy. It's said that the leaves were once used to wrap butter, hence the name. This image shows part of the canal near Hungerford where it was only just possible to peer over the great mounds of foliage to the water beyond.

Borage

Among the green patchwork of England's summer landscape it's always refreshing to see the occasional swathe of borage. Growing here in the corner of a barley field, probably as a remnant from the previous year's crop, this patch of borage was in full bloom in early June. I had the good fortune to stumble across this scene on a misty morning when exploring the network of country lanes in West Berkshire.

Borage on the margin of a barley field

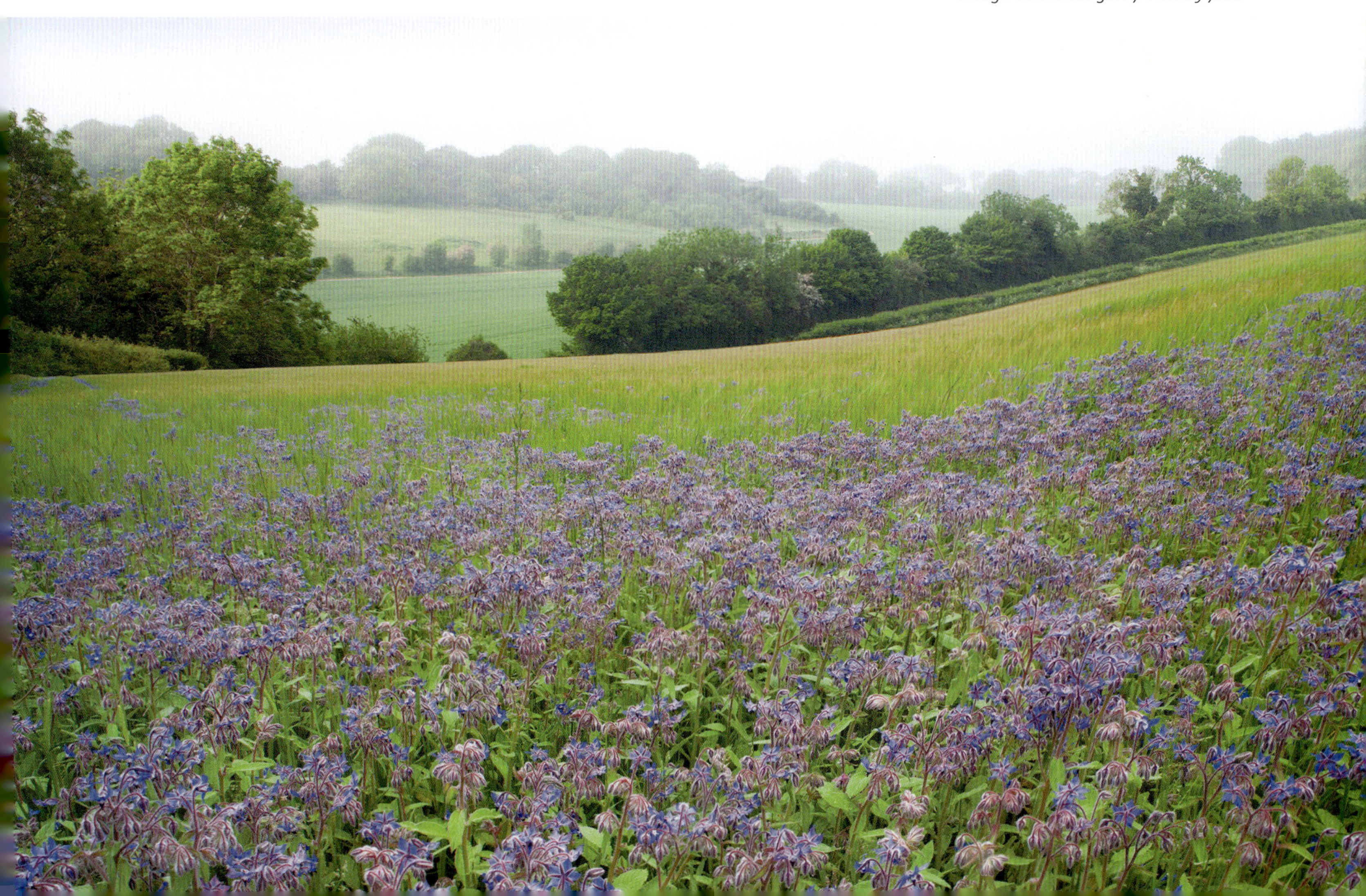

The Kennet at Marsh Benham

This tranquil view shows part of the Craven Fishery on the River Kennet near Marsh Benham, and is seen from the bridge just south of Hamstead Lock. Captured in midsummer and dominated by broad arches of weeping willow, the shallow watercourse seems almost swallowed up by the lush green foliage. I've noticed that this particular view varies greatly depending on seasonal conditions – in dry spells the water level drops sufficiently to reveal small islands of shingle, while in winter the water is deeper and the whole scene looks stark and leafless.

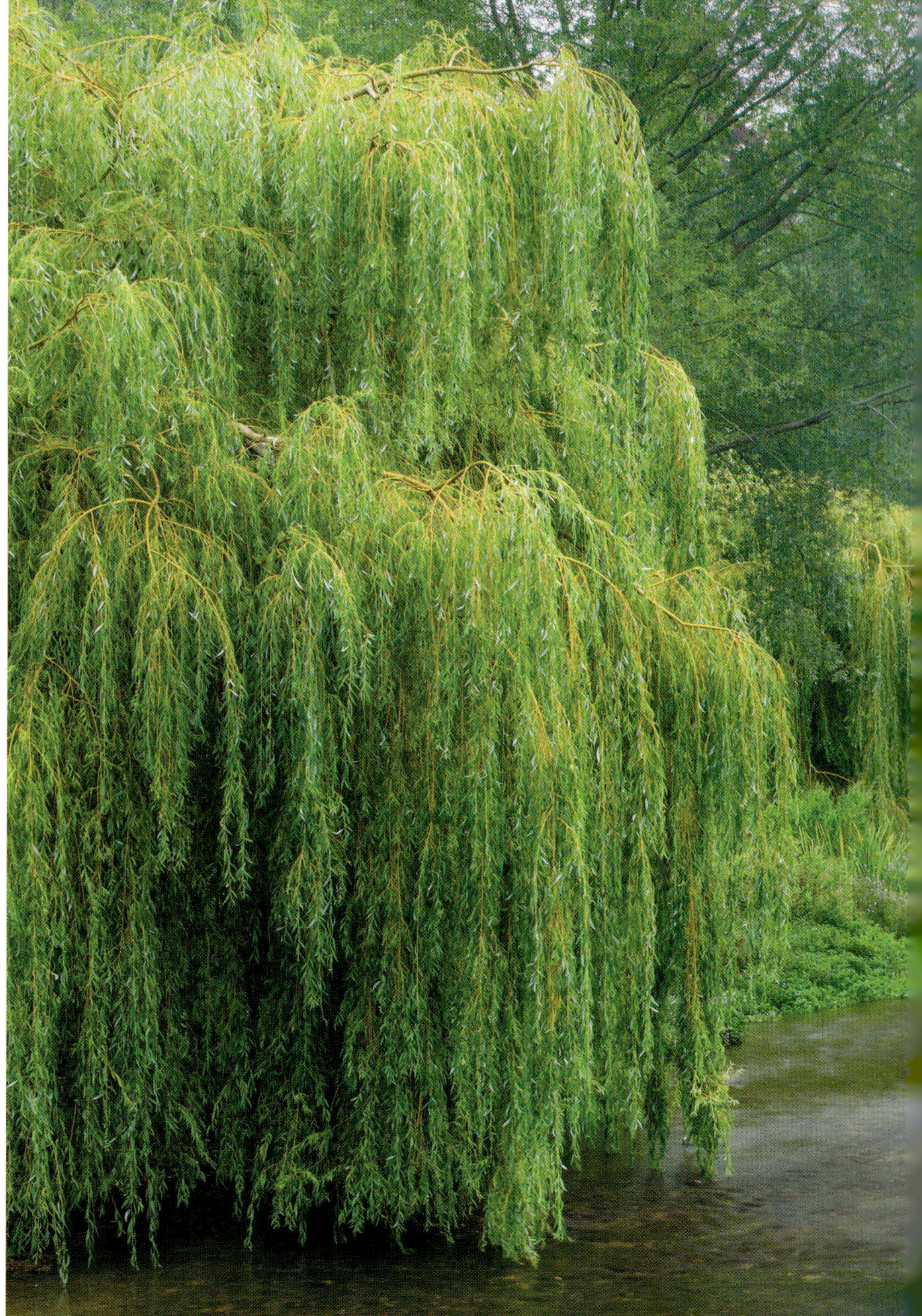

Willows along the Kennet at Marsh Benham

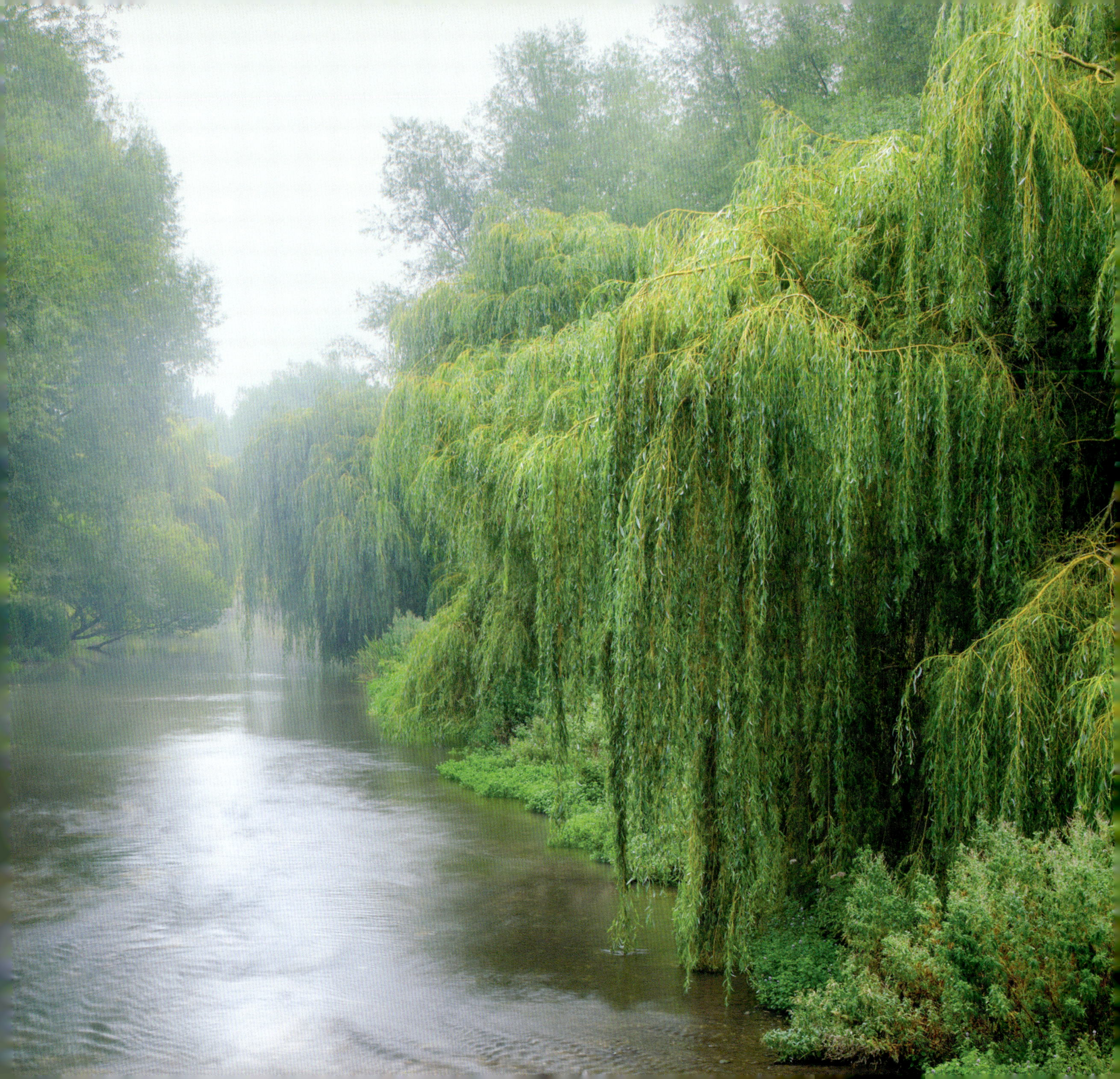

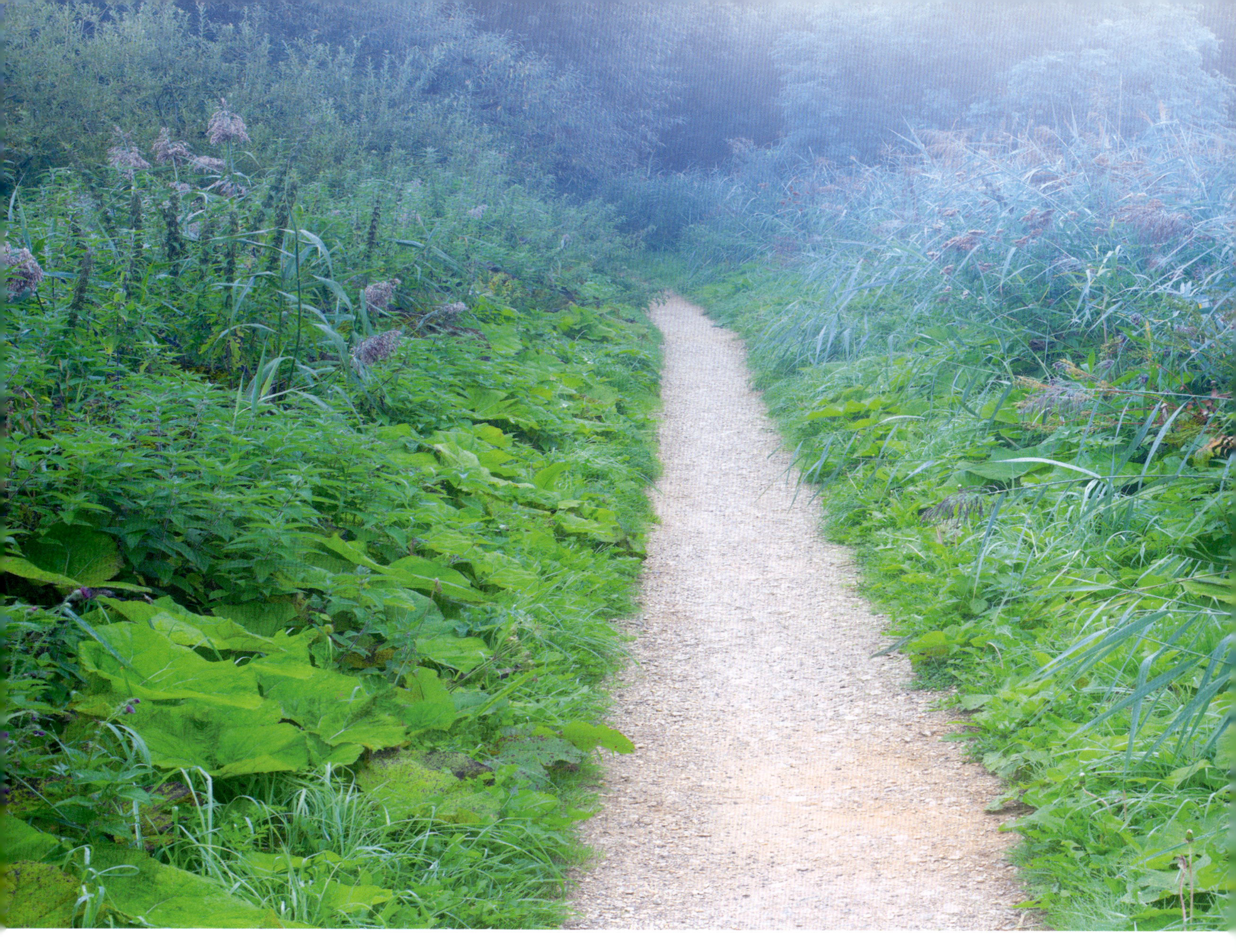

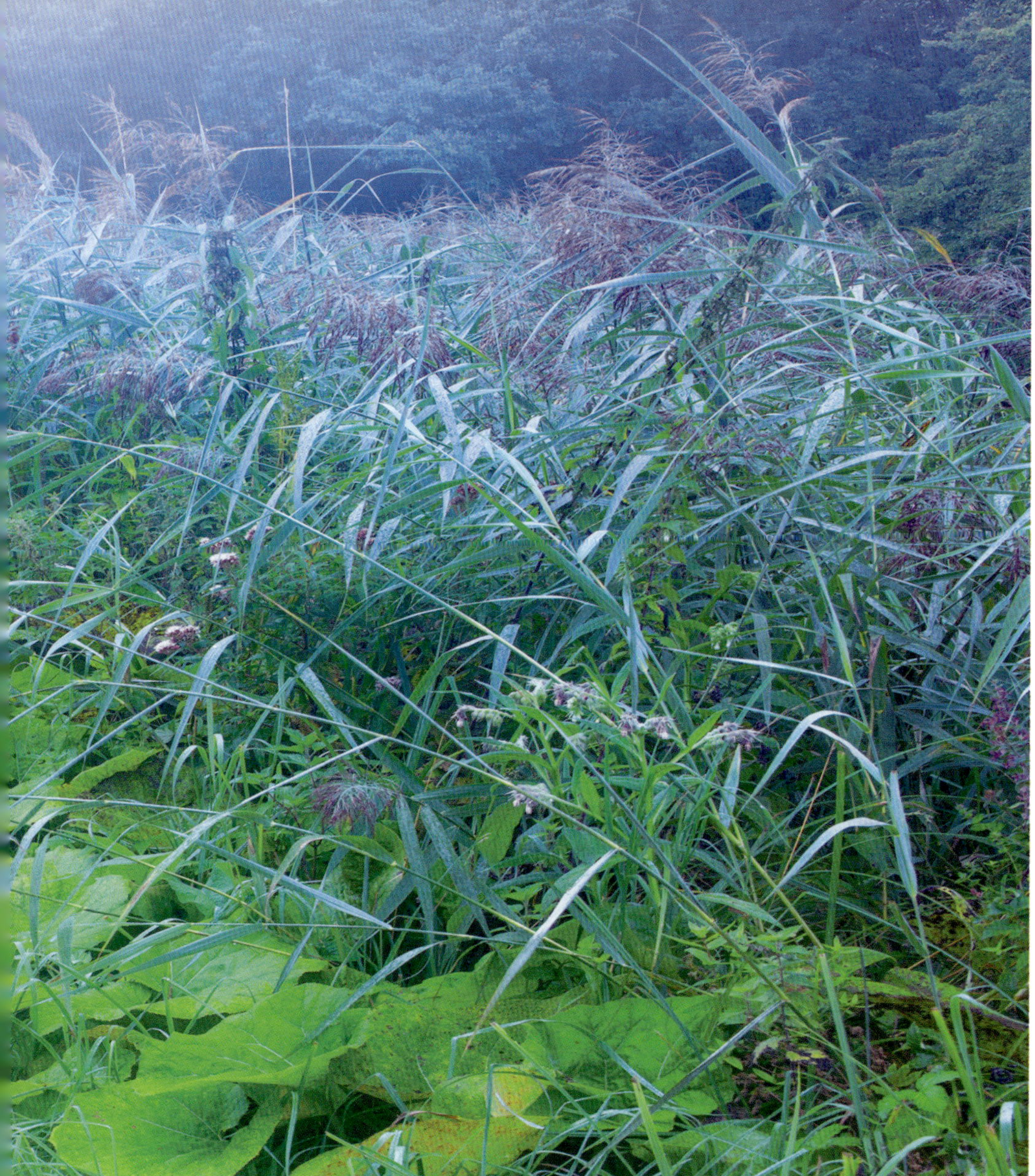

A midsummer mist in the waterlands of the Kennet

The Kennet Valley near Newbury

Between Benham Park and Enborne is a beautiful stretch of wetland, bordered by paths to the north and south. It's an area where river and canal meet, and the map shows a network of channels and pools which effectively divide the landscape into a set of islands which are connected by a host of footbridges. Much of the terrain is wooded with willow and alder; elsewhere reed-beds and marsh plants thrive in the moist, wild habitat. It's astonishing to think that the busy centre of Newbury is only a mile or so away.

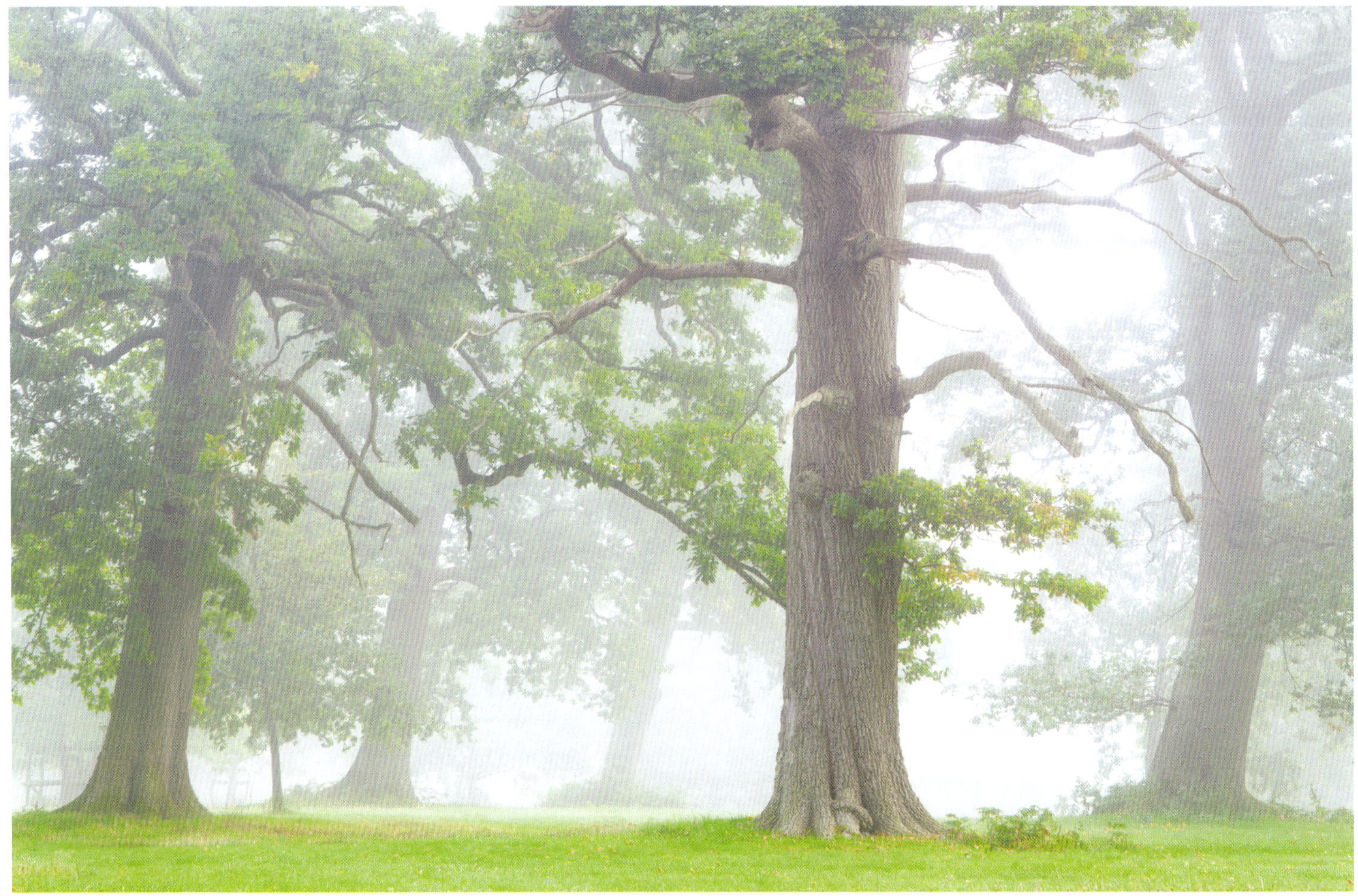

Rugged beauty – the oaks at Hamstead Park

Oak Trees at Hamstead Park

Towering cedars and a formal avenue of limes give Hamstead Park a stately aspect. But alongside this grandeur is a more humble feature – a grove of English oaks with twisted boughs and dead wood hanging here and there. There's no doubt that these old trees lack the refinement of their neighbours, but their rugged outlines are no less appealing, especially when shrouded in a morning mist.

Flax

If crops were grown for their colour then fields of flax would probably be a more common sight. Reputed to be one of man's oldest crops, the tiny flower heads of this plant are pure blue, and when grown en-masse they bring a serene look to the landscape. This photograph was taken near Swallowfield, a small village near the confluence of the rivers Loddon and Blackwater.

A landscape in blue – flax near Swallowfield in June

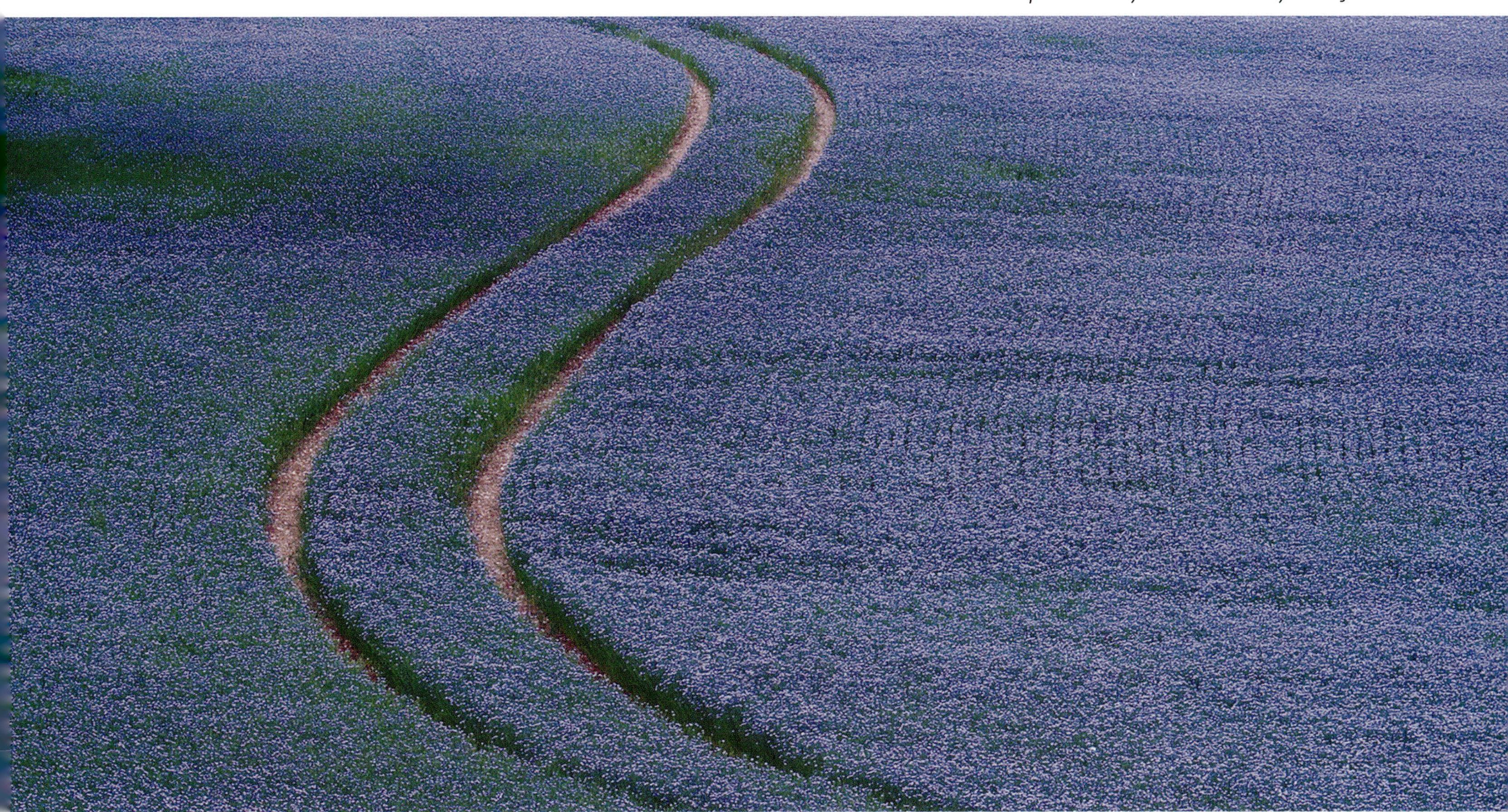

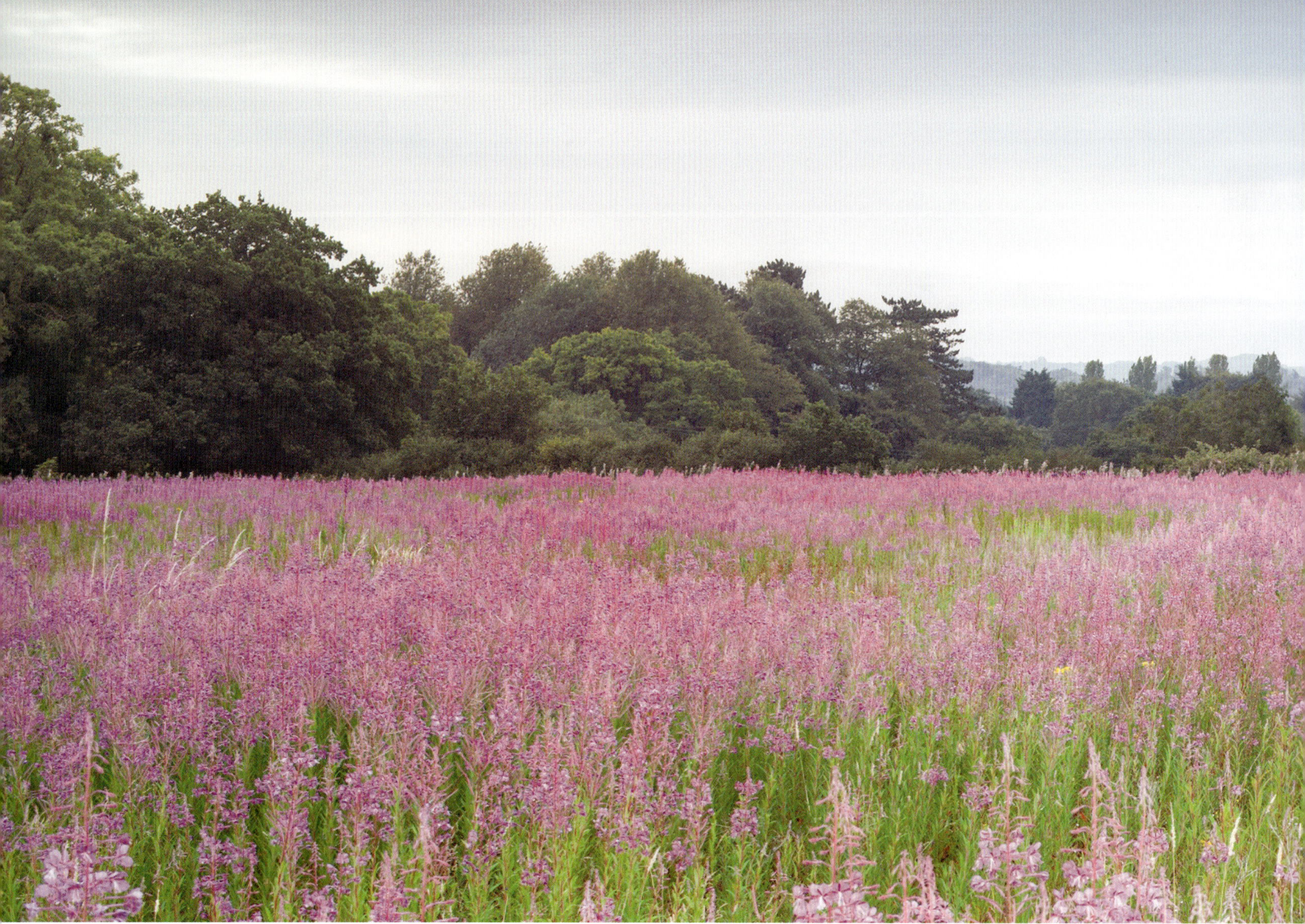

Rosebay Willowherb near Beedon Common

Near Beedon Common is a remnant of farmland – probably a disused pasture – which has been invaded by rosebay willowherb. It can be seen on the south side of the lane known as Old Street, and during July and August the deep drifts of pinky-mauve flowers cannot be missed. Sometimes known as fireweed, this plant is a familiar feature of the countryside, but only when it grows en-masse does it create such a dazzling sight.

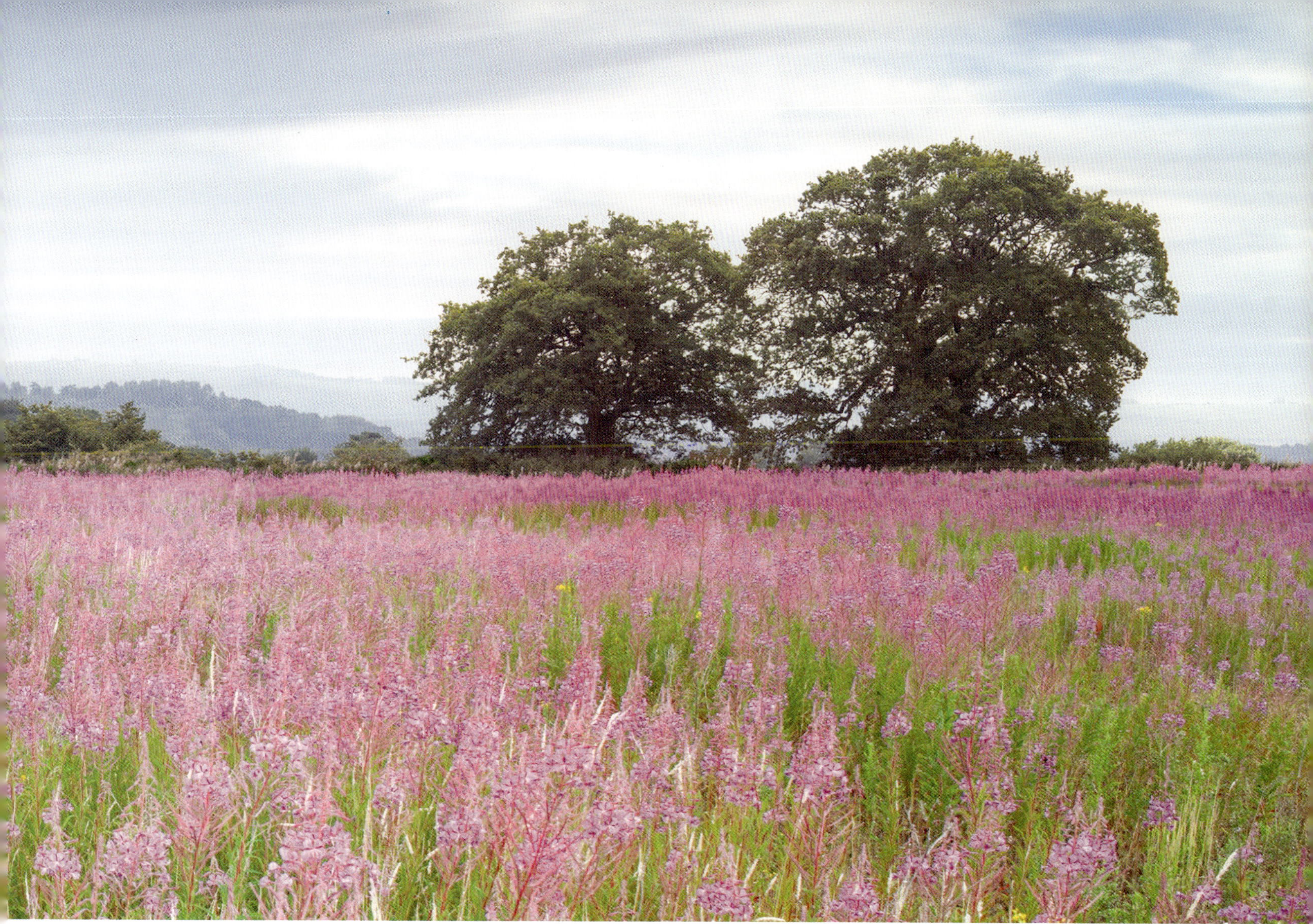

Drifts of rosebay willowherb in the Berkshire countryside

Gazing across the sea of flowers it's difficult to understand why rosebay willowherb is seen as a weed – it's almost never exploited in English gardens despite its attractive appearance. However, it seems that the plant is held in higher esteem in Canada, where it's the floral emblem of the Yukon and appears on the territorial flag.

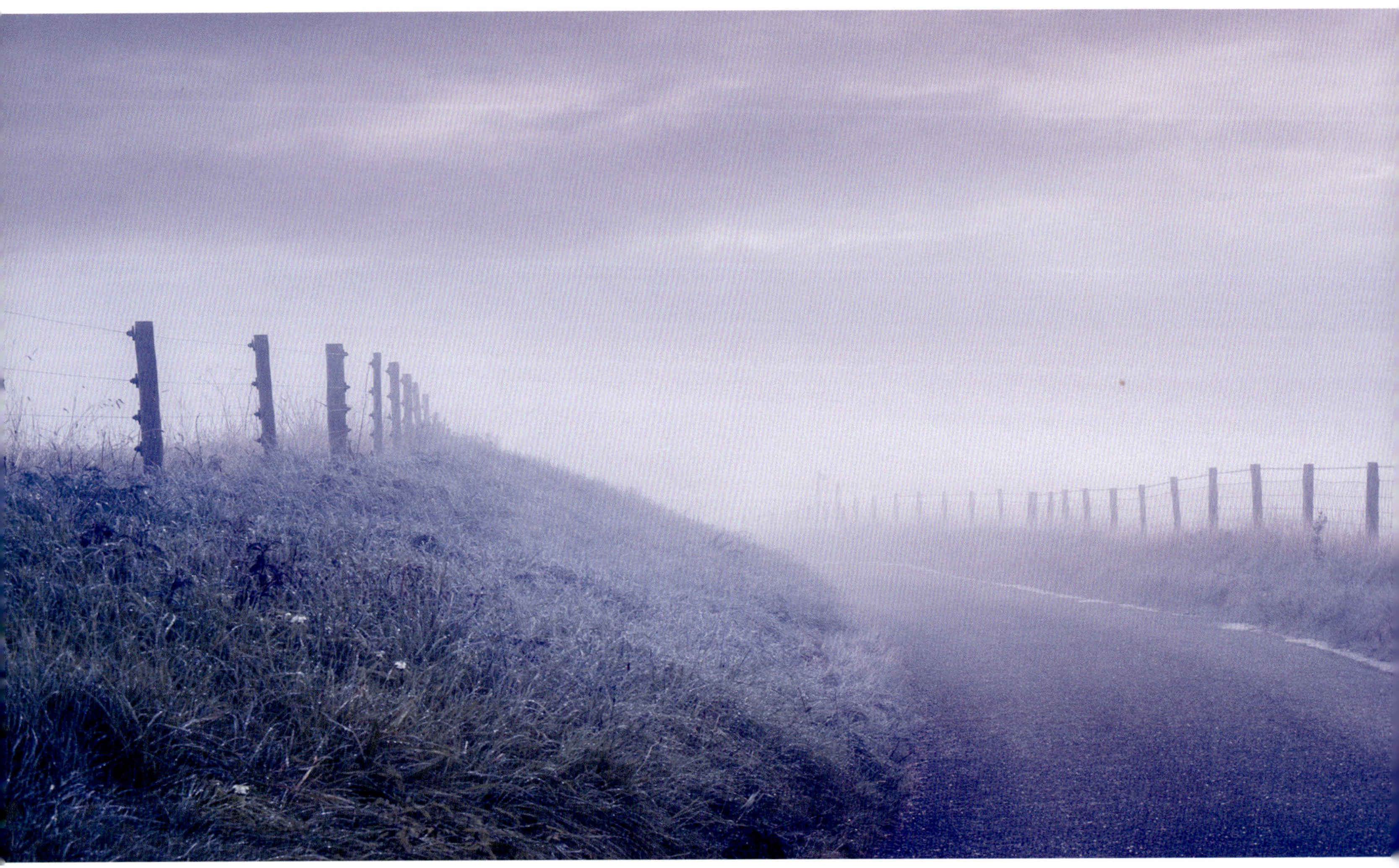

Country Lane on Walbury Hill
The lane which runs south from Inkpen Common soon reaches the foot of Walbury Hill, part of England's highest chalk upland and also the highest point in the south-east. The lane then curves across West Woodhay Down, ascending the hill to a small car park. Glancing back from this point reveals one of the best elevated views in Berkshire, a vista stretching from side to side, encompassing almost the entire western section of the county.

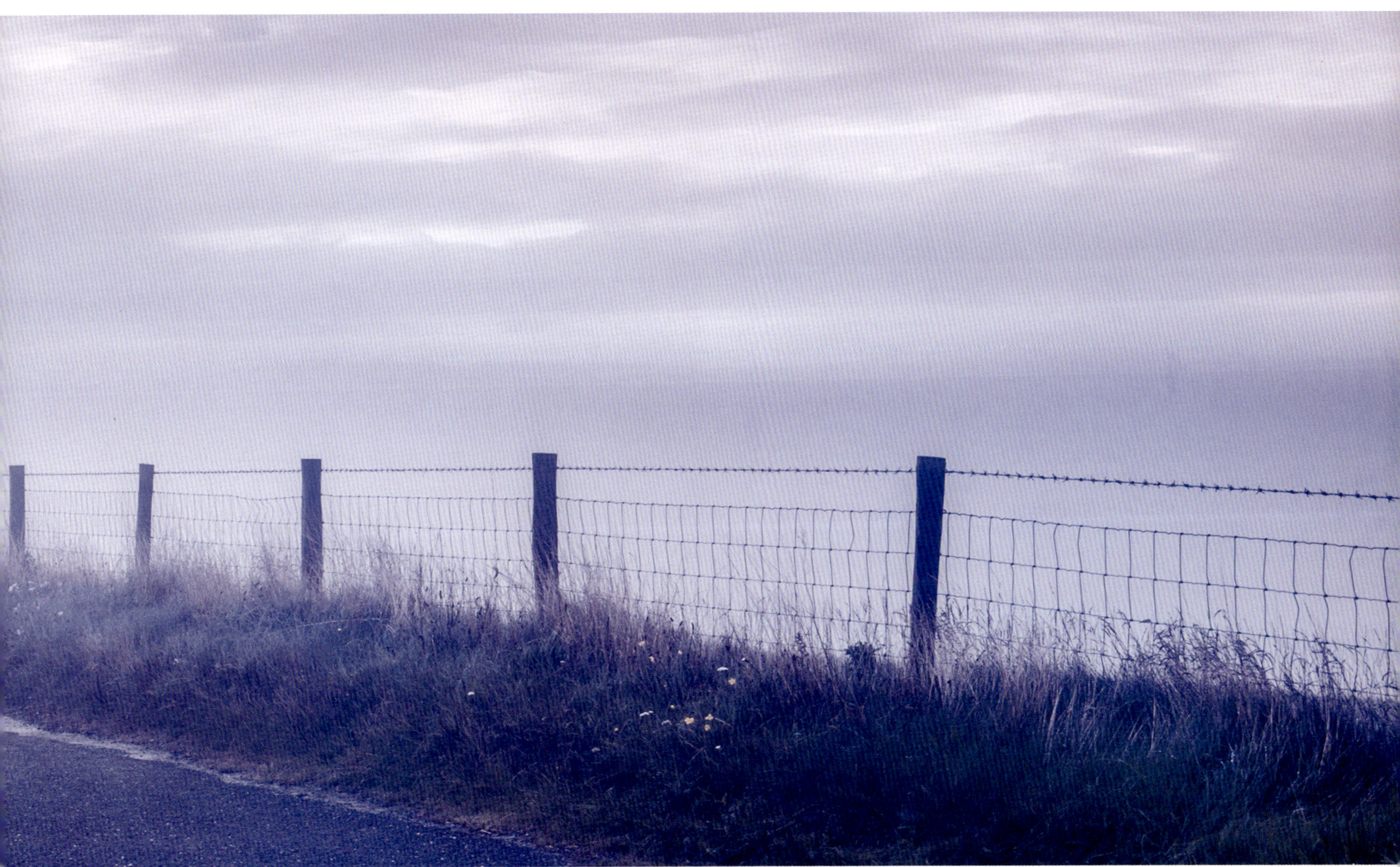

A misty descent from Walbury Hill

However, atmospheric conditions meant that none of this was visible when this photograph was taken – but the view of the lane vanishing into the summer mist was beautiful nonetheless.

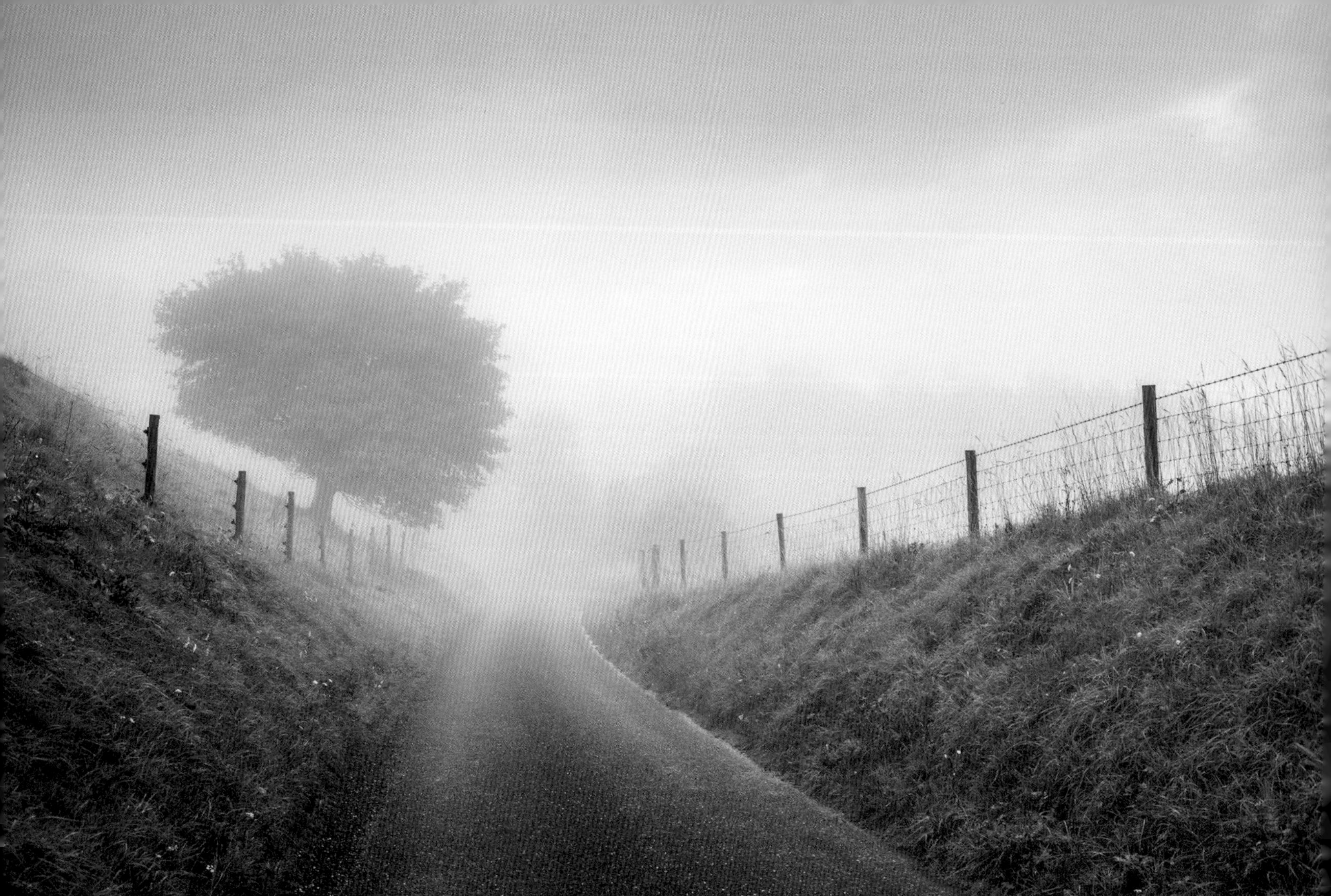

A tilting oak tree above the lane on West Woodhay Down

Oak Tree on West Woodhay Down

At the edge of West Woodhay Down is an oak tree which leans gracefully towards the lane. Its shape is well-defined, being round-topped but neatly trimmed below by nibbling livestock. It's a feature which could easily go unnoticed, except on foggy mornings when its dark profile stands out against the pale backdrop.

This image shows the view looking down the lane in late summer; the atmosphere was intense, and the silence broken only by the occasional sound of sheep.

Meadow Cranesbill near Farnborough

Leading south from Farnborough village is an unfenced country lane with wide sloping verges which are left uncut for much of the summer. The result is an ideal wild flower habitat, and one which is dominated year after year by meadow cranesbill, a wild geranium with exquisite blue petals. The location is open and exposed, and the flowers tend to suffer in wet and windy weather; but the plant is not as delicate as it appears and soon recovers.

This is the best show of cranesbill I've come across in Berkshire, although I have noticed a similar display a few miles away on the lane-side at Beedon Common.

Stalks of cow parsley among meadow cranesbill

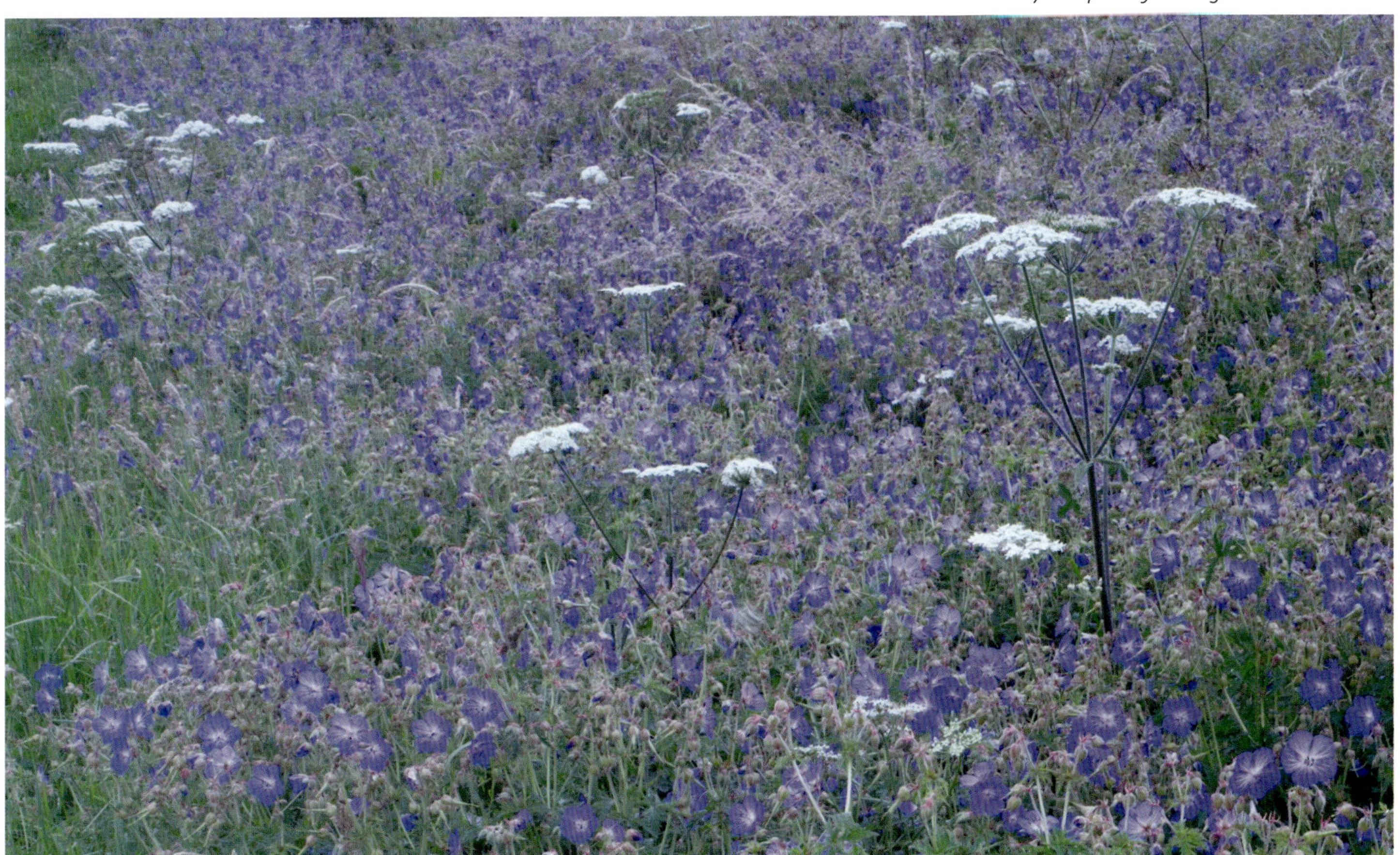

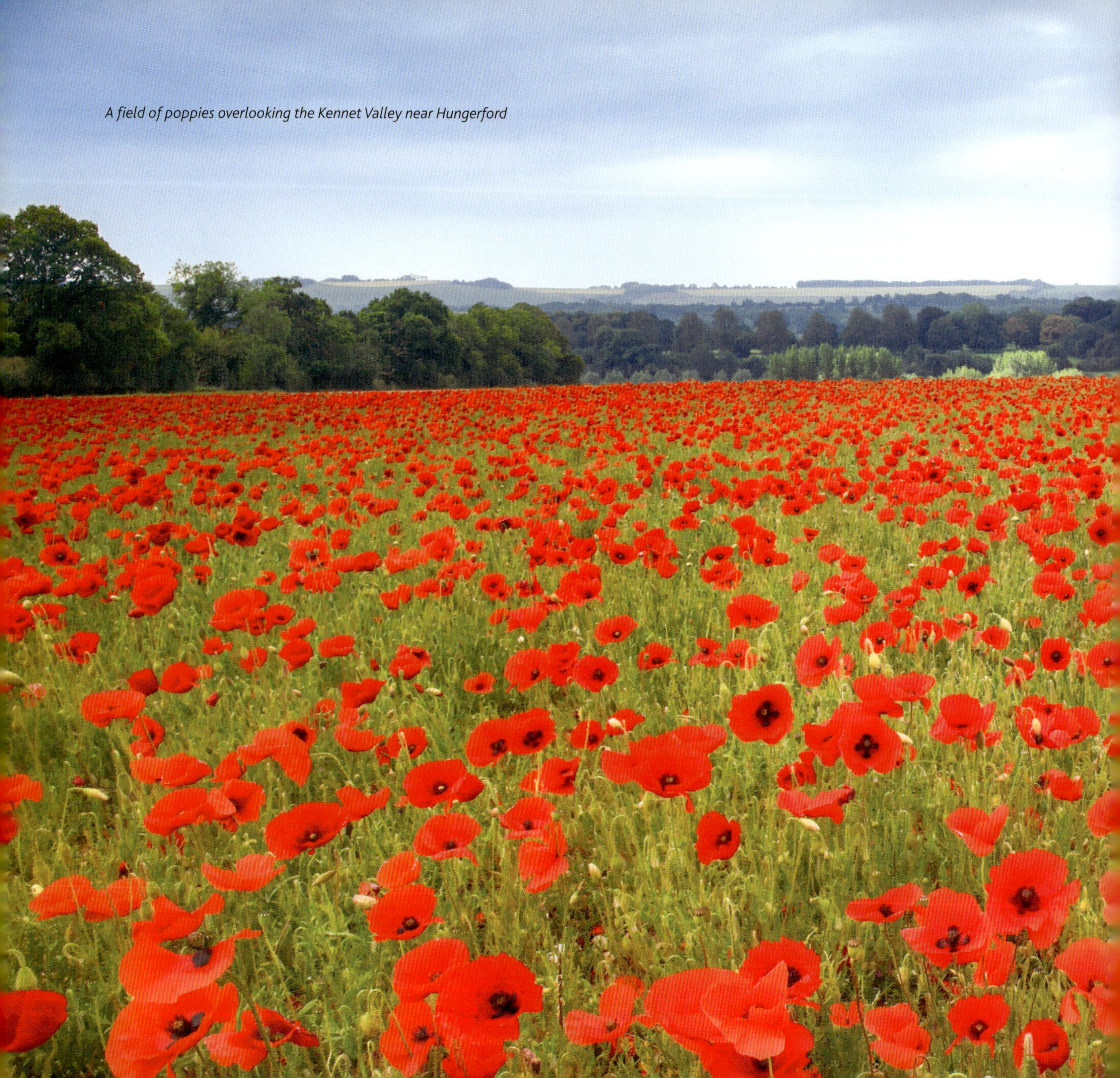

A field of poppies overlooking the Kennet Valley near Hungerford

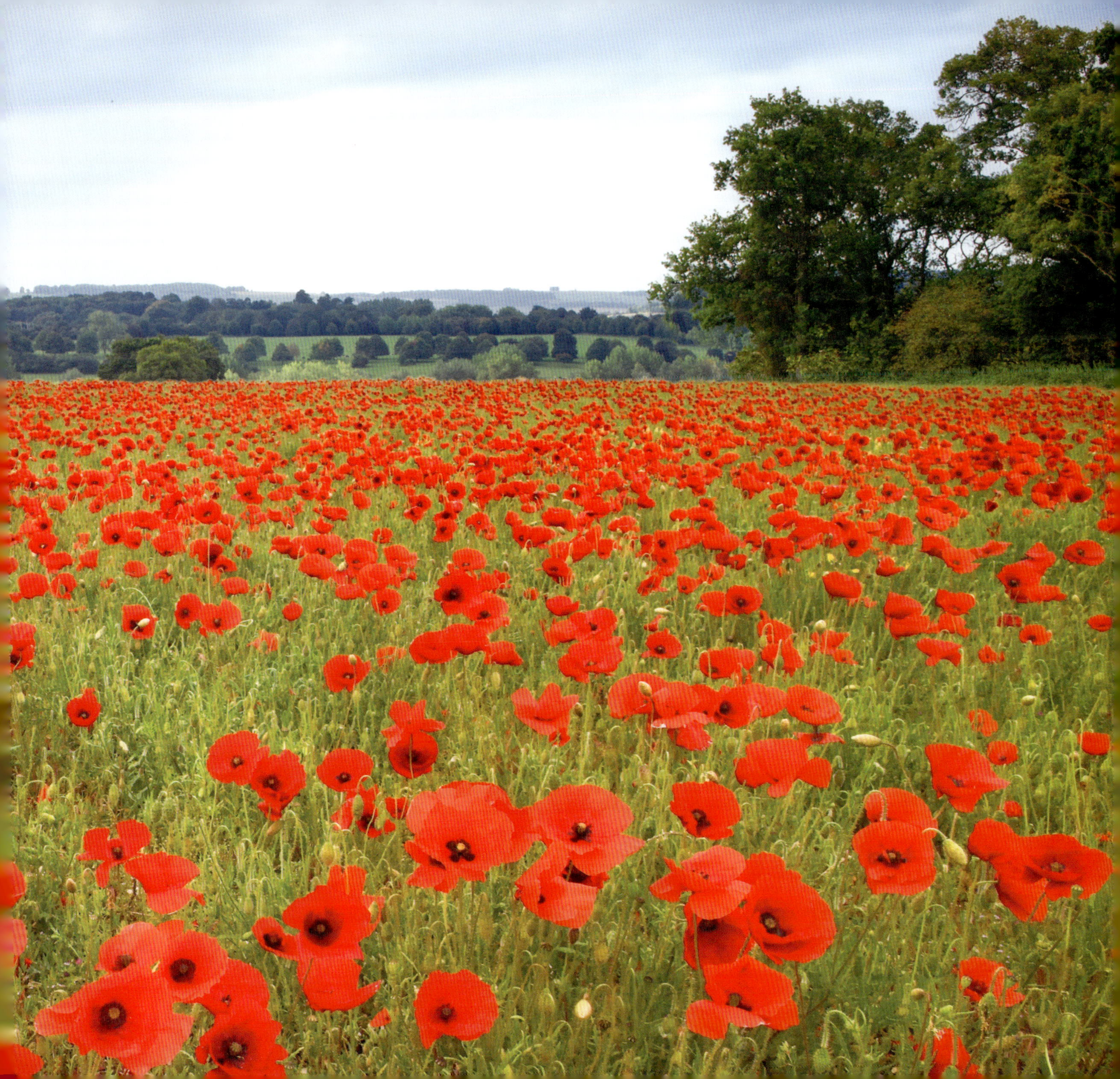

Landscape near West Ilsley

The undulating landscape surrounding West Ilsley is classic chalk country: never harsh or dramatic, but rounded and gently sweeping – features which have probably been accentuated by centuries of ploughing. A few lanes and hedges, and the occasional isolated copse are all there is to break the sequence of vast open fields.

This lack of prominent features and the monotone of the crops creates a landscape with an abstract quality which can be appealing to photographers and artists alike. This panoramic image is a study of lines and curves, and shows a side-lit view of a distant wheat field.

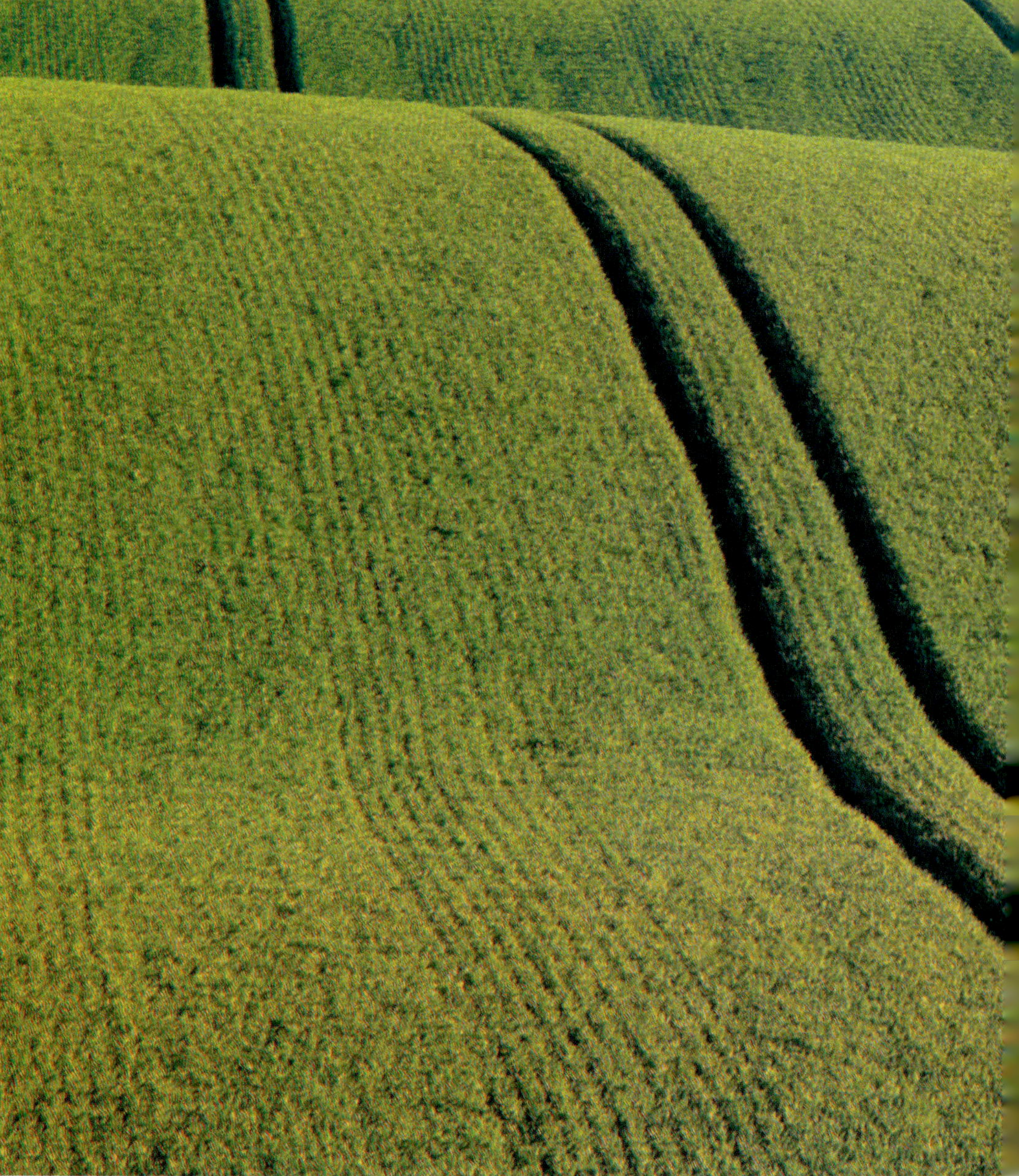

Lines and curves in the landscape near West Ilsley

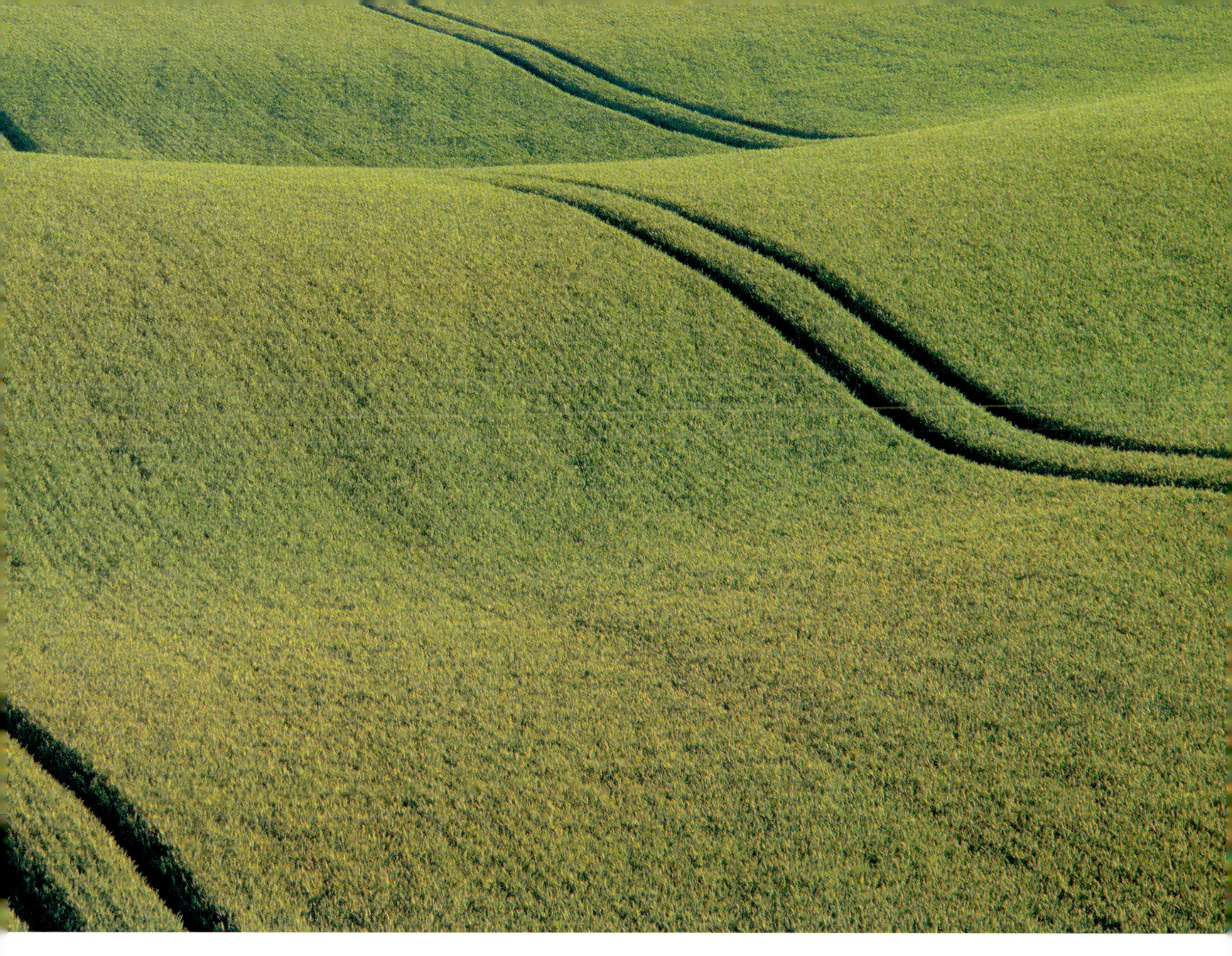

Misty Landscape from Walbury Hill

The morning view from the lofty heights of Walbury Hill depends greatly on the combination of weather and season. On clear summer mornings the rising sun cuts right across the scene, picking out the highpoints one by one. In winter the sun is obscured by the ridge, and much of the landscape remains in shadow until late morning. But the most atmospheric view comes when the lowlands are cloaked in mist with only the tallest trees rising above. These were the conditions when this image was taken in July; the view, looking roughly north-east in the direction of Hamstead Park, shows the many woods and copses beyond West Woodhay.

Islands of trees in the mist

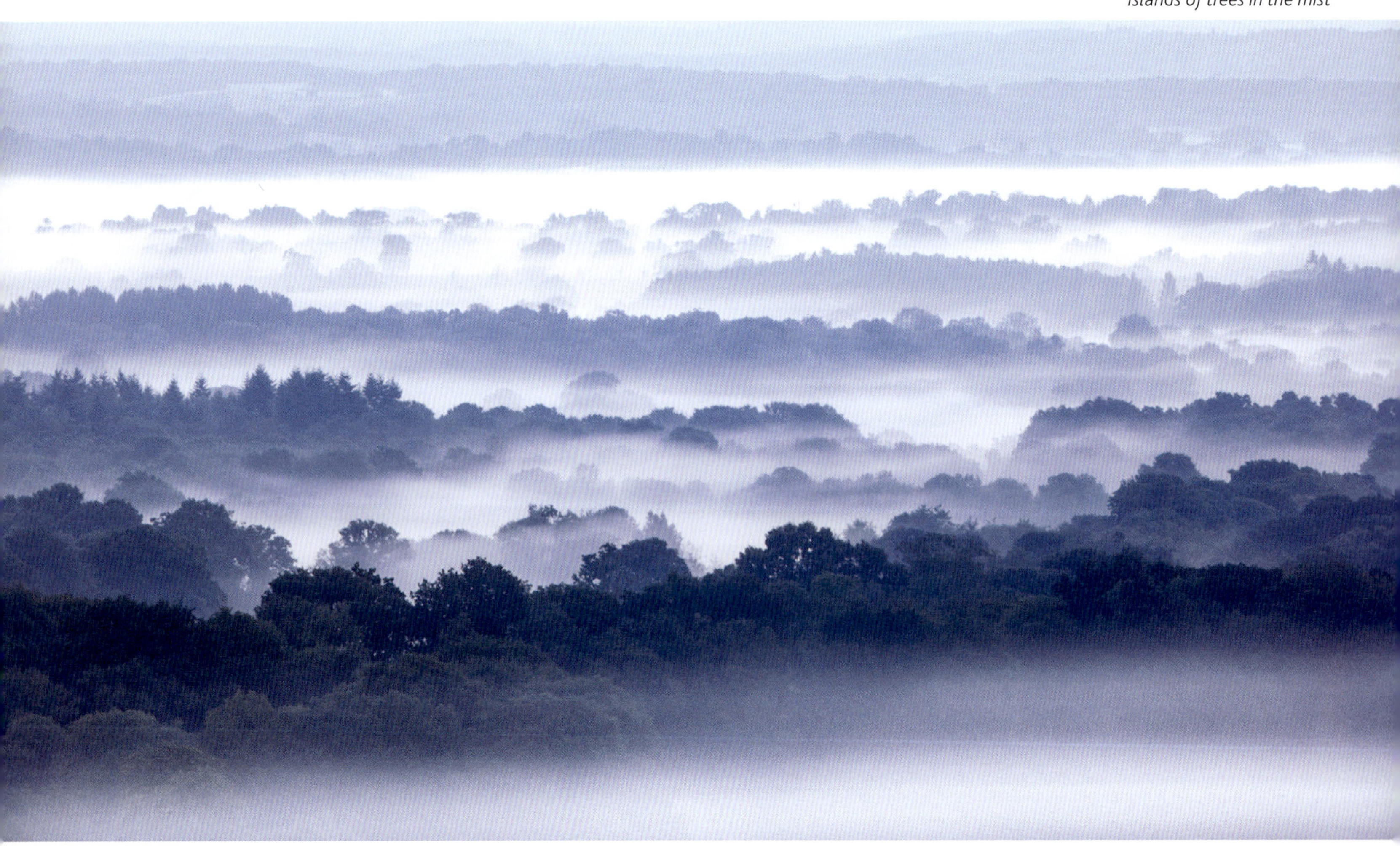

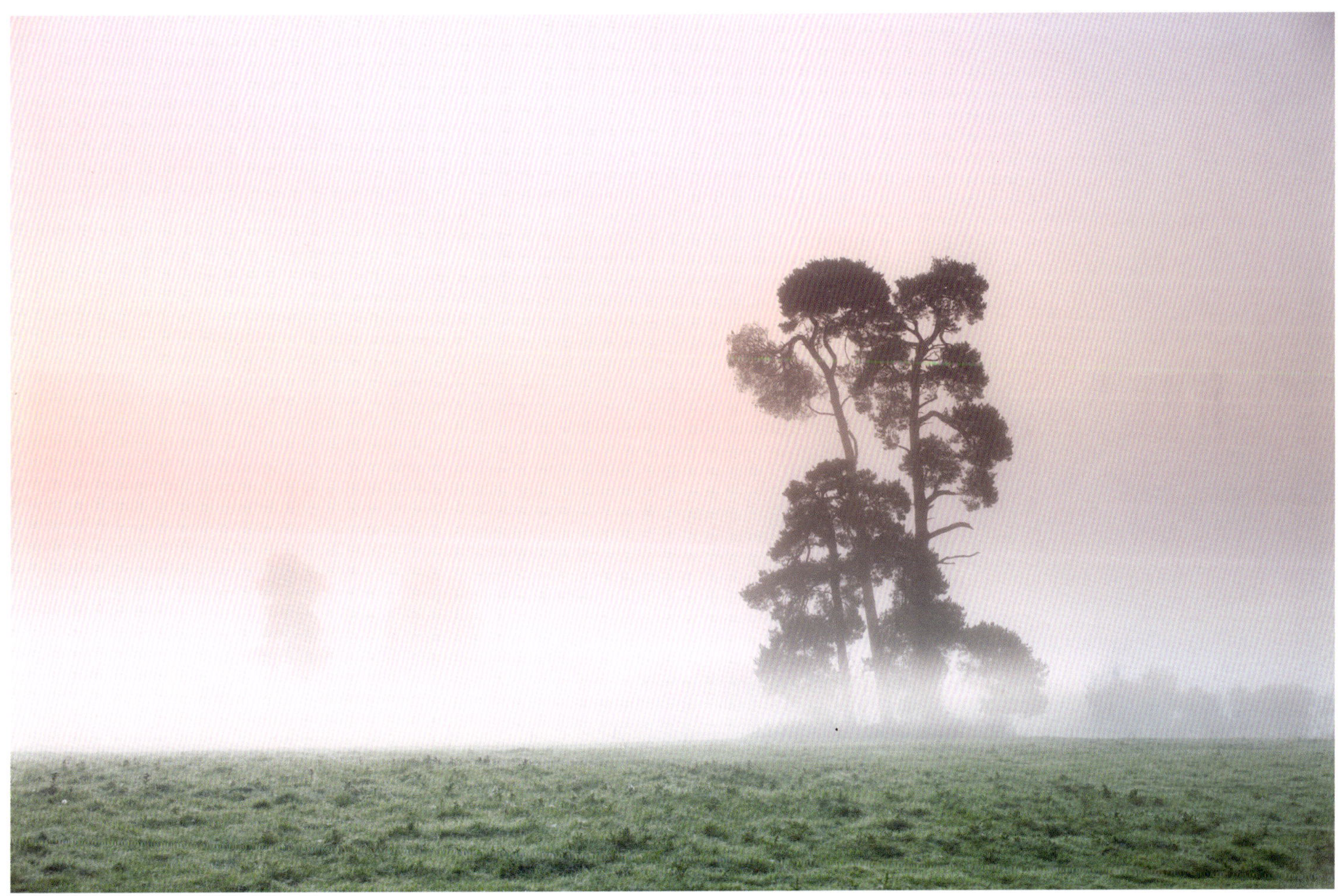

Pine trees billowing out of the mist at Winterbourne

Landscape at Winterbourne

This small stand of Scots pines can be seen from the lane between Boxford Common and Winterbourne. They grow in a field over-looked by the tower of St James the Less Chapel, and are just one of a number of isolated tree clumps in the area. Snelsmore Common lies just beyond, although on this morning almost everything other than the pines was swallowed up in a thick mist.

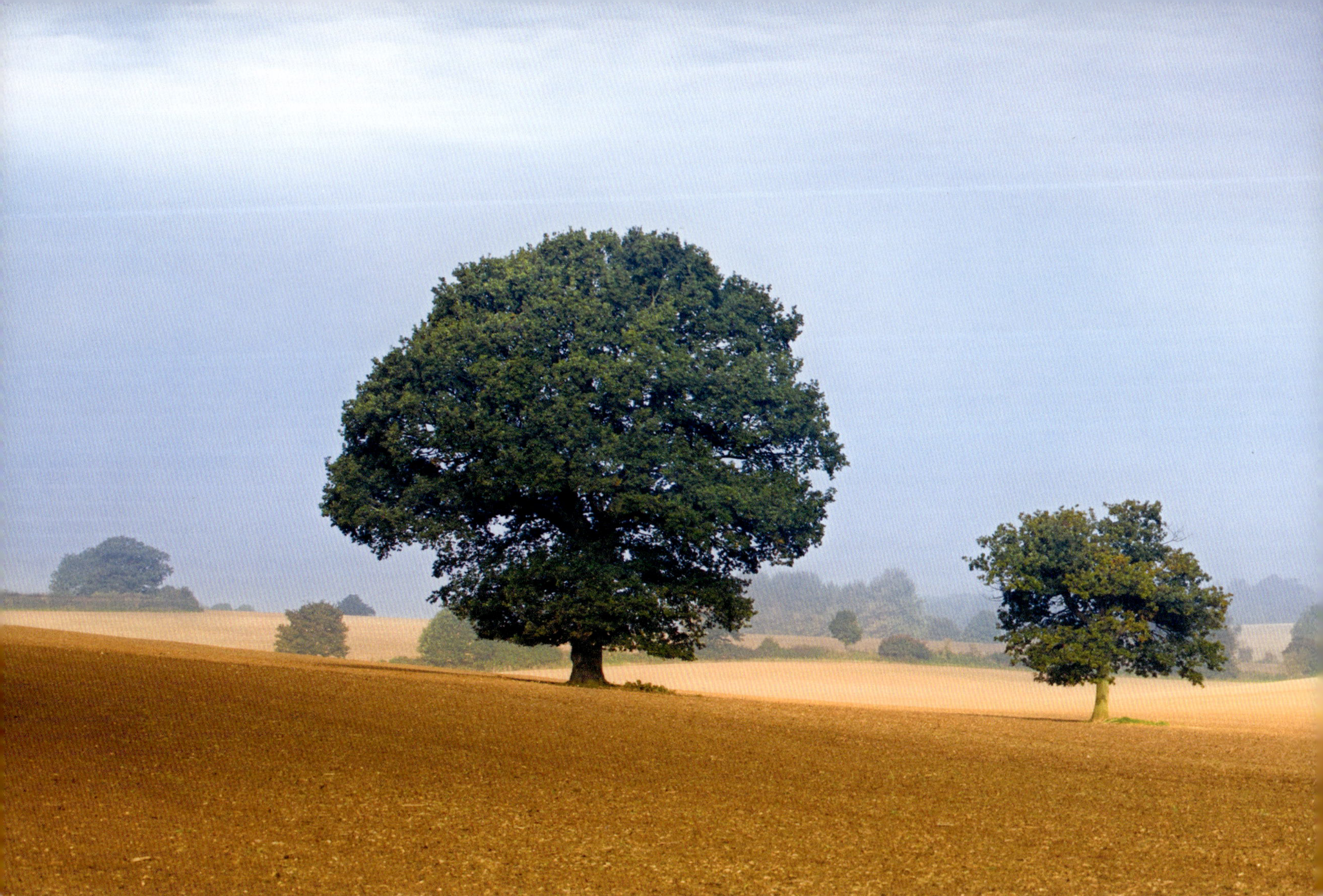

Brightwalton

Fields laid bare by the plough are a feature usually associated with winter, though in fact some landscapes are ploughed as soon as summer begins to wane. This view of two oaks at Brightwalton was taken in the first week of September, when the trees and hedges were still heavy with late summer foliage. The morning sun, slowly burning through an early mist, was casting a soft sidelight across the newly-ploughed soil.

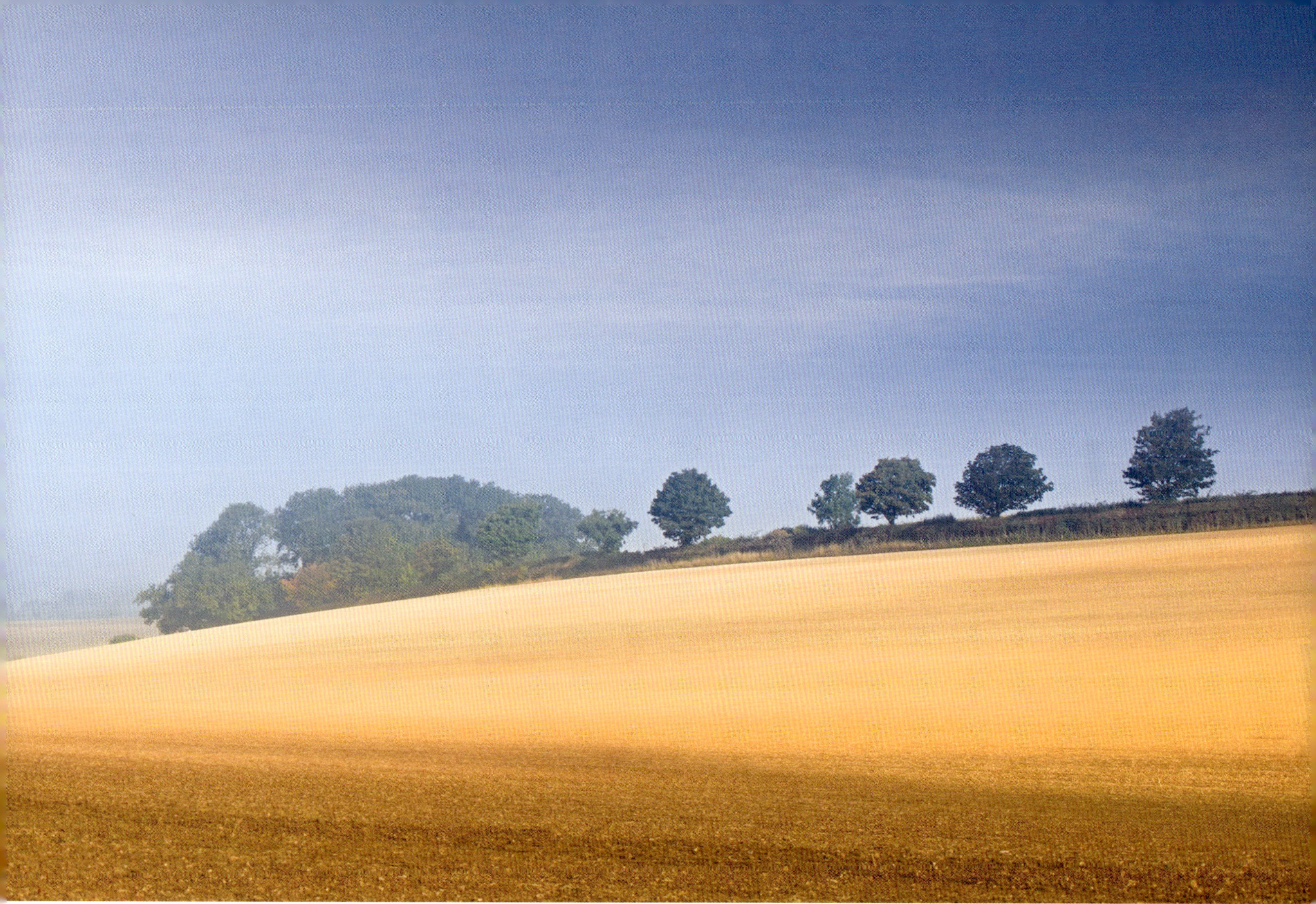

Field oaks at Brightwalton in September

The downland scenery in this area is particularly attractive with its gently flowing contours and tree-studded fields. It's also an area with many evocative place names – 'Nightingale Farm' and 'Sparrowbill Copse', among others.

Harvest at Thorn Hill

The main route from Aldworth to Hampstead Norreys is quiet enough, but an alternative one – quieter still – is along the narrow twisting lane from Pibworth Farm to Milkhill Farm. It descends into a small valley near the source of the River Pang and is hemmed in by hedges for much of its route, but just below Thorn Hill a gateway gives a sudden glimpse of the rolling countryside to the south.

The image on this page shows the view from this spot at the time of summer harvest, when dozens of straw bales were scattered like bobbins across the field. On this particular morning a receding bank of cloud was suffused with shades of pink as the sun began to rise in the east.

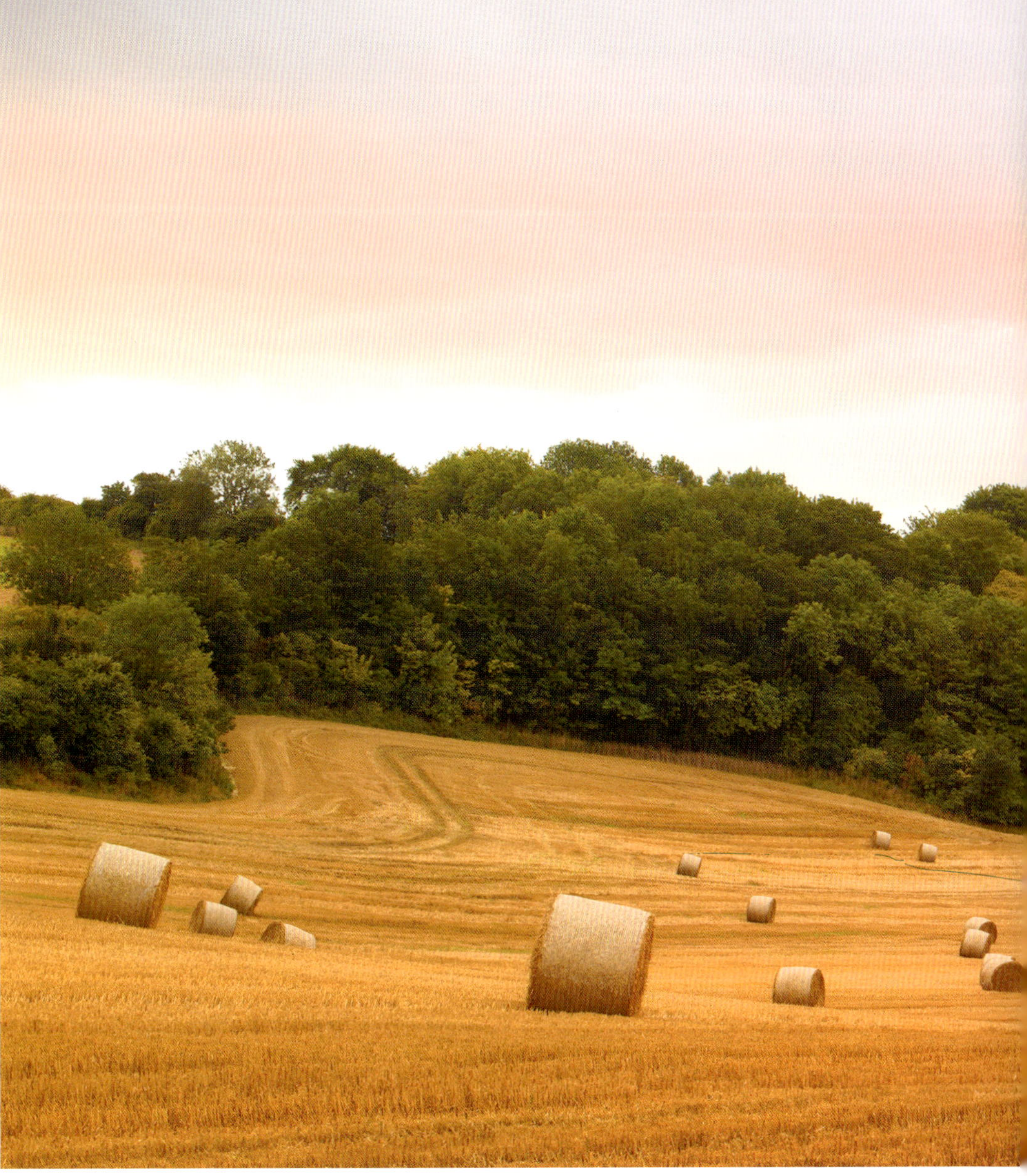

Straw bales in the West Berkshire landscape

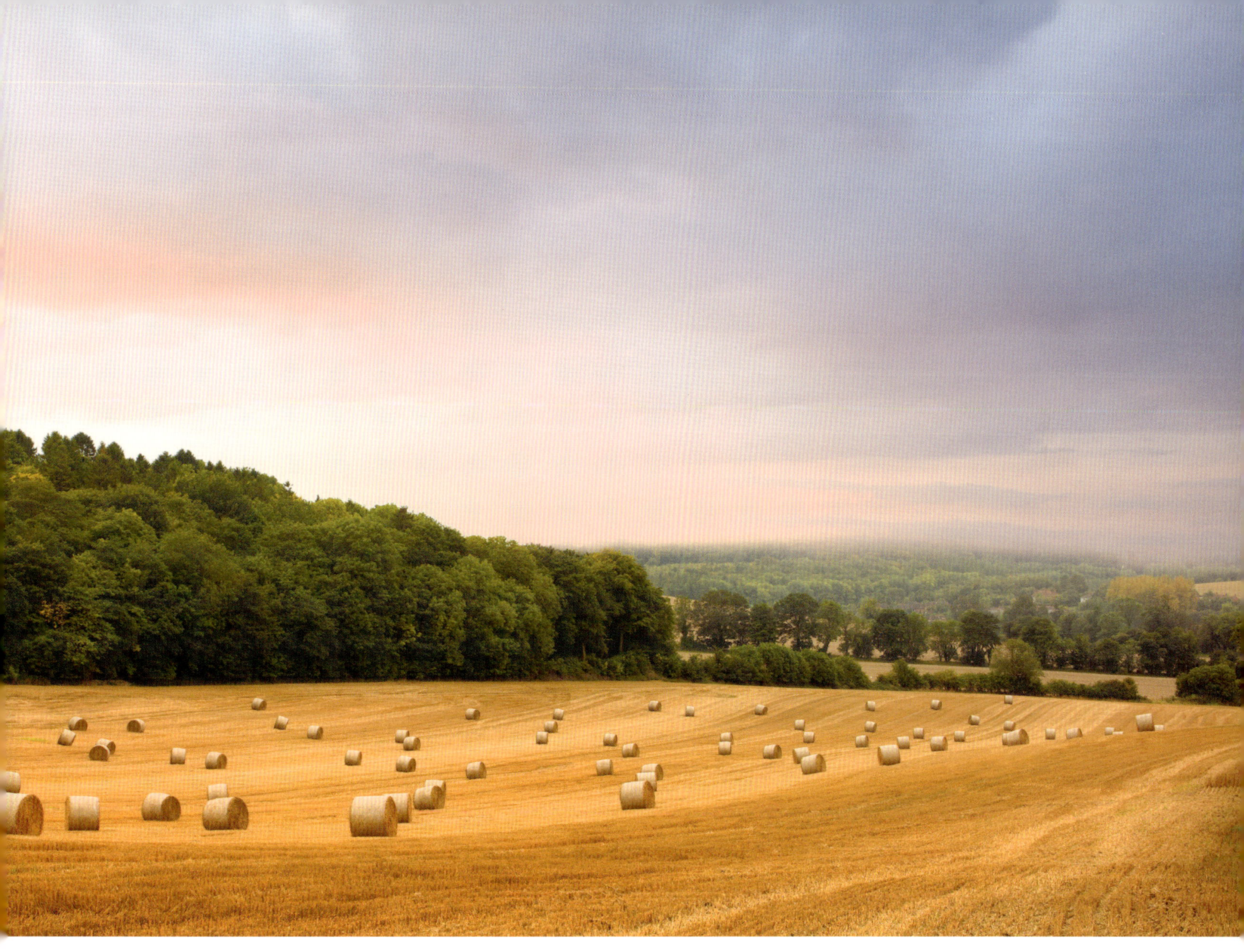

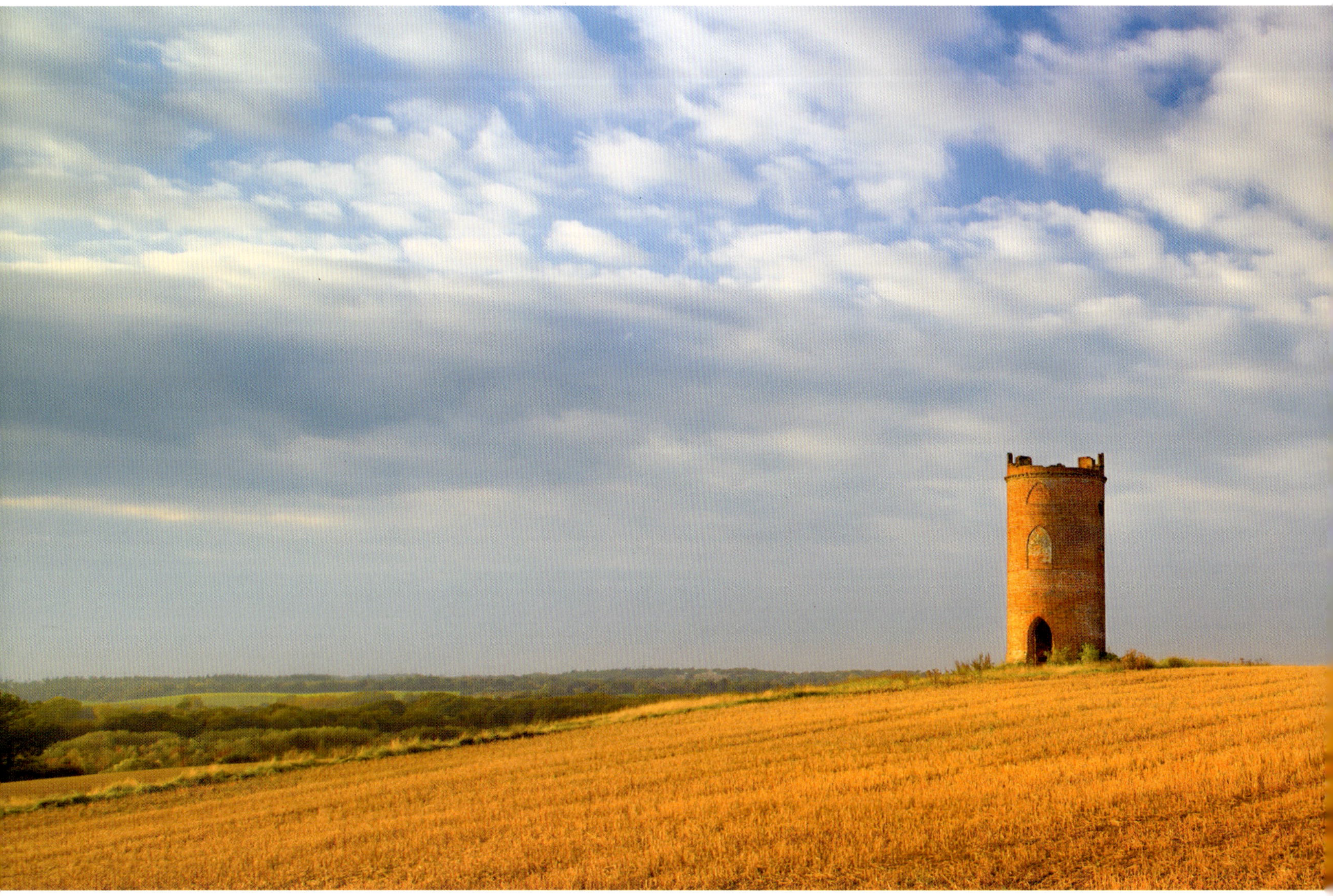

Wilder's Folly near Sulhamstead

The enchanting ruin which sits on the open landscape above Nunhide is known as Wilder's Folly, or 'The Pigeon Tower'. It was built in the eighteenth century by Henry Wilder when he was courting Joan, daughter of William Thoyts of Sulhamstead House, and was located in such a position that both could see it from their respective homes. They married in 1768.

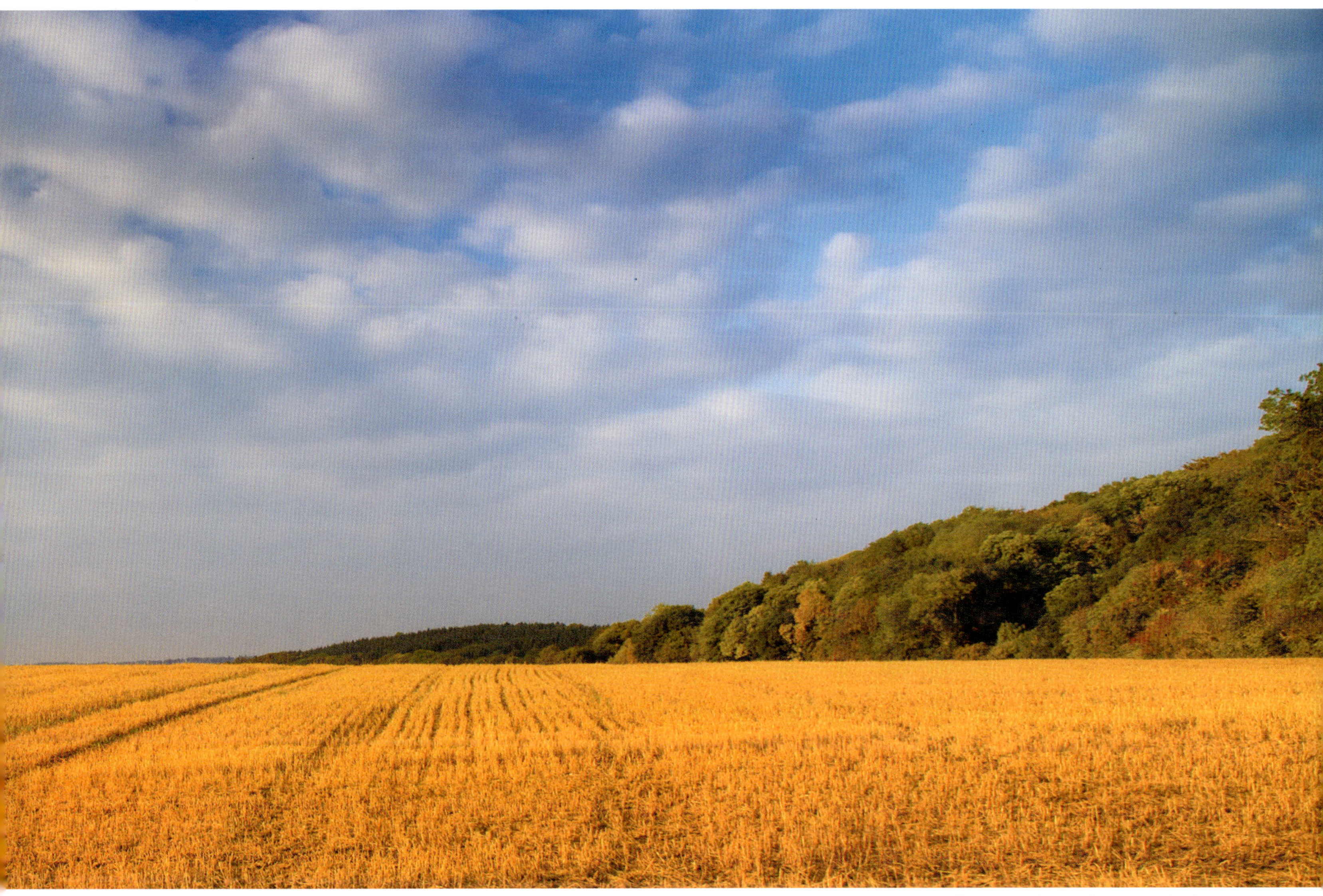

Wilder's Folly – now a haven for nesting birds

A small permissive path leads to the monument, which has a number of nest boxes built into the brickwork of the top section. This image shows the tower in September, side-lit by the evening sun.

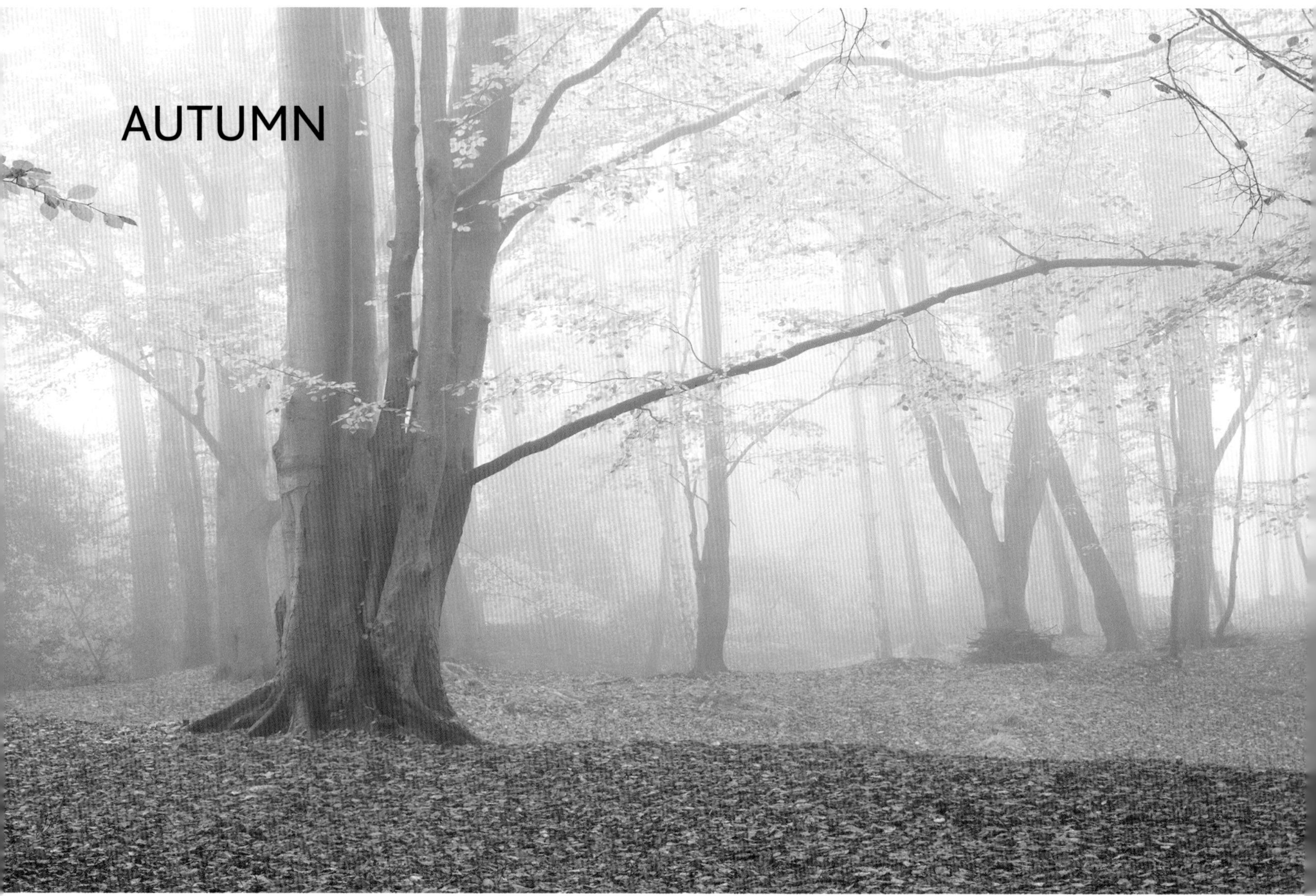

AUTUMN

Frilsham Common

A striking contrast between wilderness and modernity is experienced at Frilsham Common. Here, on the northern fringe of the wood, beech trees young and old grow unchecked – as they have probably done for generations – in a scene reminiscent of the New Forest in

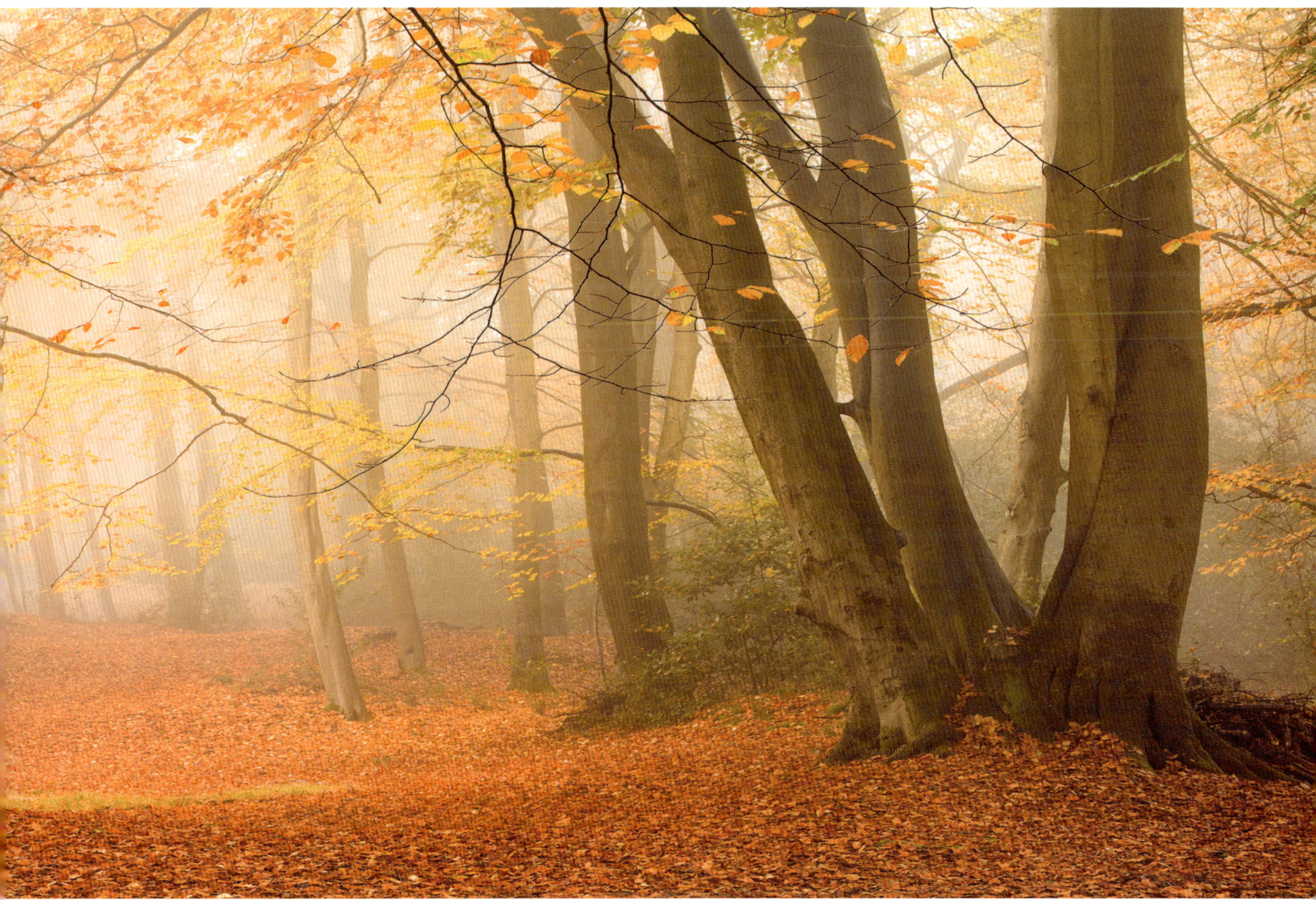

Autumn under the beech trees at Frilsham Common

Hampshire. Yet barely a stone's throw away is the busy M4 motorway, the noise from which continually echoes into the wood. Nonetheless, the fine trees and leafy landscape make the place appealing, and the hum of traffic can't spoil the magic on a misty autumn morning.

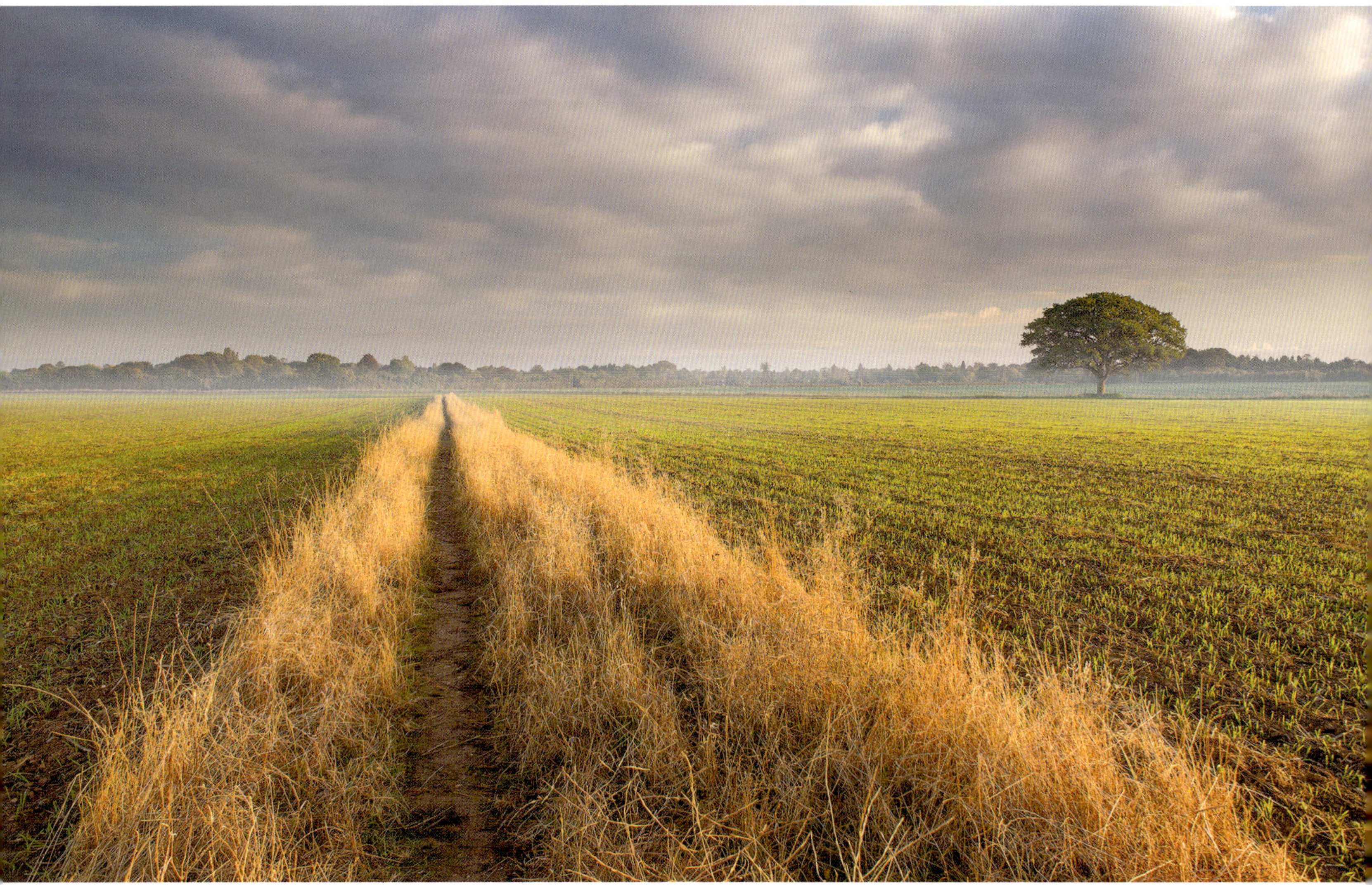

The grassy path near Littlewick Green in October

Landscape near Littlewick Green

To the south-west of Maidenhead Thicket is an area of open landscape, a place of big skies and wide horizons. It's best enjoyed from a footpath which runs due south from Littlewick Green, and joins a lane which leads to White Waltham. There are few natural features other than a solitary oak tree which stands mid-field to the east of the path. This image shows the scene on an October morning when the early sunlight was sweeping through the golden grasses which line the path.

Greenham Common

Cloud patterns are always fascinating and make an ever-changing backdrop to the landscape. Throw in some evening sunlight, and it's clear how a relatively featureless scene can become something more dramatic. This photograph shows a remote pool on Greenham Common near Newbury, a location where I was able to capture the reflected drama of an evening sky.

The area is now a nature reserve, but is perhaps best remembered as an airbase and the site of a long-term peace protest by women in the 1980s. The base closed in 1997, and the remains of military occupation are now being invaded by beds of moss and wild flowers.

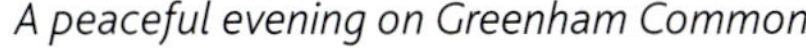

A peaceful evening on Greenham Common

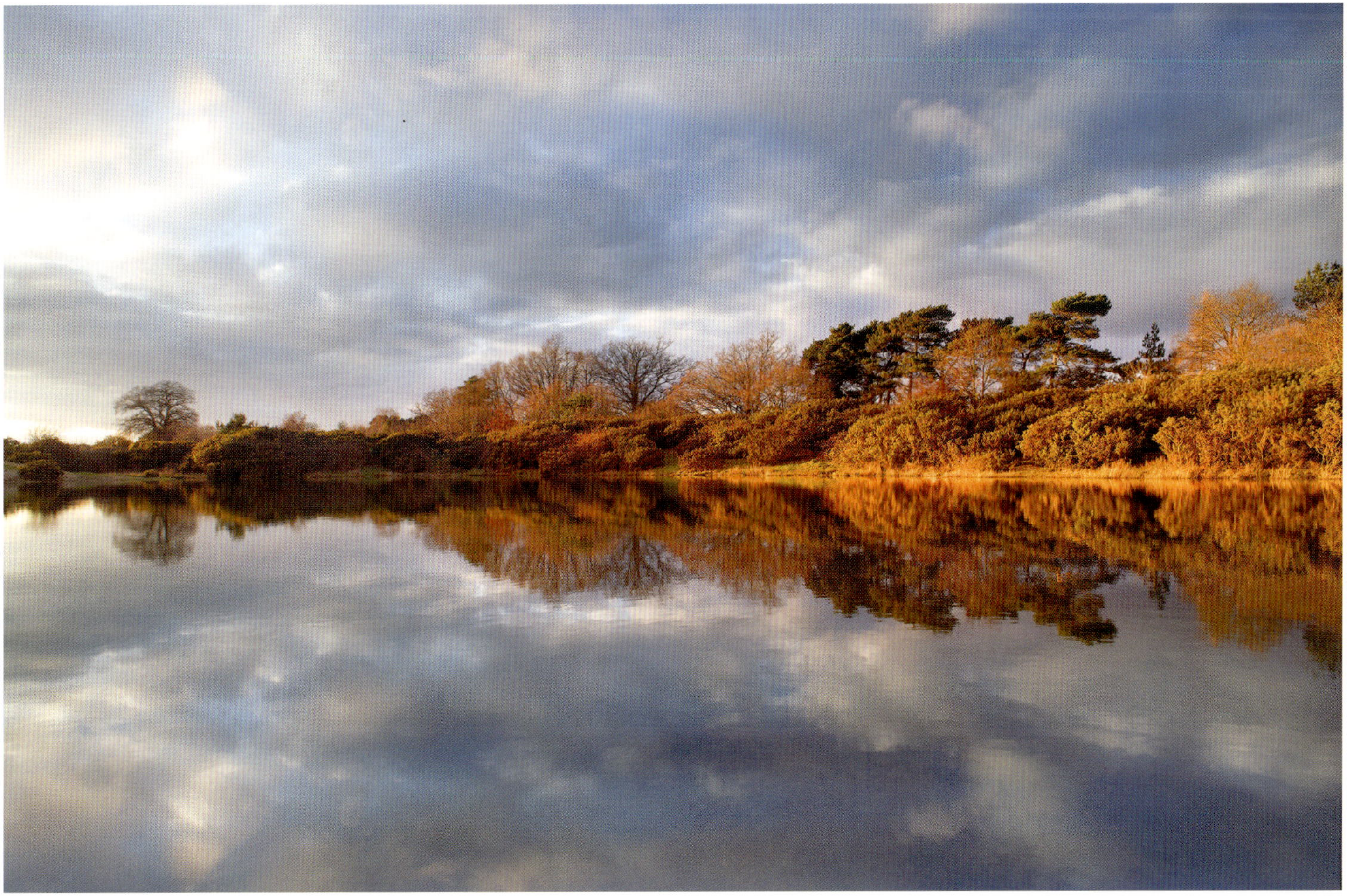

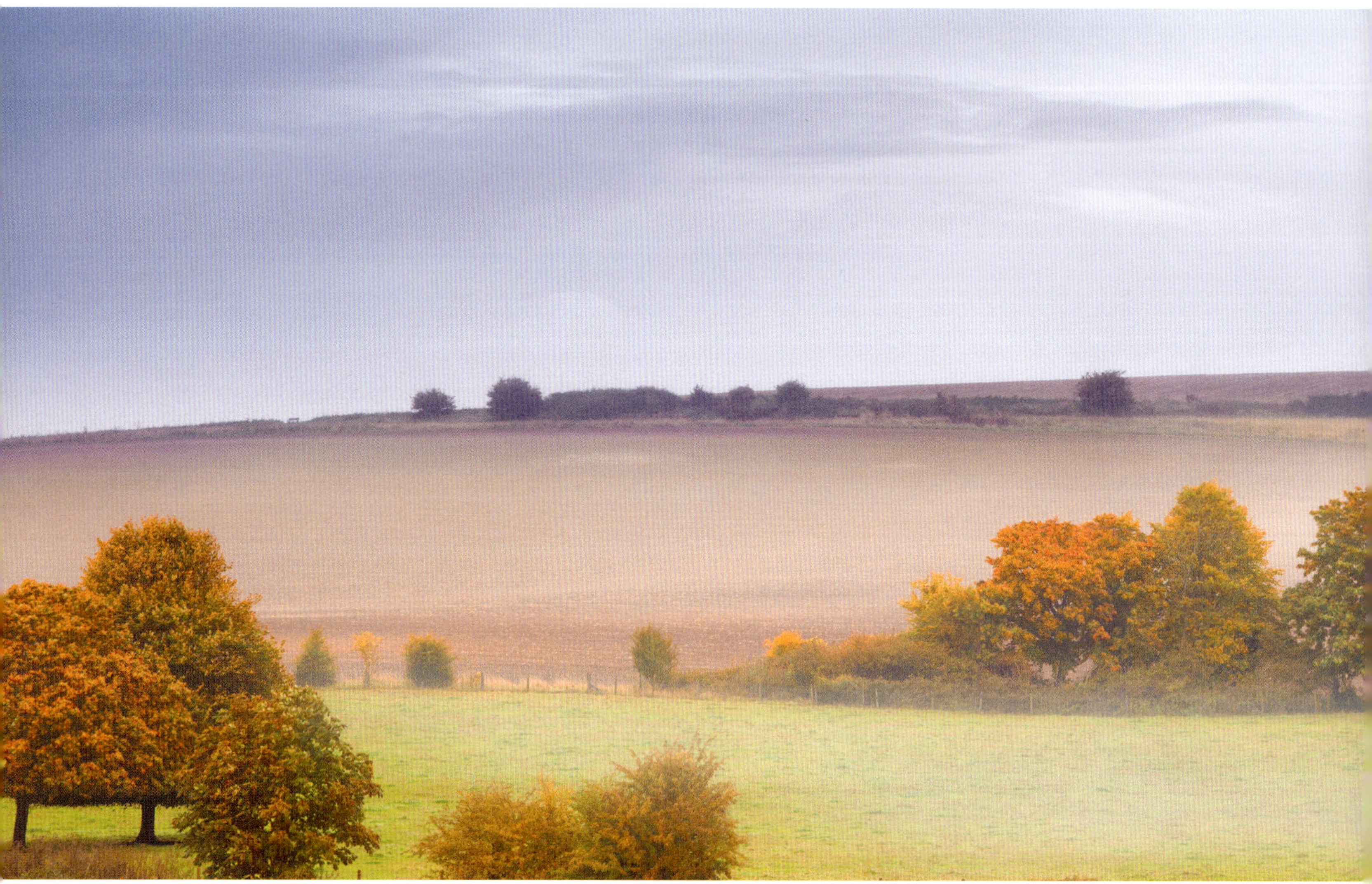

Maidencourt near Great Shefford

The course of the River Lambourn can be traced for some 15 miles down to its junction with the Kennet at Newbury. Maps indicate its source as being in the region of Upper Lambourn, but in this area it's a seasonal water which disappears in dry spells – only below Great

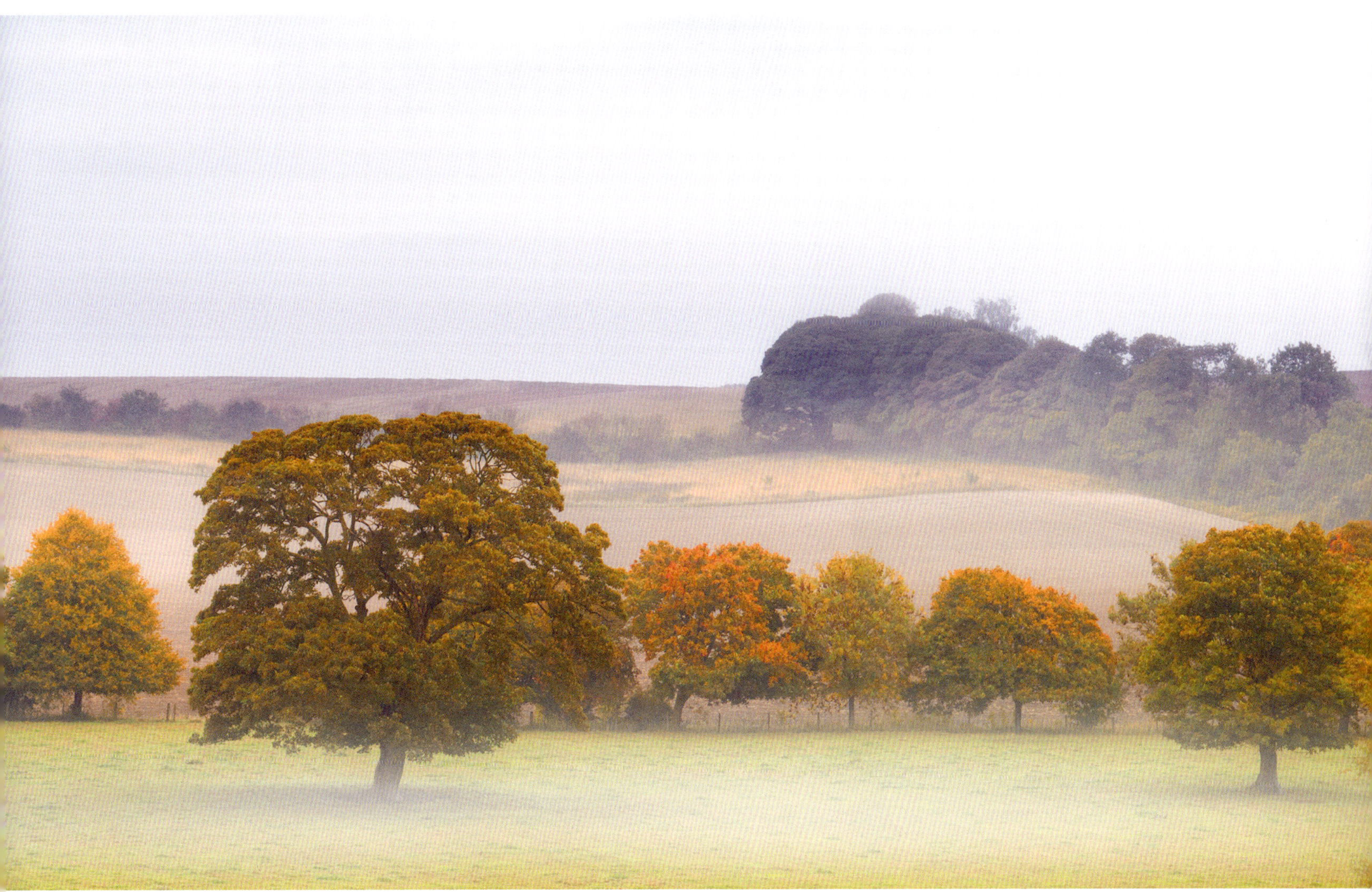

A pastoral scene in the upper Lambourn Valley

Shefford does it become a more permanent feature, forming a delightful chalk stream which passes through a string of charming villages. This image shows the view looking across one of the upper sections of the valley at Maidencourt, where a large rounded sycamore stands in a livestock field.

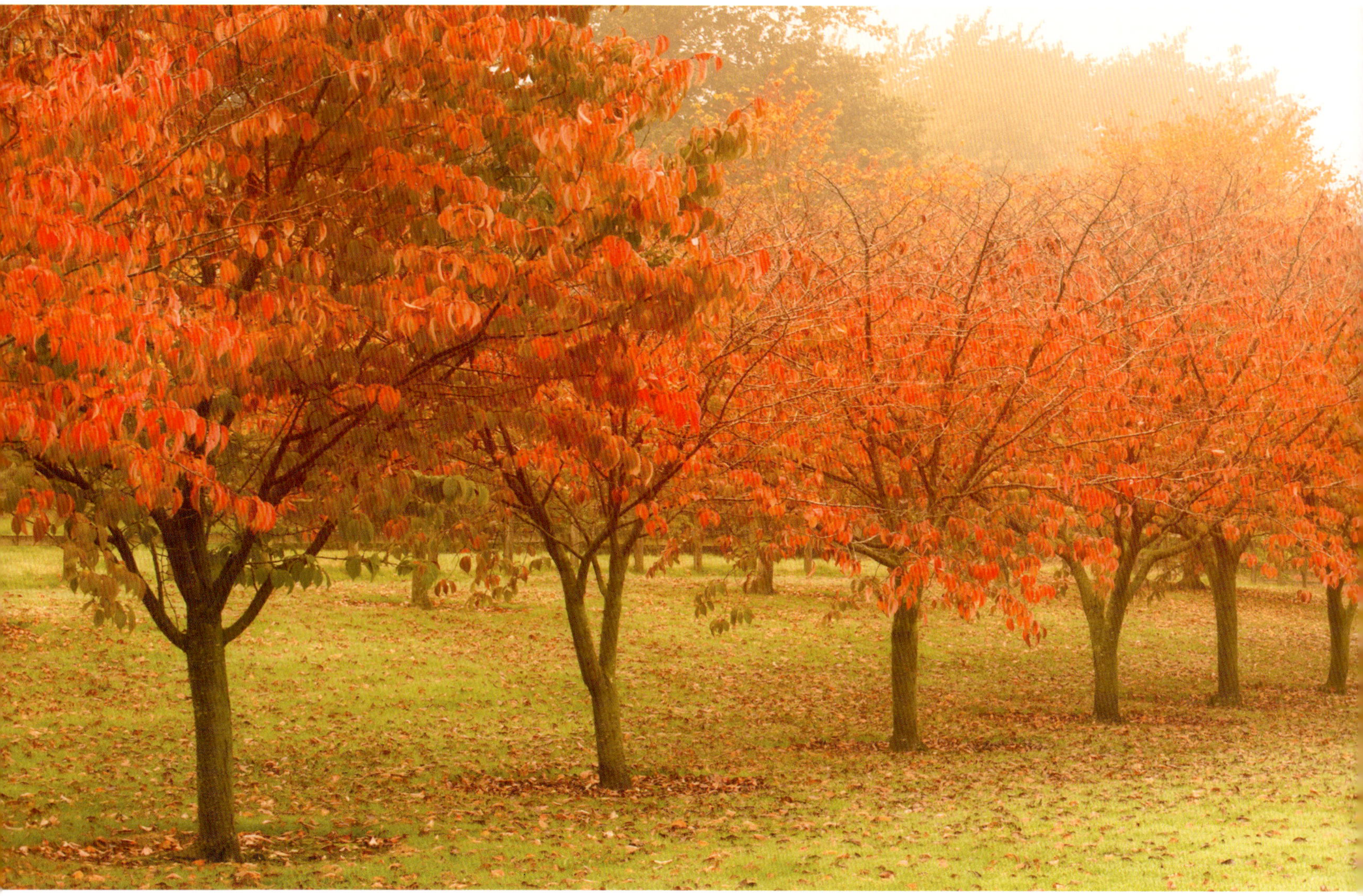

West Woodhay

The landscape of southern England shows little sign of autumn colour until late October, and it's usually well into November before the native trees reach their peak. But the first flash of colour comes much earlier at West Woodhay, where an avenue of ornamental cherries runs alongside the lane. Numbering some 40 or more trees, their fiery display can be seen in late September and makes an inspiring sight for passers-by.

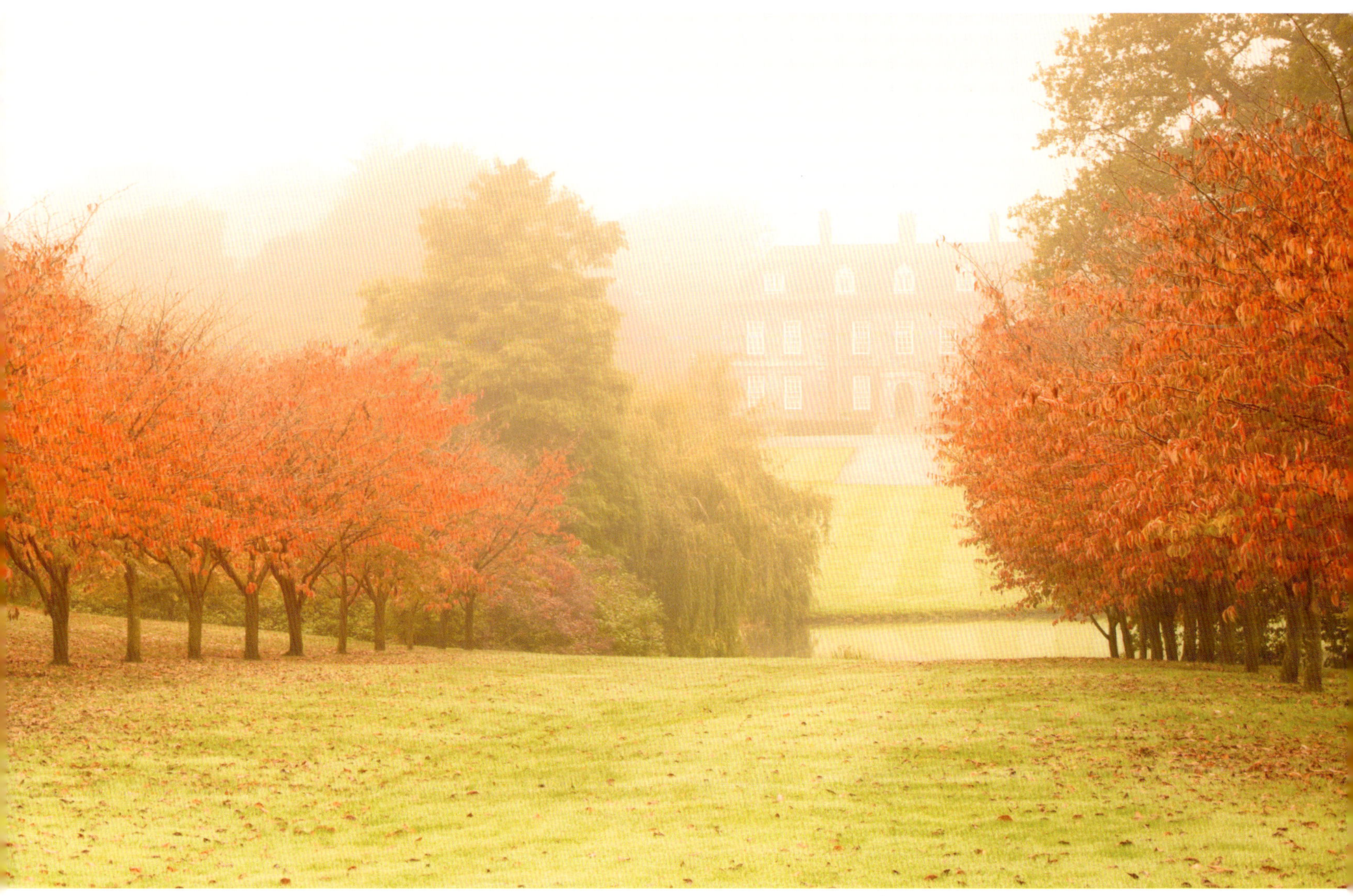

Cherry trees at West Woodhay in late September

The lines of trees dip down to a small lake which stands in front of West Woodhay House, built in 1635. The remains of the former parish church stand within the grounds of the house; a new church was built on a different site in 1883.

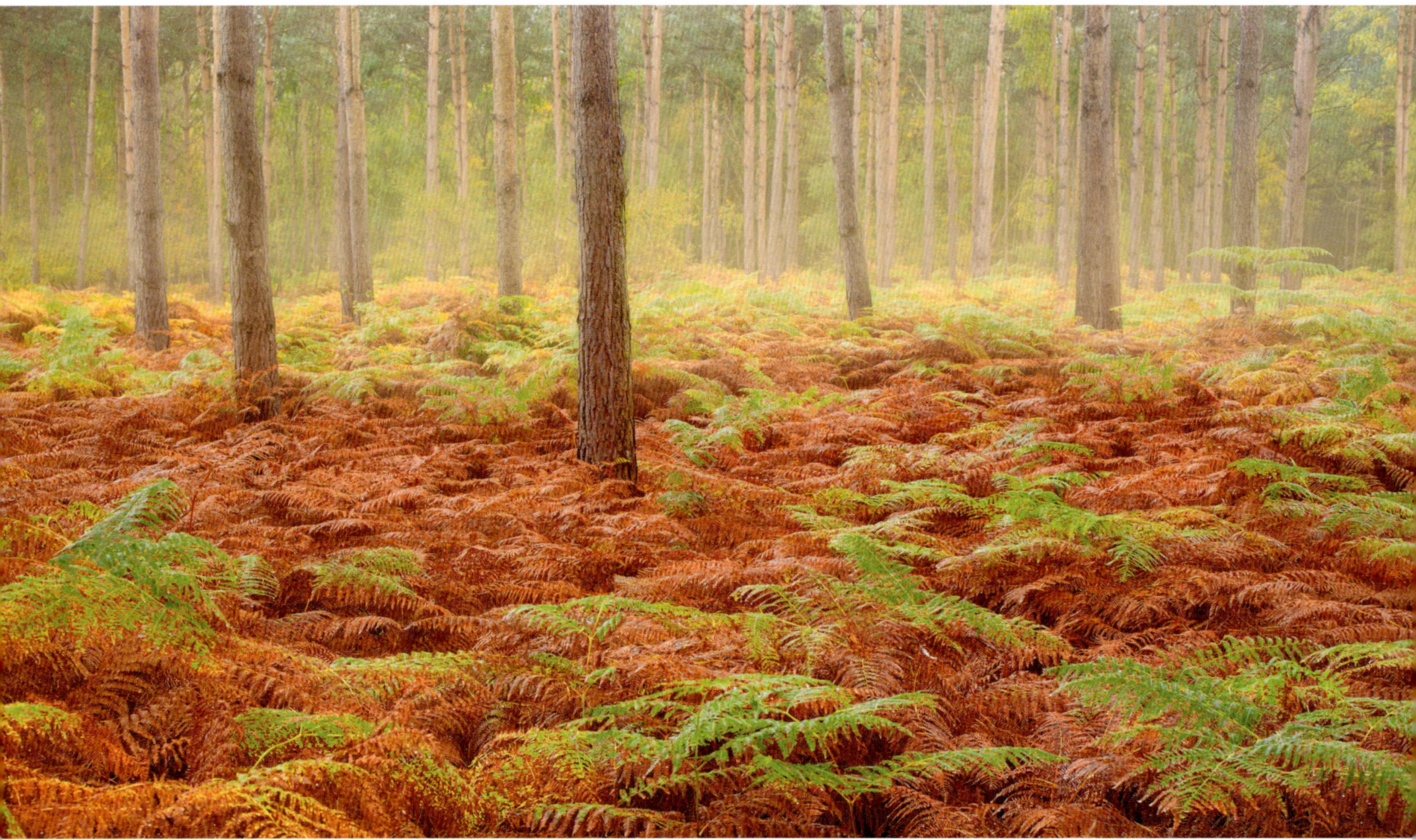

Beds of ferns under the pines at Scotch Wood

Scotch Wood near Stockcross

Between Stockcross and Wickham Heath the road passes through Scotch Wood, a small forest which is dominated by pine plantations. Unfortunately this type of coniferous monoculture offers little in the way of habitat for wildlife, owing to the absence of undergrowth on the dark and shady woodland floor. But as the trees mature and are thinned out, light levels begin to increase and smaller plants begin to spread in, such as the ferns shown in this picture.

While the pines offer nothing in terms of seasonal colour, this is made up for by the mosaic of fern fronds which turn from pale green to deep brown as autumn takes hold.

Bisham Woods

Across the Thames from Marlow a lane zigzags its way up the steep valley side towards Cookham Dean. The route cuts through Quarry Wood, part of the more extensive Bisham Woods, an ancient habitat managed by the Woodland Trust, and one which may possibly be a surviving fragment of Britain's original virgin forest.

Apart from its 'wild wood' appeal, the area has a rich human history, being the site of the bygone Bisham Quarry which supplied stone for the building of Windsor Castle. It is also home to an eighteenth-century ice house, and a number of small ponds which have formed from disused clay pits. The photograph shows a glade on the north-west hilltop which is part of an area dedicated to the businessman Lord Marshall of Knightsbridge.

An autumnal glade in Quarry Wood

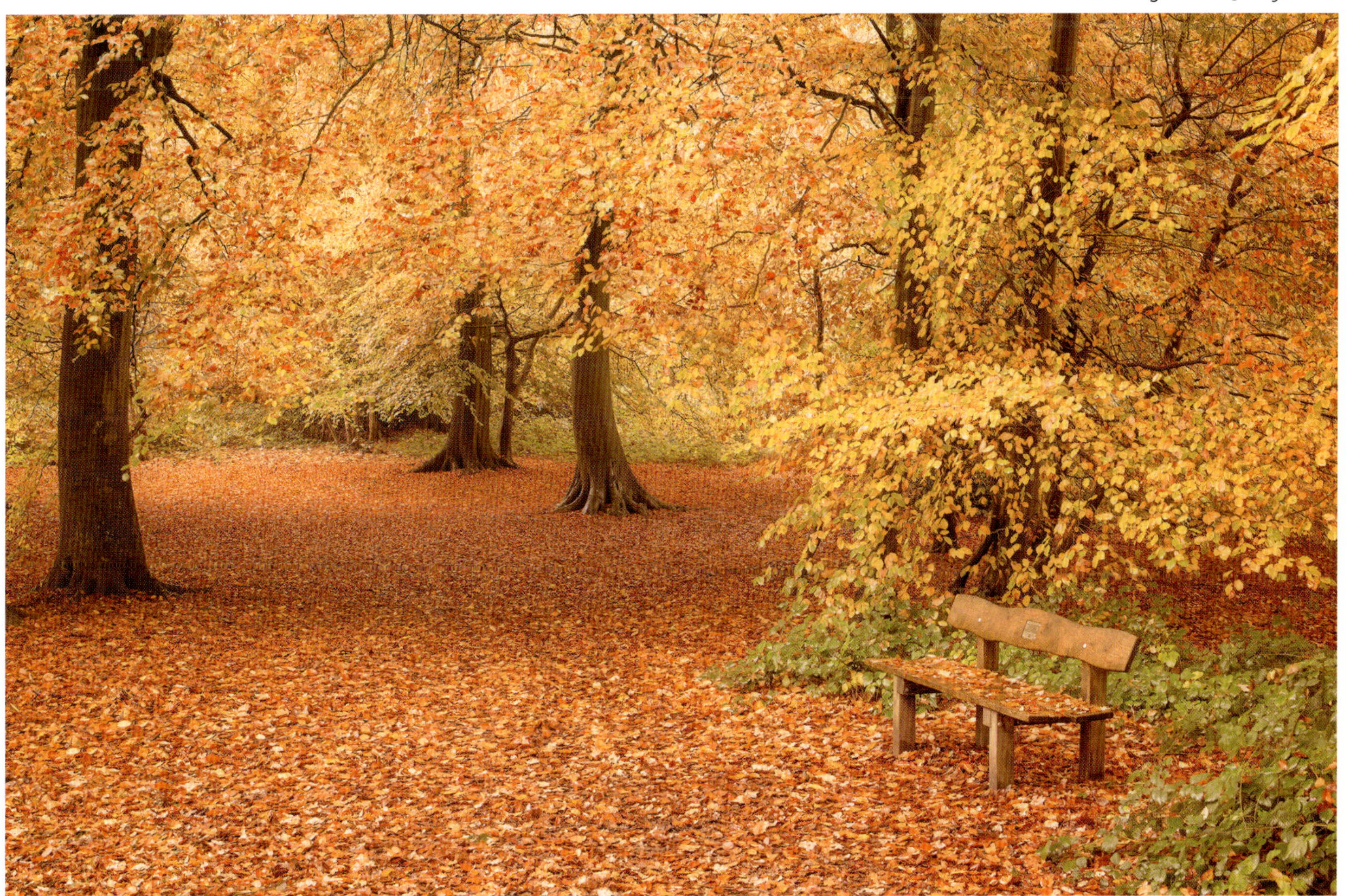

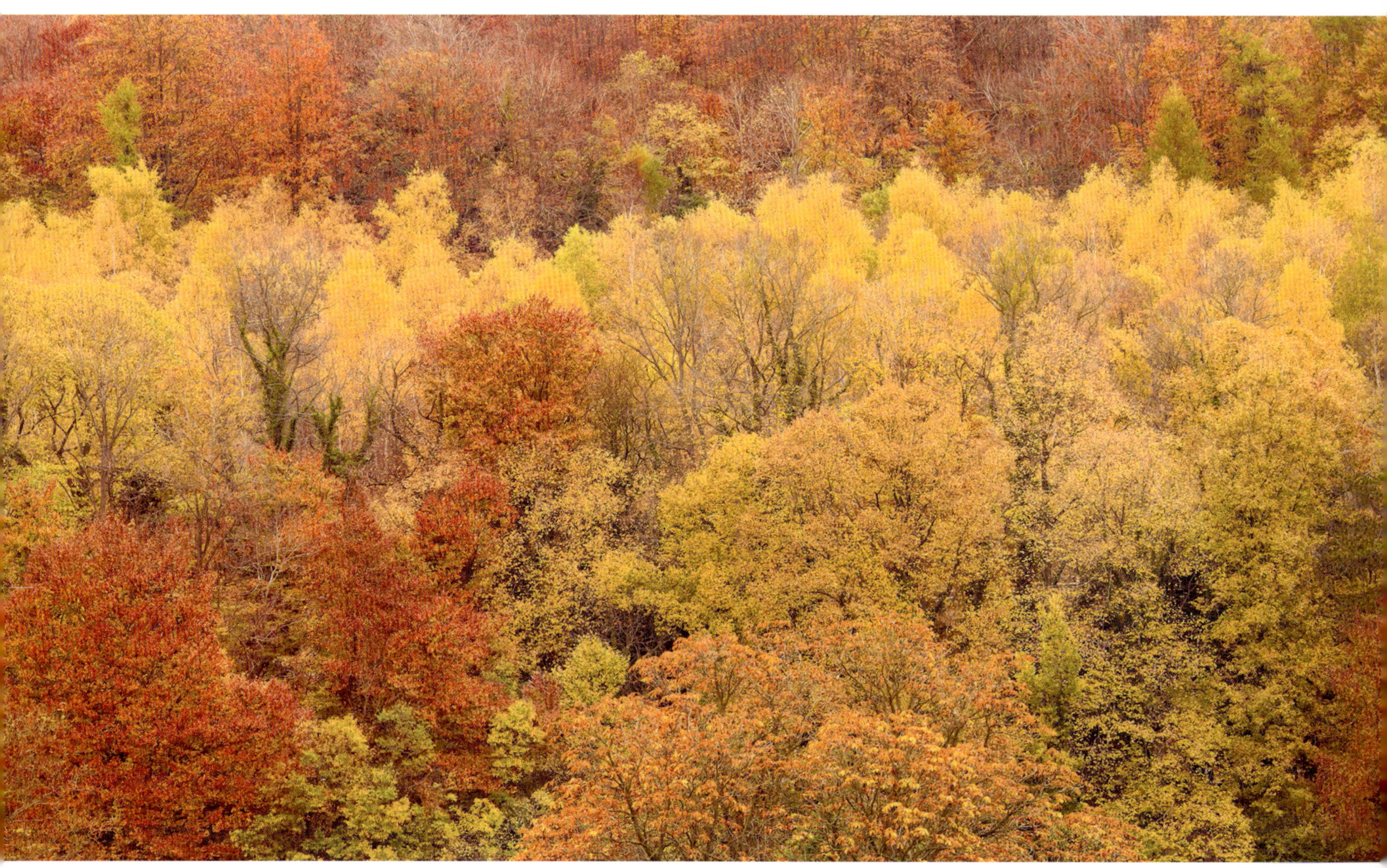

Dungrovehill Wood near Hurley
It seems remarkable that one of Berkshire's most spectacular autumn sights is not found in an arboretum or forest park, but stands either side of a busy dual carriageway. This image shows the lower section of Dungrovehill Wood; the A404 passes through from left to right, though it is screened by the riot of colourful foliage.

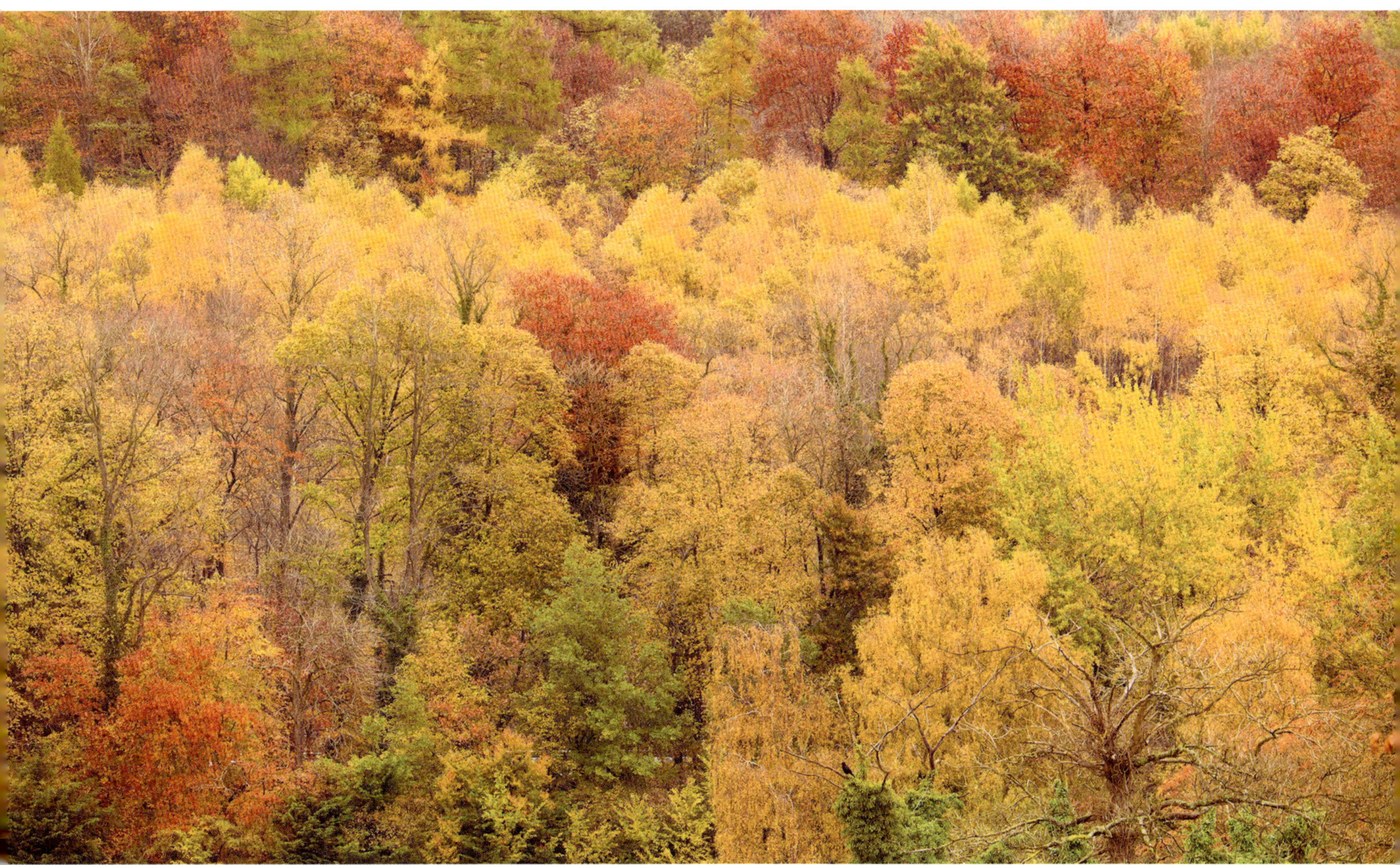

The colourful canopy of birch and beech at Dungrovehill Wood

This was the scene in mid-November when a spell of calm weather had allowed the leaves to develop their full colour while still on the trees. The best vantage point is from the footpath which crosses Temple Golf Course, giving a bird's eye view from the side of Speen Hill.

Poplar Trees at Boxford

In the syncline between Hoar Hill and Boxford Common is a parade of poplar trees; they number around 400 in all and line the footpath which leads from Boxford Farm to Bagnor Wood. As a fast-growing species they must be a relatively recent addition to the landscape, probably planted within the last twenty years or so. Of all Berkshire's tree-lined routes, this is one of the longest and straightest outside Windsor.

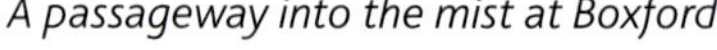

A passageway into the mist at Boxford

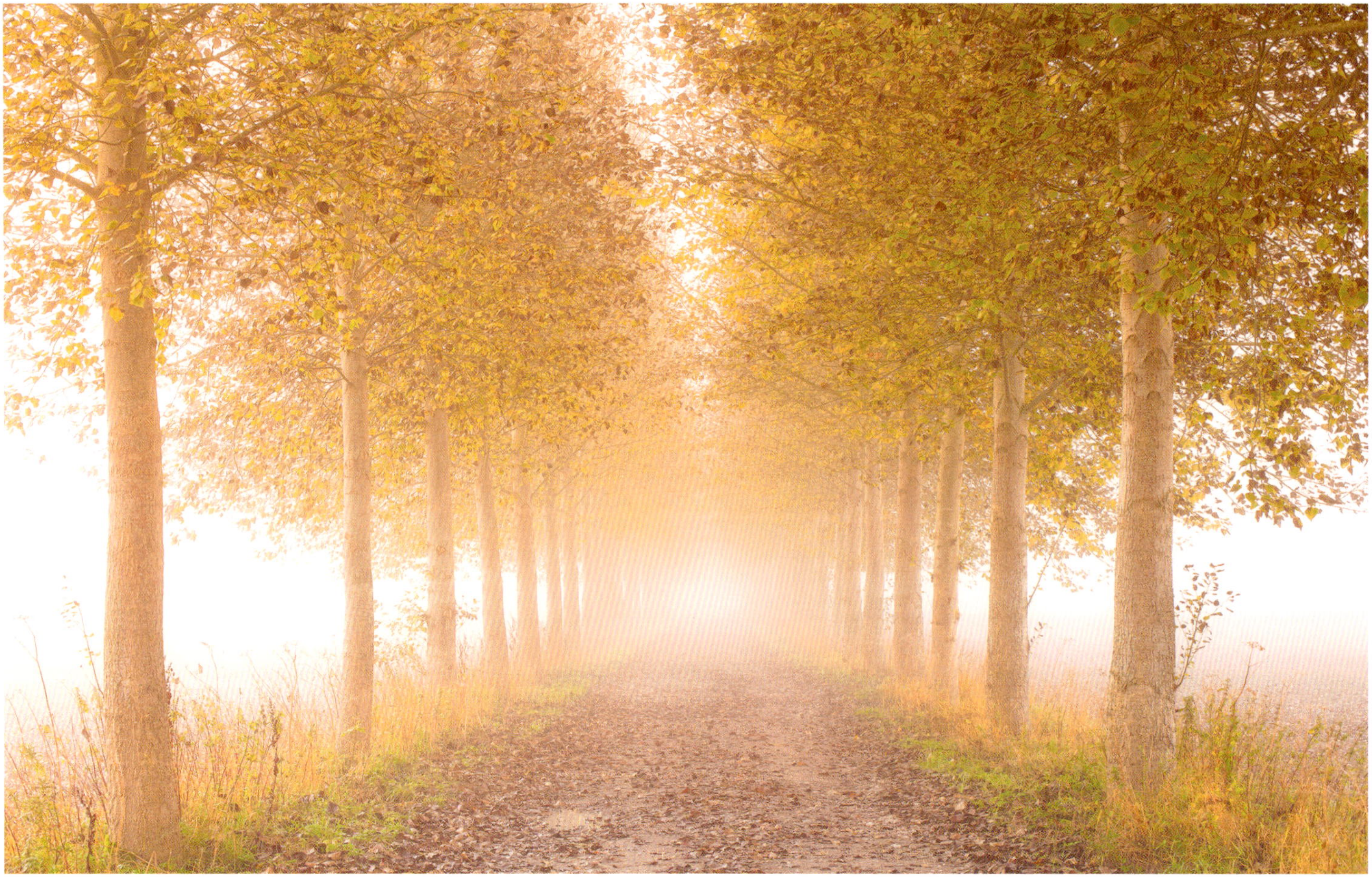

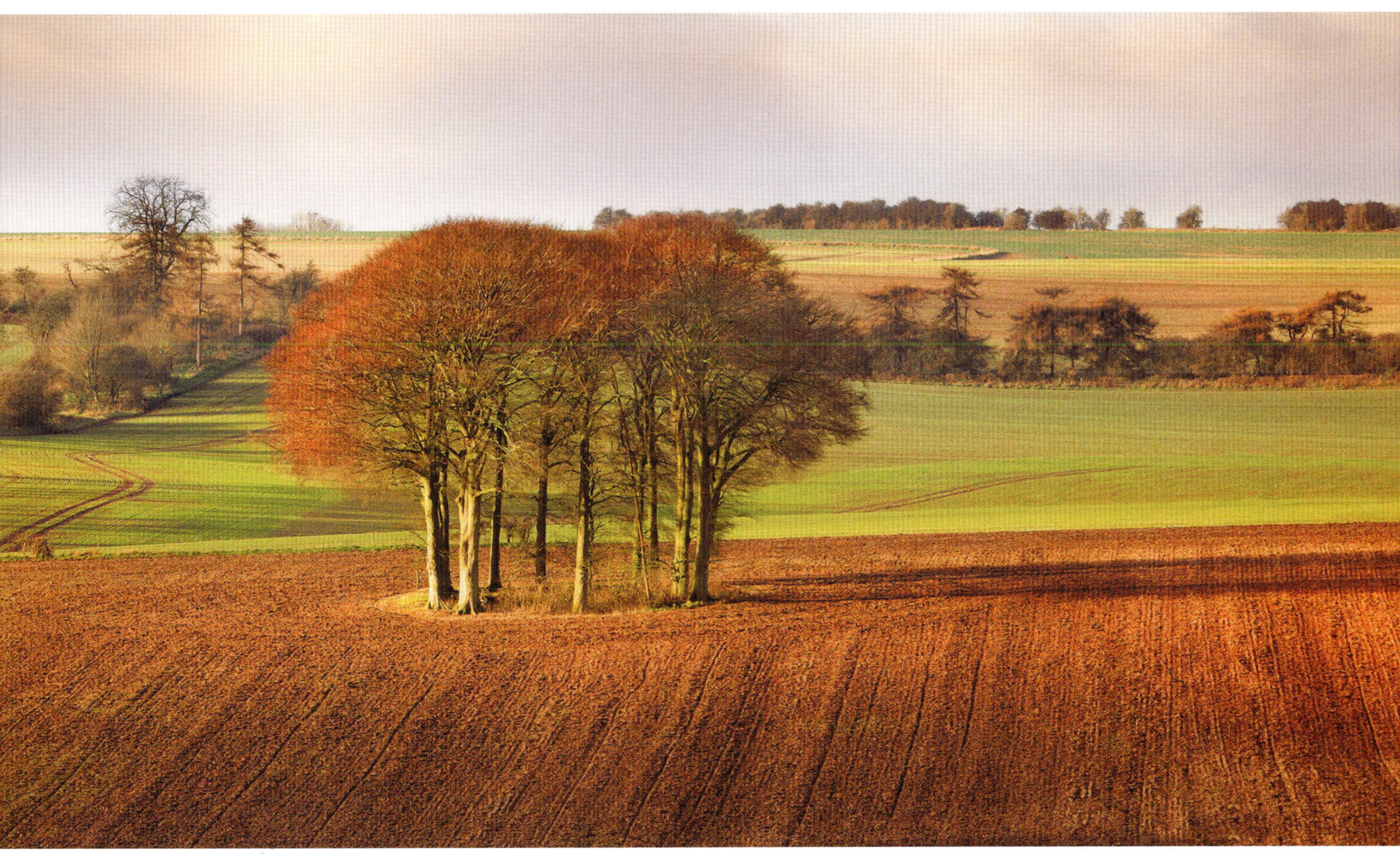

A crowd of beeches on Angeldown

Angeldown

Angeldown is a rolling farmscape which straddles the border between Berkshire and Oxfordshire. It can be seen south of The Ridgeway as it approaches Segsbury Castle, and to the west of the main road which leads to Wantage. Although on a bedrock of chalk, the landscape here is overlaid with clay, giving the fields a rich brown hue when first ploughed. The down's most conspicuous feature is a stand of beech trees in the centre of a field – this view shows them on a fine morning in late autumn.

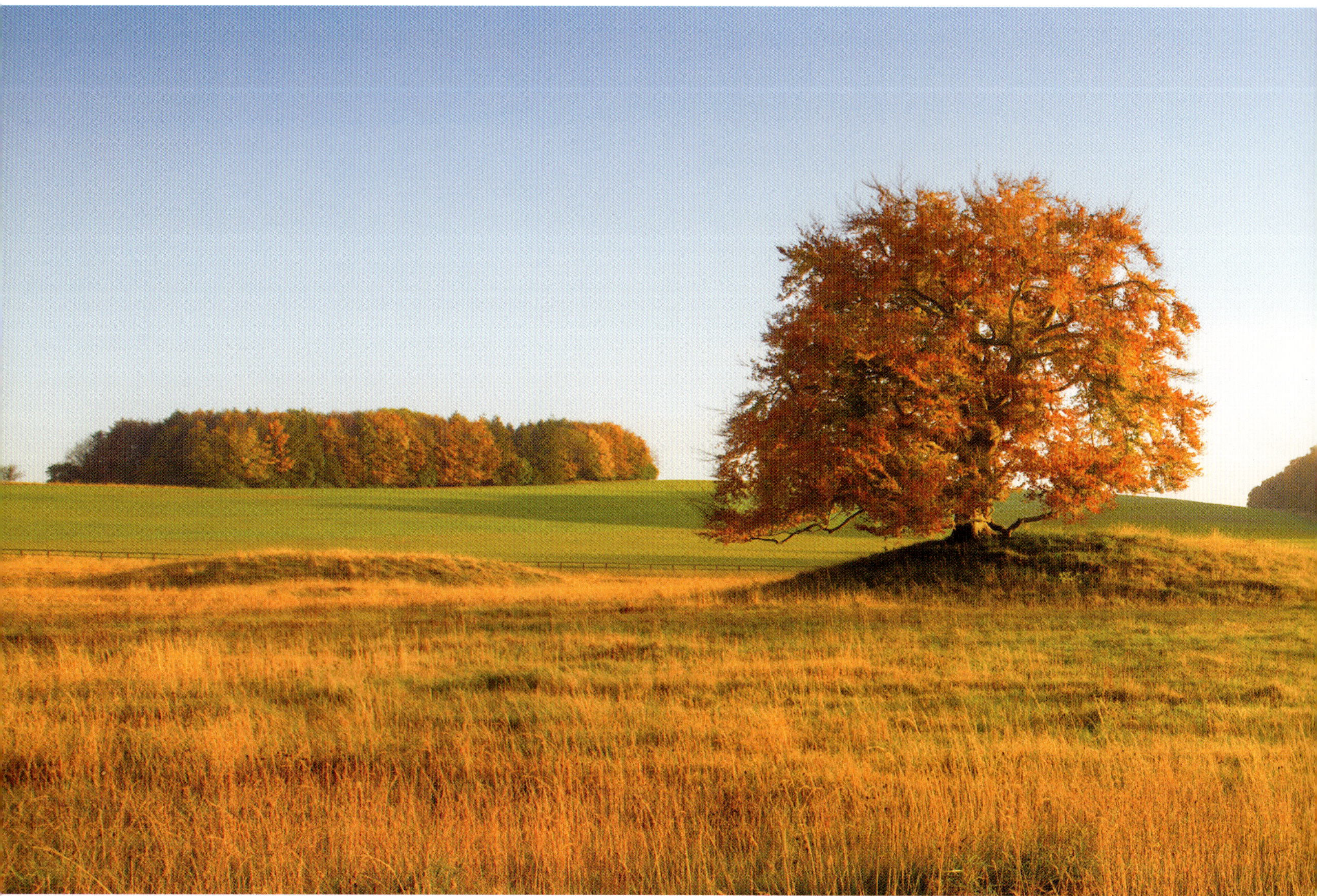

Seven Barrows near Lambourn

Lying at the very north-west tip of Berkshire are the remains of a Bronze Age cemetery; a group of burial mounds known as Seven Barrows. There are many more of these earthworks in the vicinity, so there's no doubt that the area was the site of a significant settlement around 3500 years ago.

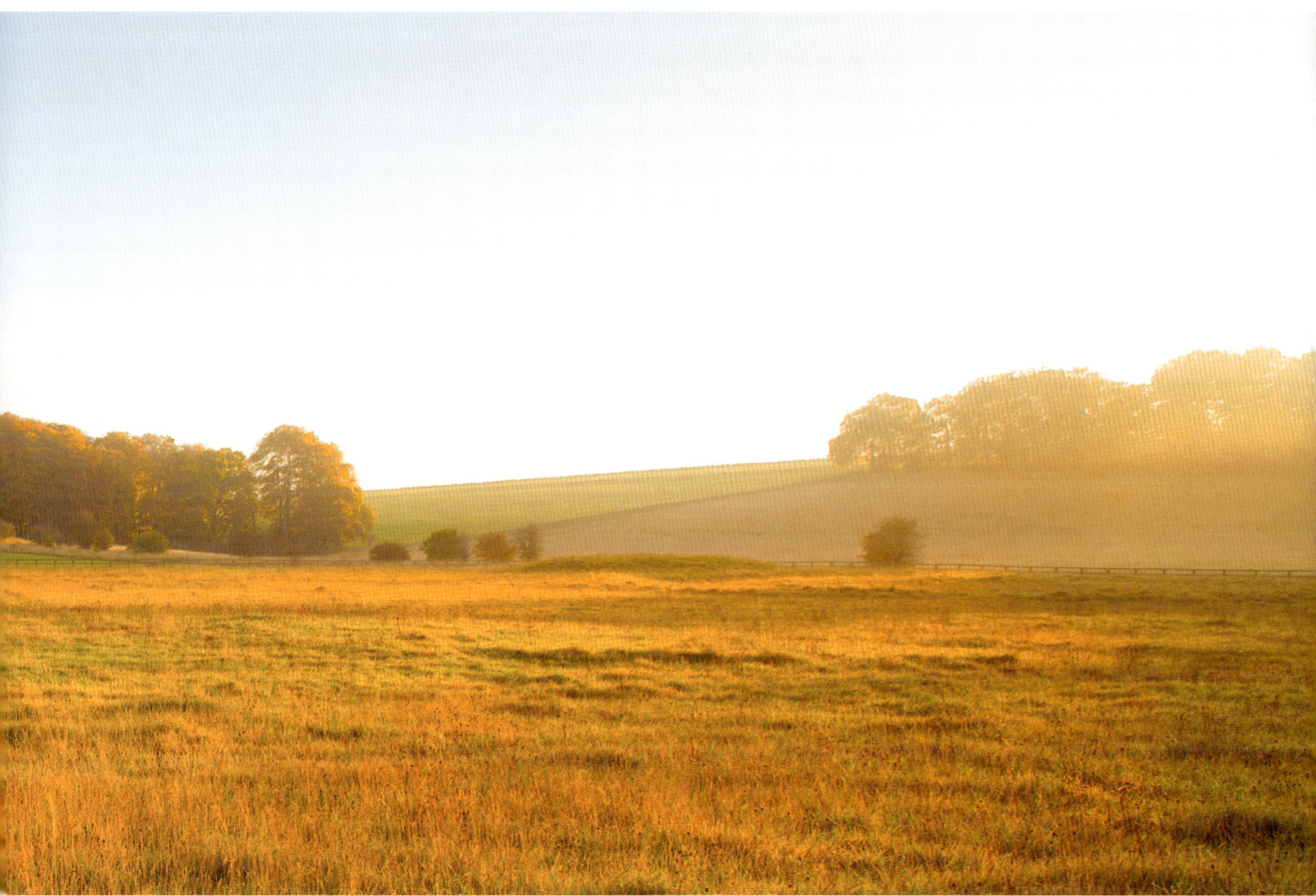

The solitary beech tree at the centre of Seven Barrows

All is quiet today, and this stretch of wild chalk grassland is cared for by the local Wildlife Trust. There is only one tree on the site – a small rounded beech which sits on top of the central mound. The wild flowers had gone to seed when this photograph was taken in late October, but with autumn at hand the golden beech leaves brought a new splash of colour to the landscape.

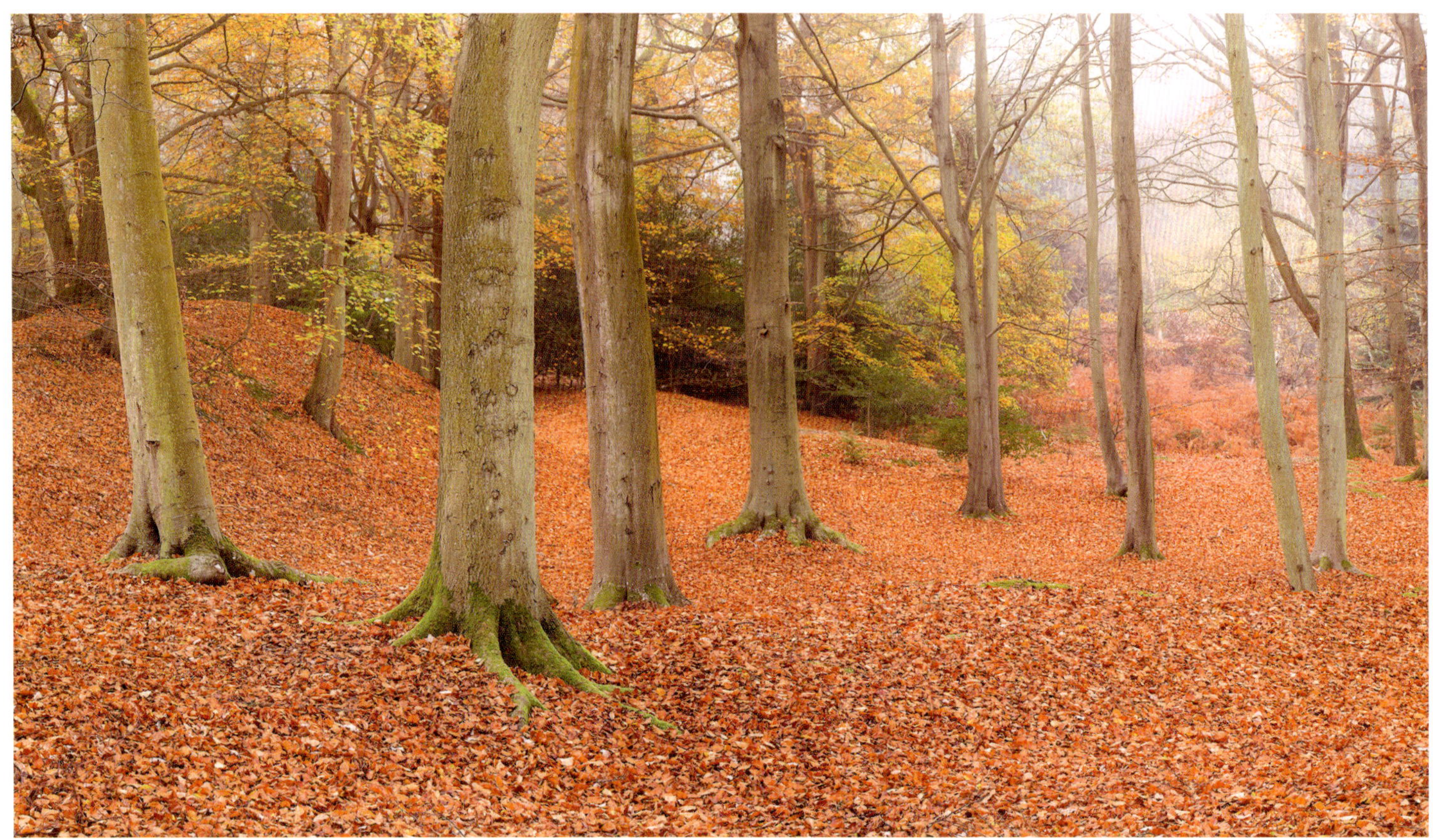

A leafy clearing on the west side of the hill-fort

Grimsbury Castle near Hermitage

There are around 800 hill-forts in England, many of which are prominent monuments that give commanding views of the surrounding countryside. And there's no doubt that the builders of Grimsbury Castle hill-fort near Hermitage chose a location which would allow them to keep watch over the surrounding area. But at some point over the centuries trees have invaded the abandoned site, and today there are no views from the steep ramparts which are traversed by a quiet wooded lane.

However, the seclusion and silence brought about by the canopy of beech and oak gives the site a great atmosphere, and one which is no doubt more peaceful than that which it knew in the past.

Steeped in mist – one of the many elegant beech trees on the ramparts

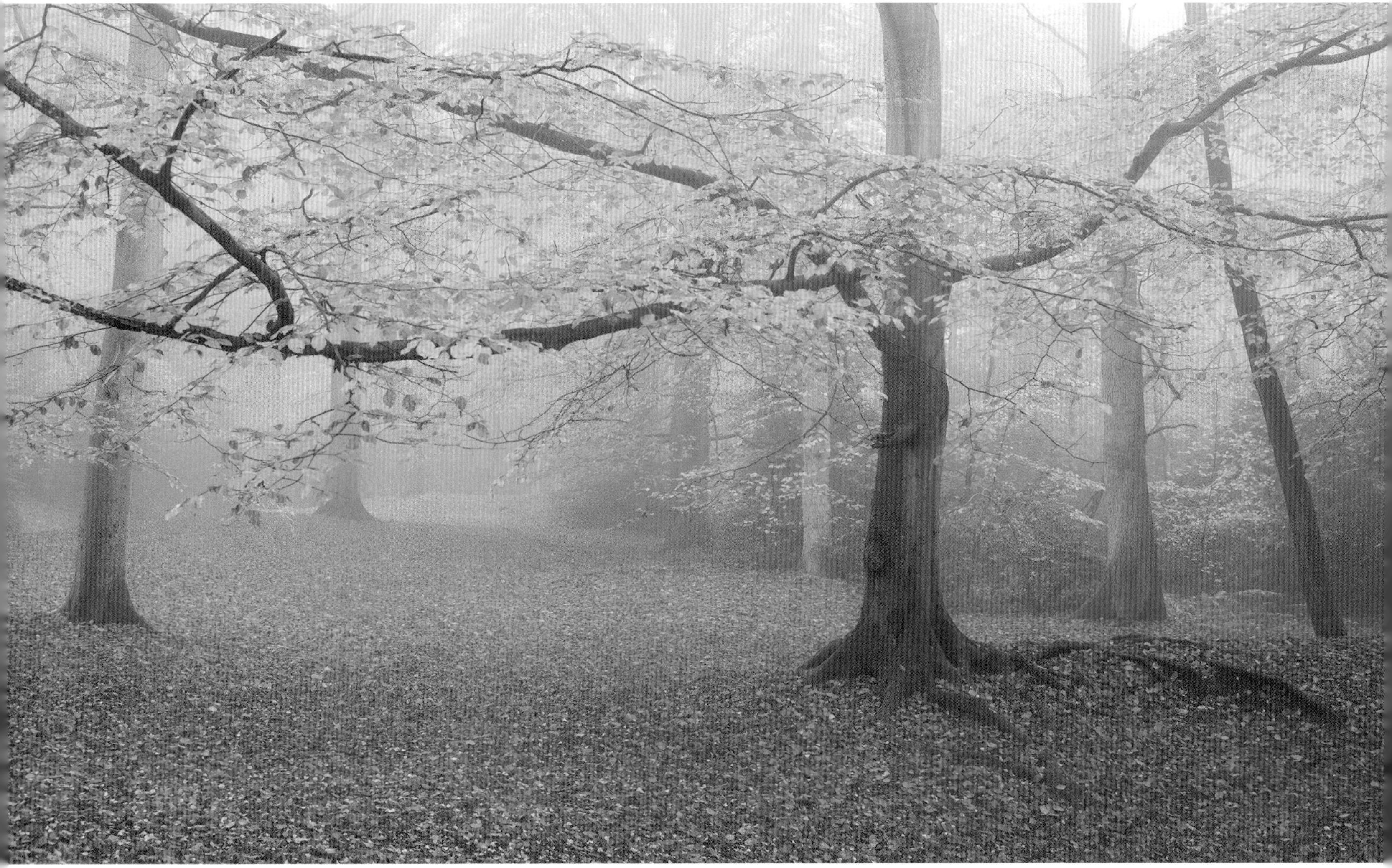

Fawley Church

Set among the high fields of north-west Berkshire is the small village of Fawley. Woolley Down can be seen across the dry valley to the east, while to the west a footpath leads towards the Lambourn Downs. The grey stone church with its eighteenth-century tower, in many ways the centrepiece of the village, stands elevated above the surrounding buildings, most of which are screened by trees. Its position makes it a focal point visible on the skyline from a number of distant locations, and it makes an impressive sight – especially at first light in November when its easterly walls reflect the rising sun.

The picturesque setting of Fawley church

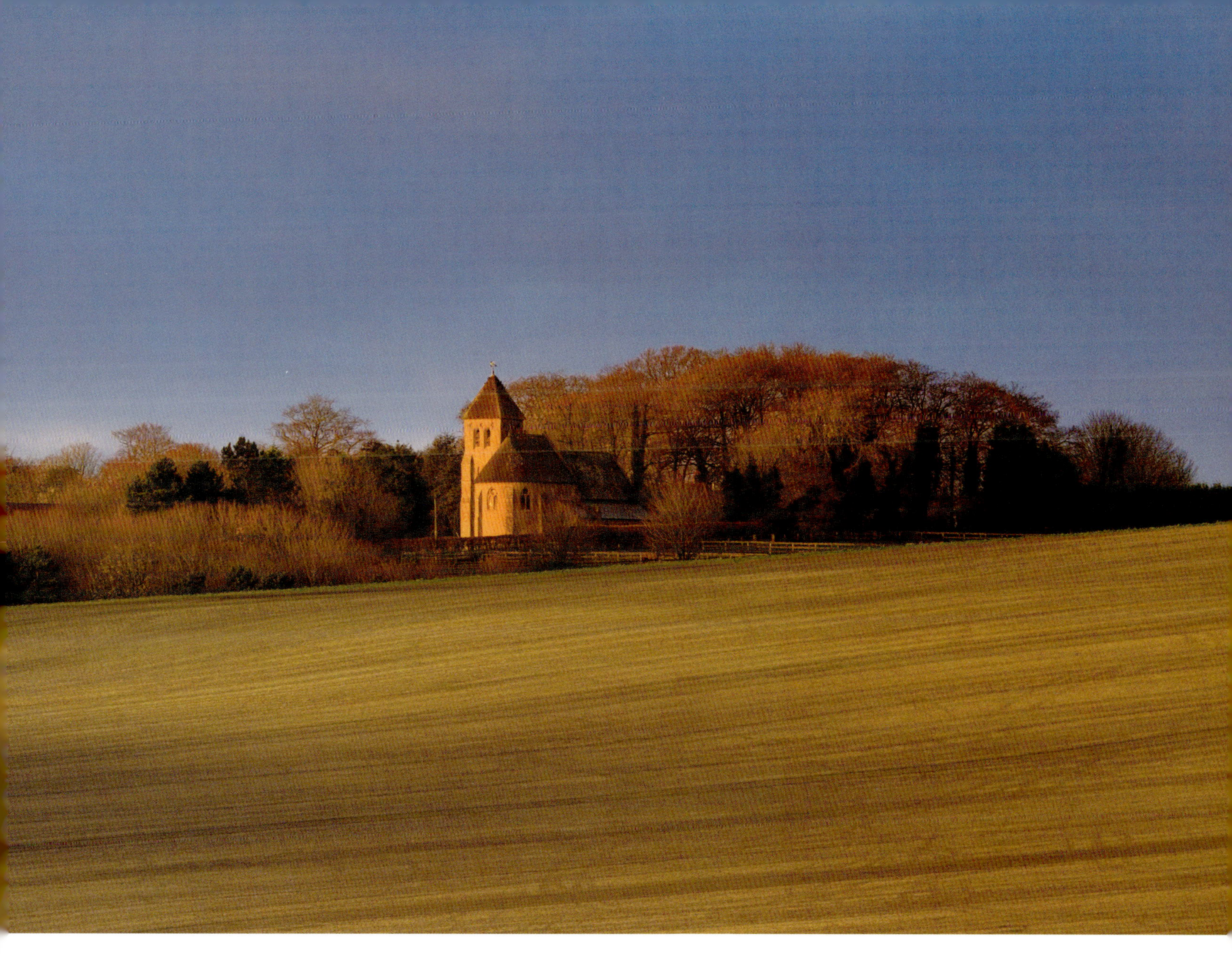

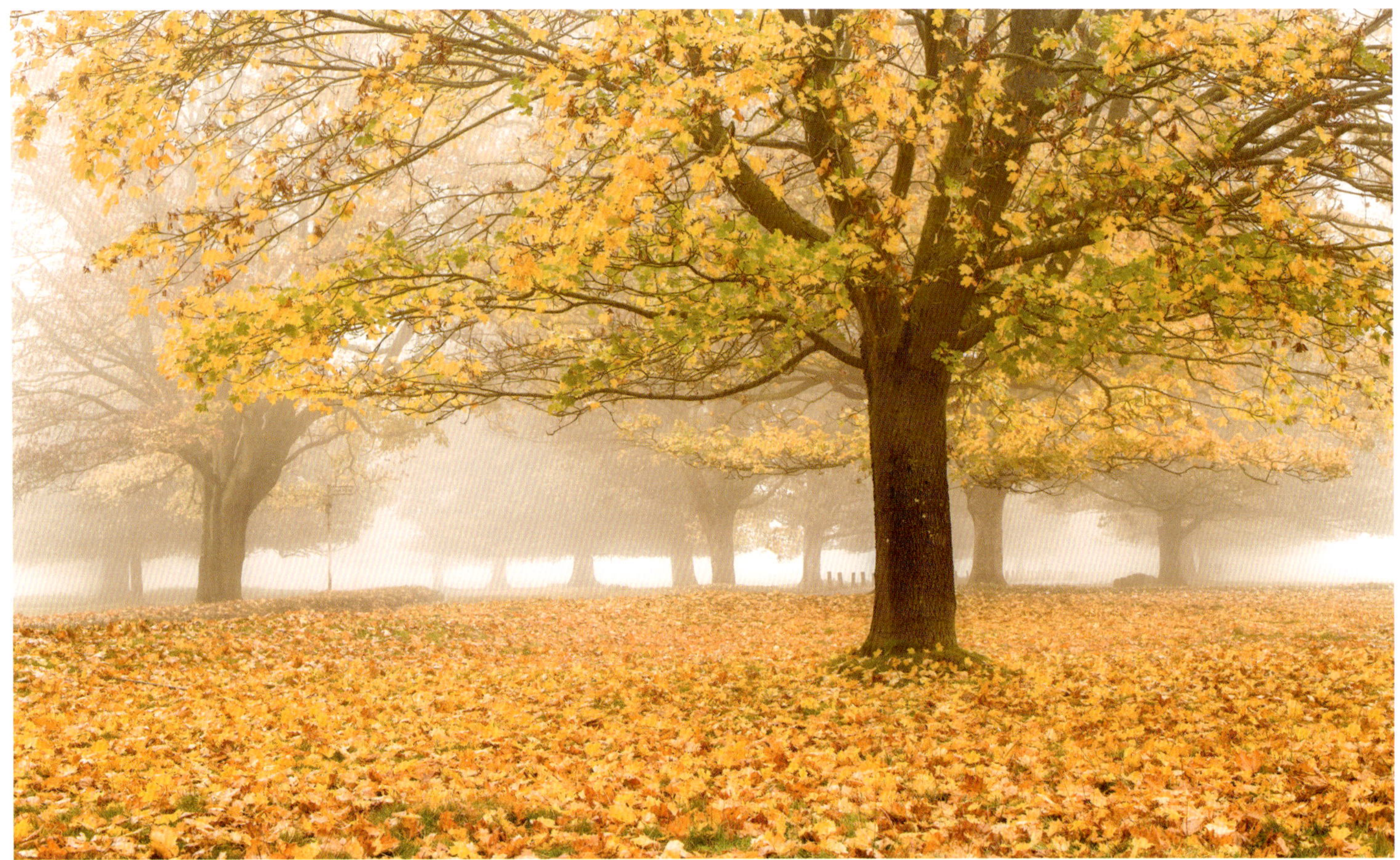

A carpet of maple leaves on the common in November

Hungerford Common

Known also as Hungerford Port Down, this stretch of land covers around 200 acres to the south-east of the town, with a slope overlooking the Kennet Valley. It's an attractive green space, partly tree-lined and sometimes grazed by cattle, which was recently enhanced by the removal of overhead power cables that were re-routed underground.

Six public footpaths criss-cross the area, though in reality people are free to wander unrestricted across the landscape. This photograph shows a colourful maple which stands where three lanes meet at the centre of the common – the signpost to Inkpen is just visible on the left side.

Tree-lined Lake near Bradfield Southend

On top of a wooded hill above the River Bourne is a small lake, shown on maps but without a name. It is certainly man-made, probably created as a fishing water at some point in the last few decades, complete with two small islands. It is situated alongside the footpath between Ufton Wood and Ham Copse, and was looking particularly colourful when I passed this way on a damp afternoon in late autumn. The trees which surround the banks and crowd the islands were glowing yellow, and all this was reflected in the calm turquoise water.

A lake with no name – the beautiful tree-lined water by Ufton Wood

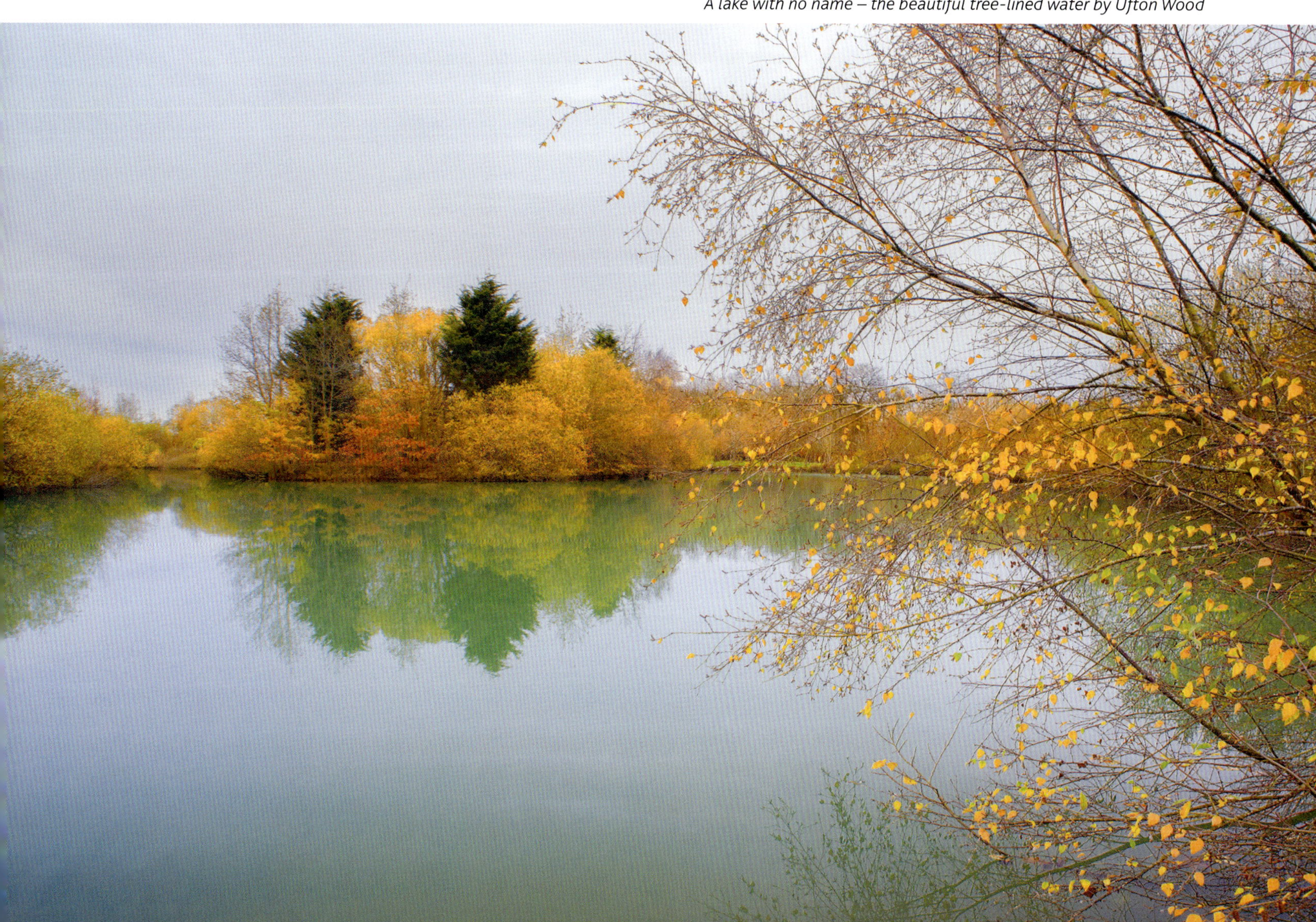

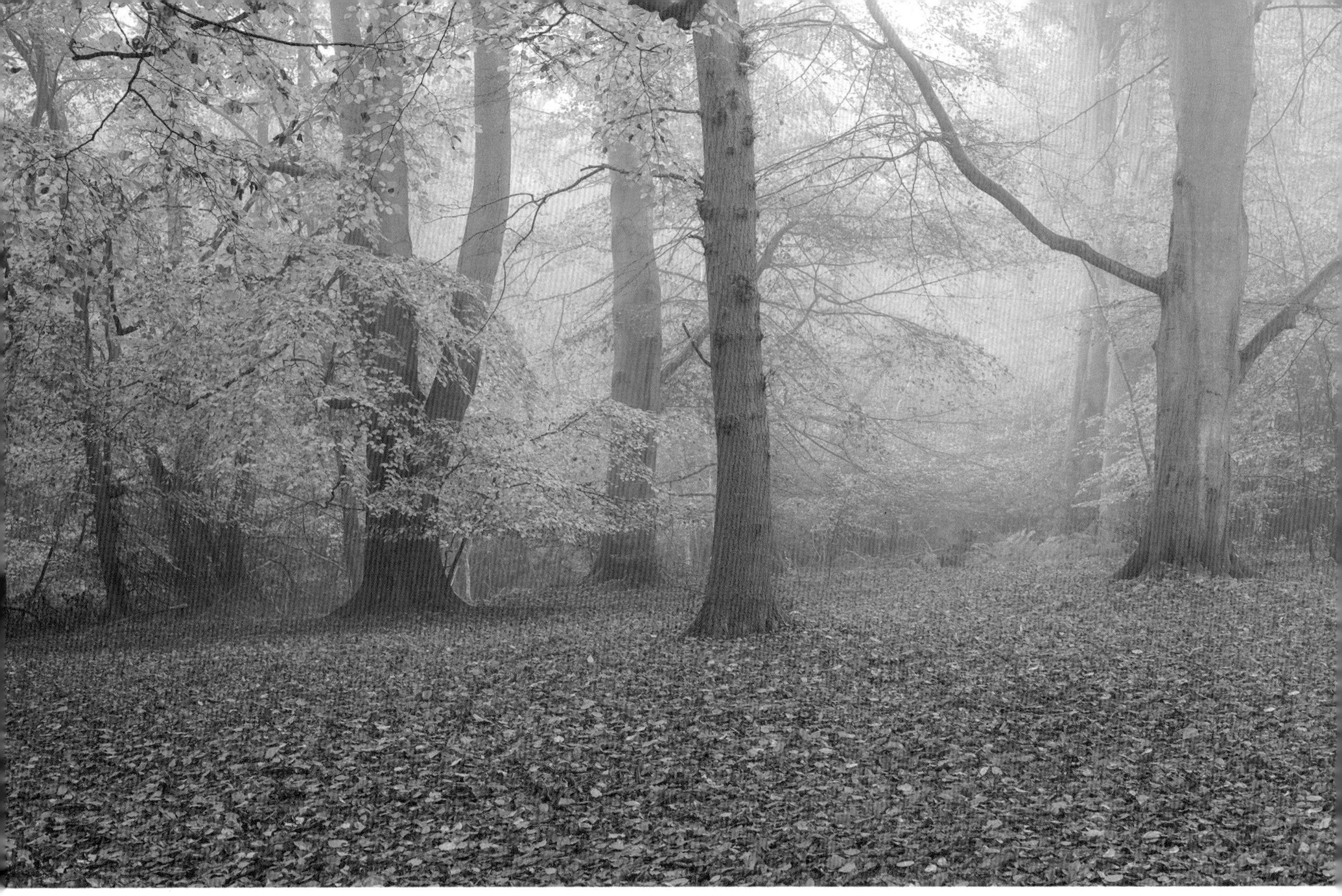

The Slade near Bucklebury

Bucklebury Common extends for some 900 acres and is one of the largest commons in southern England. The habitat consists of both forest and heathland, with a notable avenue of oaks at Chapel Row – the oldest of which were planted in the late sixteenth century to commemorate a visit by Queen Elizabeth I.

Elsewhere on the common the woodland scenery is diverse – on one side may be a tangled thicket of birch; on the other, a larch

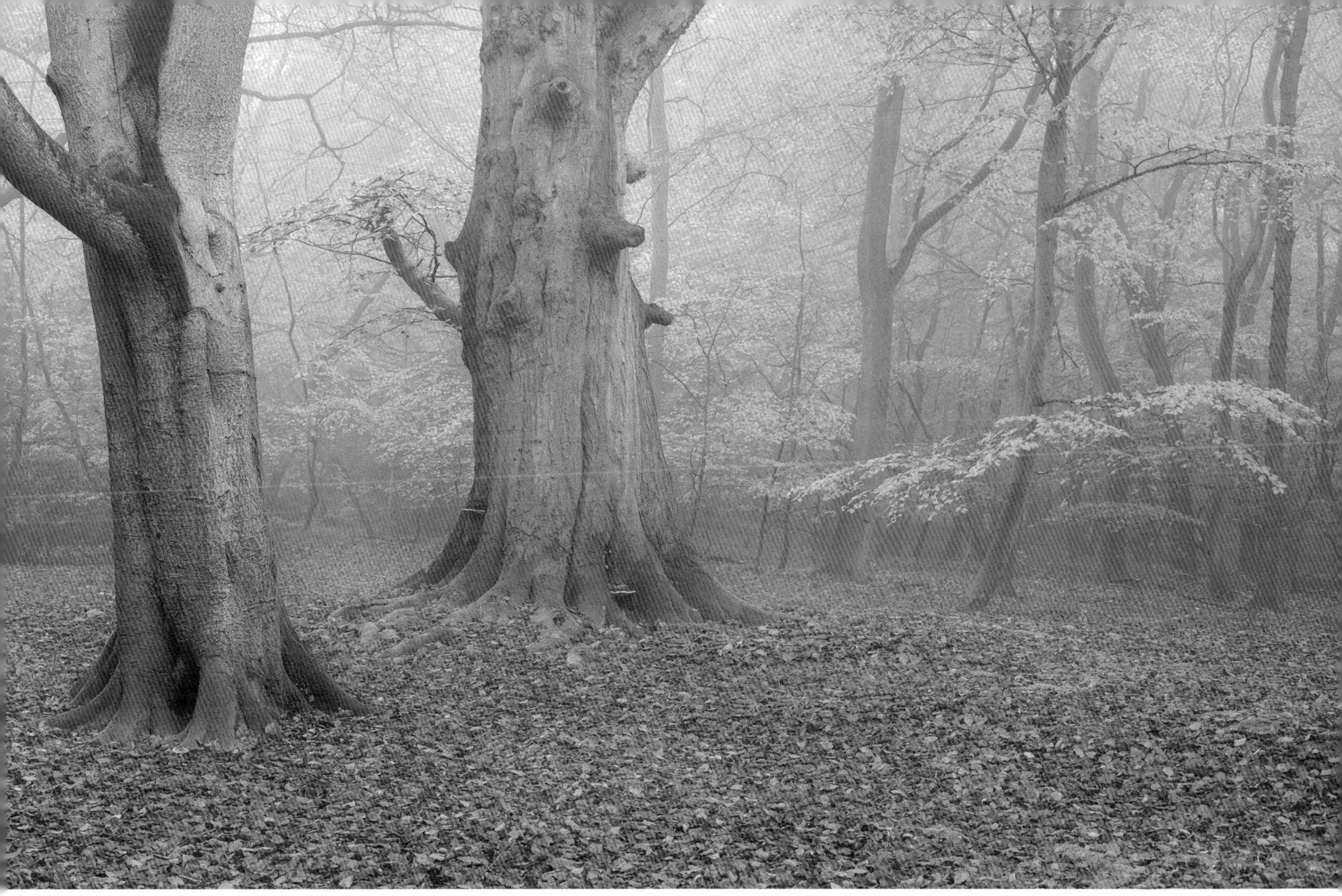

A woodland vista near The Slade

plantation with its mossy trimmings. But for the most part the dominant trees are the beeches which, in autumn at least, are the most spectacular.

This photograph was taken near The Slade – a small hamlet on the north side of the common – where a stand of older trees has shaded out the undergrowth, leaving just a clear leafy carpet on the woodland floor.

Combe Gibbet

A gibbet has existed on this site since the seventeenth century, when it was used to display the bodies of a murderous couple. Although it was never used again the structure has been maintained (and replaced a number of times) over the centuries, and its haunting outline is still visible from much of the surrounding area.

It stands on top of an ancient long barrow on the crest of Inkpen Hill, close to the plunging northern slopes. But despite its dark past the site has become a focal point for sightseers and passing ramblers, not to mention a host of hang-gliding and paragliding enthusiasts in fine weather. This image shows the gibbet in the pre-dawn light of early autumn.

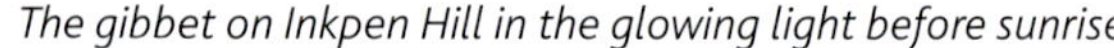

The gibbet on Inkpen Hill in the glowing light before sunrise

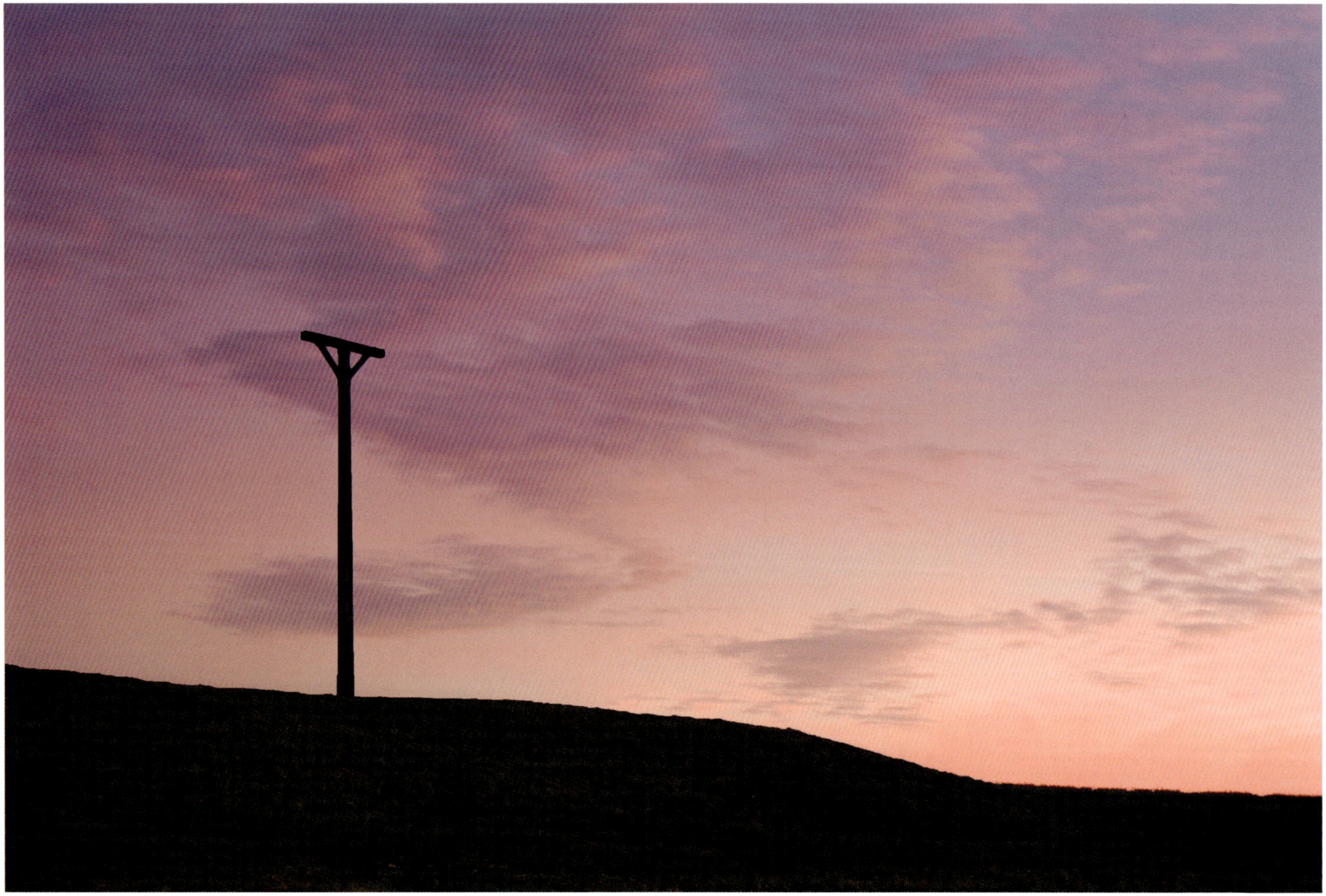

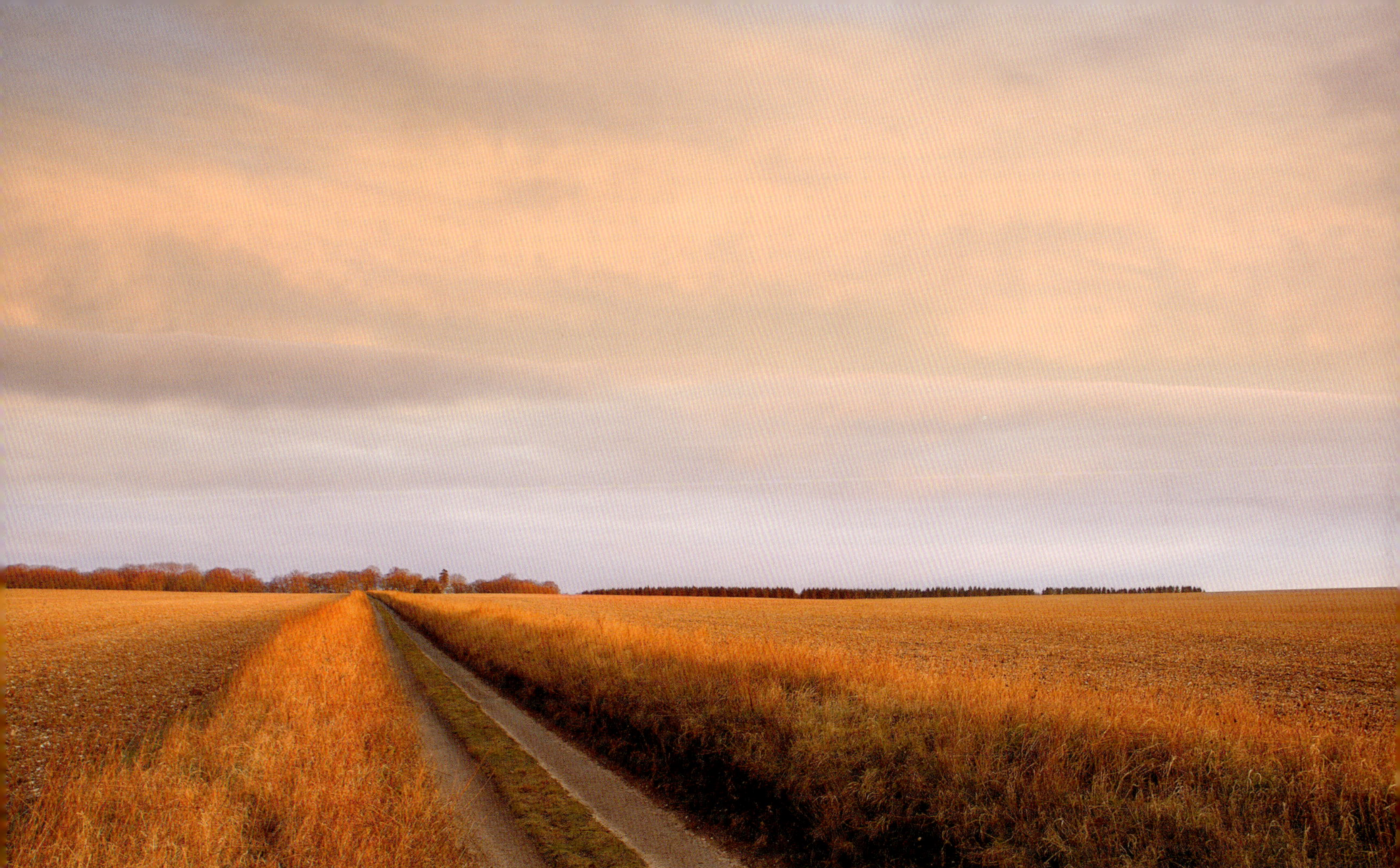

Golden light over the trackway to Brick Kiln Copse

Landscape near Hungerford

North-west of Hungerford is a small deciduous wood known as Brick Kiln Copse which is shared between two counties – the border cuts right through it, with Wiltshire to the north and Berkshire to the south. My interest in the area centres on the grassy trackway from Hopgrass Farm which leads across the fields towards the wood – I have a liking for simple, open landscapes, so this location has caught my eye a number of times.

This photograph was taken in very transient light on a mostly cloudy morning, but the brief flash of sun was enough to bring out the colours in the autumnal landscape.

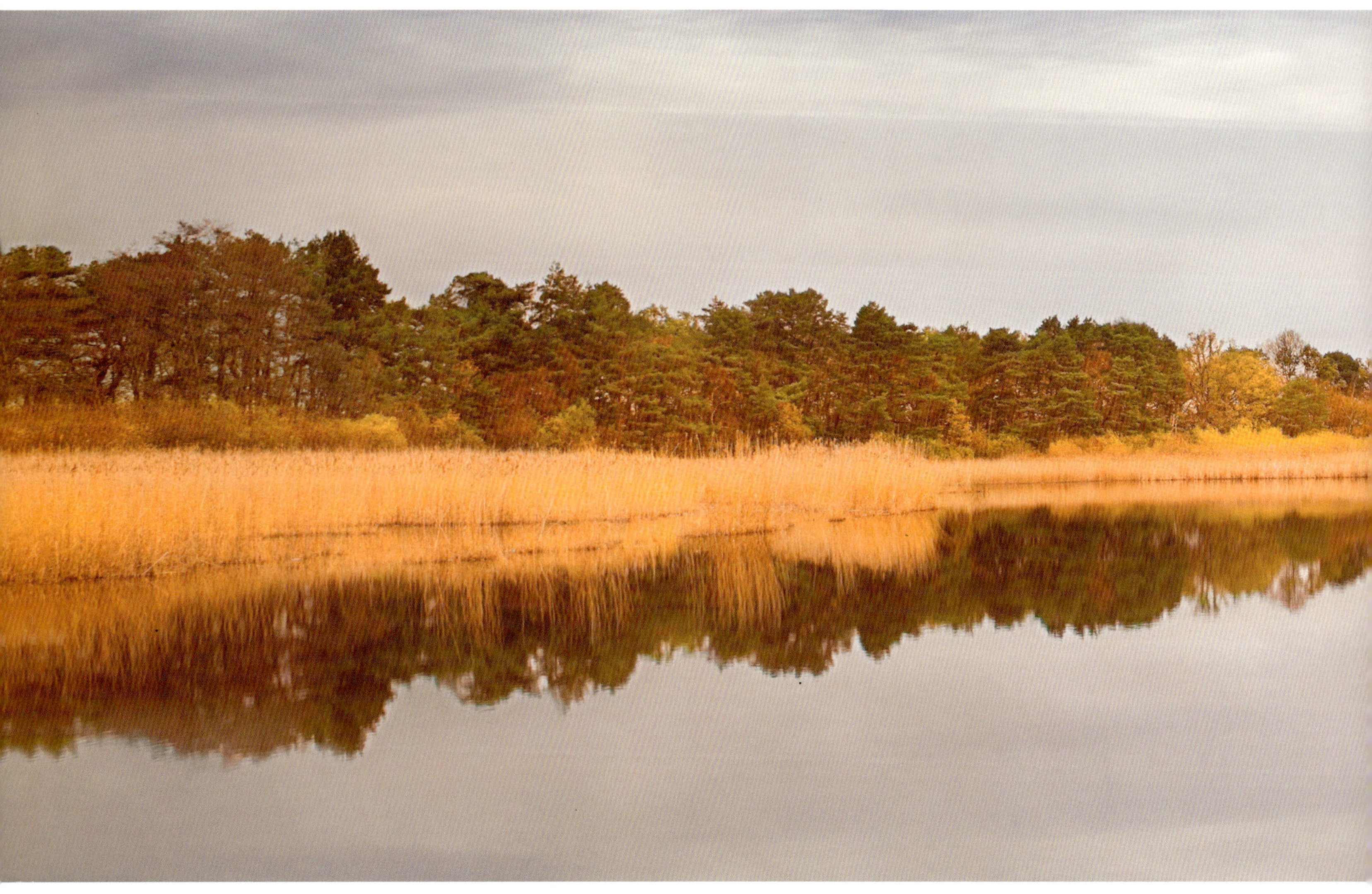

Englemere

Englemere Pond, the site of a nature reserve, is a prime example of how a wild habitat can survive amidst urban surroundings. It's enclosed in a triangle of main roads – an area of less than a square mile – which it shares with a railway line. The buildings of North

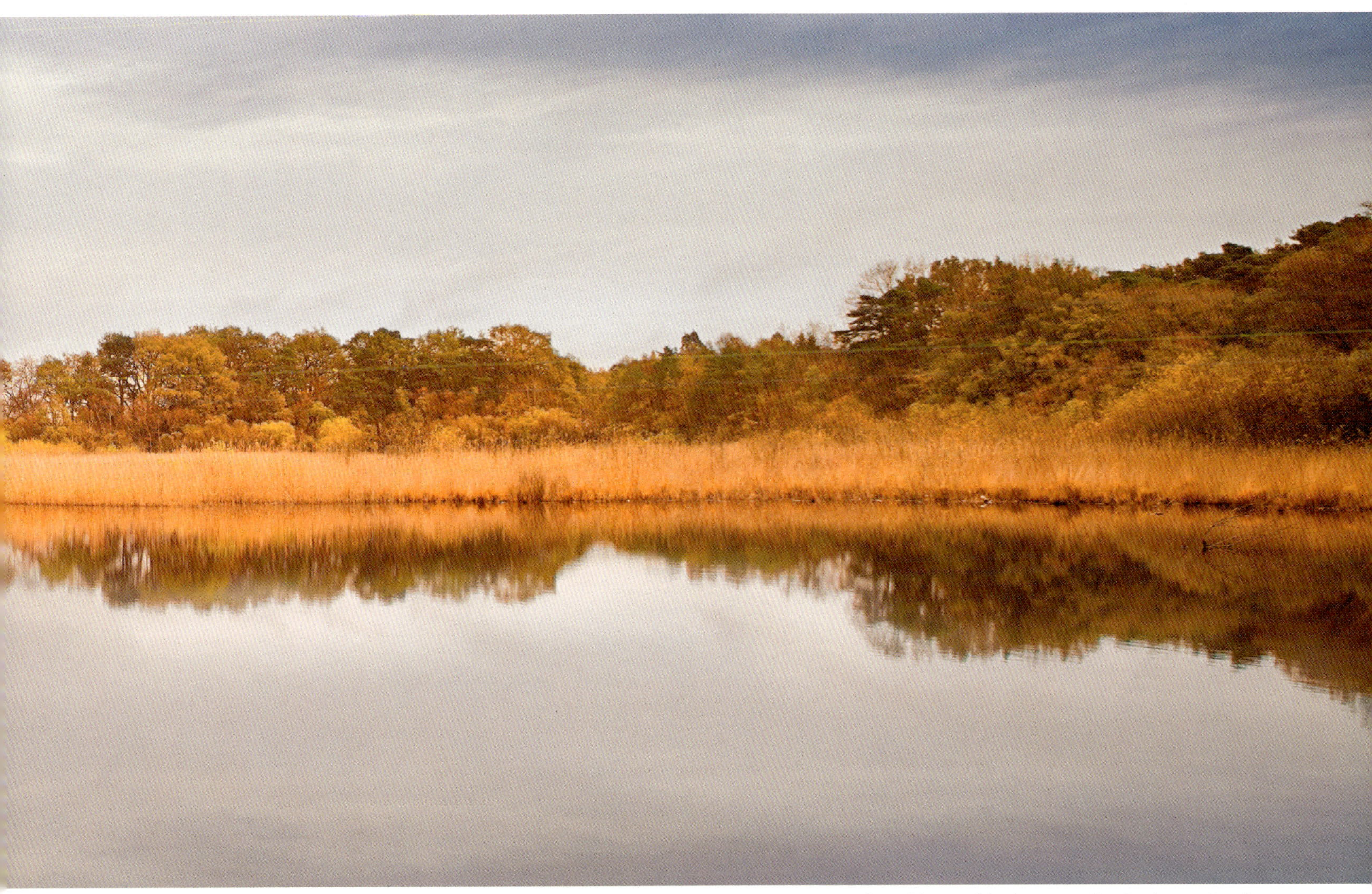

The golden reed-beds surrounding Englemere Pond

Ascot are just yards away, and the busy centre of Bracknell just 2 miles. However, the water itself is screened by trees, and below their branches grow deep beds of reeds, so extensive that a clear view of the pond can only be seen from one place – a wooden platform on the southern shore. I visited the site on a calm day in late November to capture this wide panoramic view of the autumnal scene.

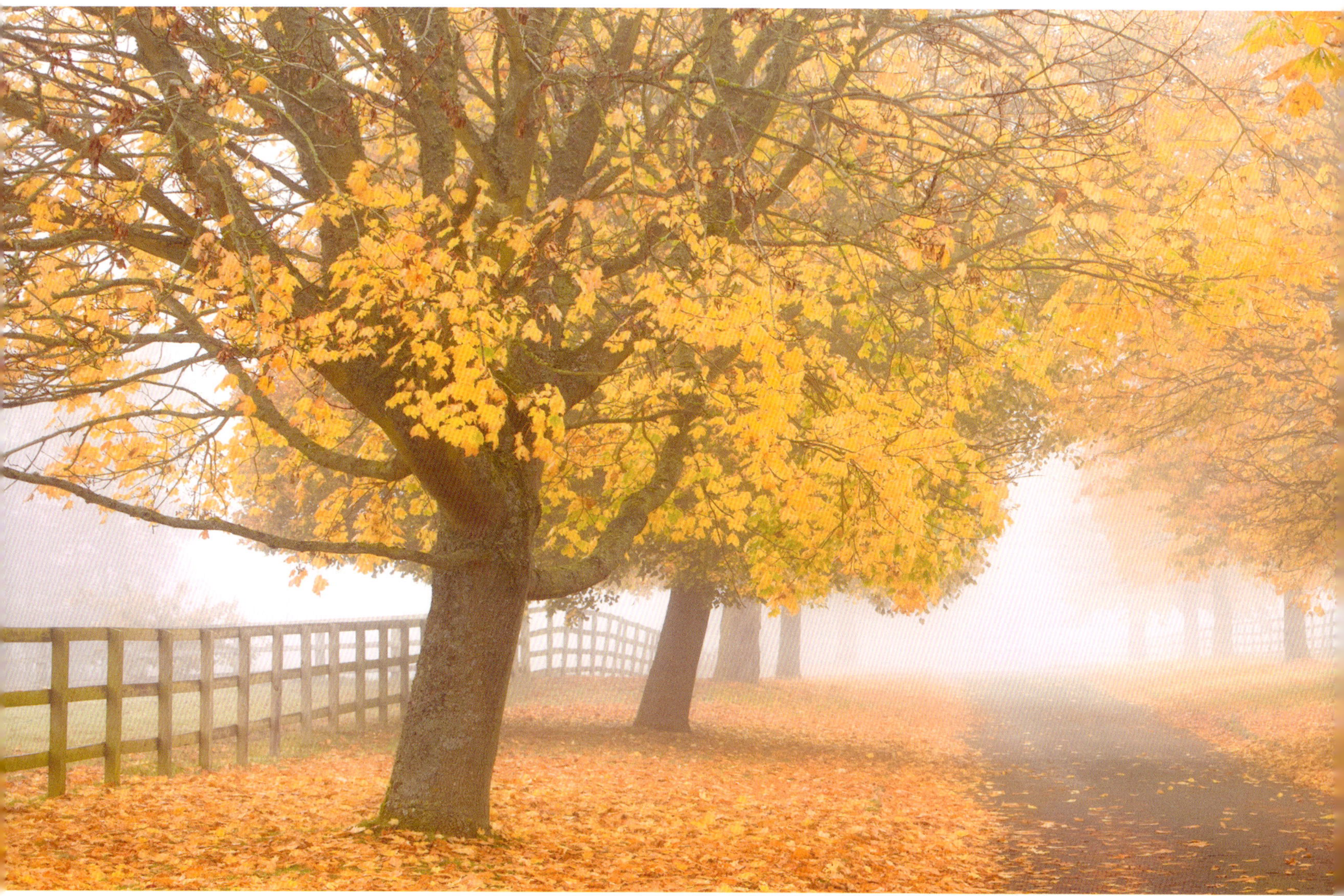

Avington near Hungerford

As the Kennett flows east from Hungerford to Kintbury it passes Avington, a small riverside hamlet surrounding a church and manor house. The place shares its name with another tiny village in central Hampshire which stands near the River Itchen not far from

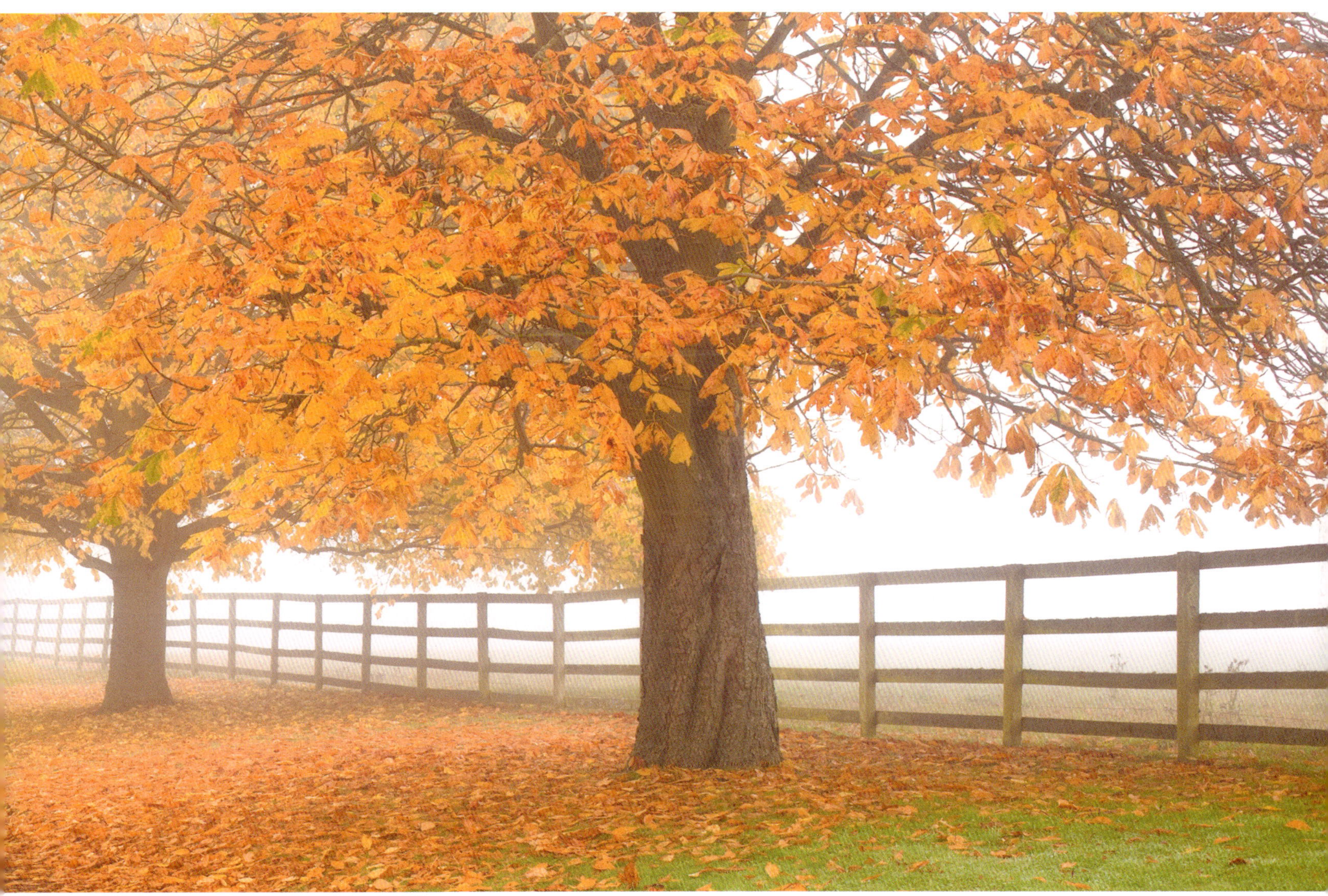

Maples and chestnuts on the approach to Avington

Winchester. Interestingly, both places share another feature: tree-lined avenues which look marvellous in autumn. Avington in Hampshire has one of lime trees leading to a mansion; at Avington in Berkshire the avenue is less formal – a mix of maples and chestnuts which grow on either side of the lane.

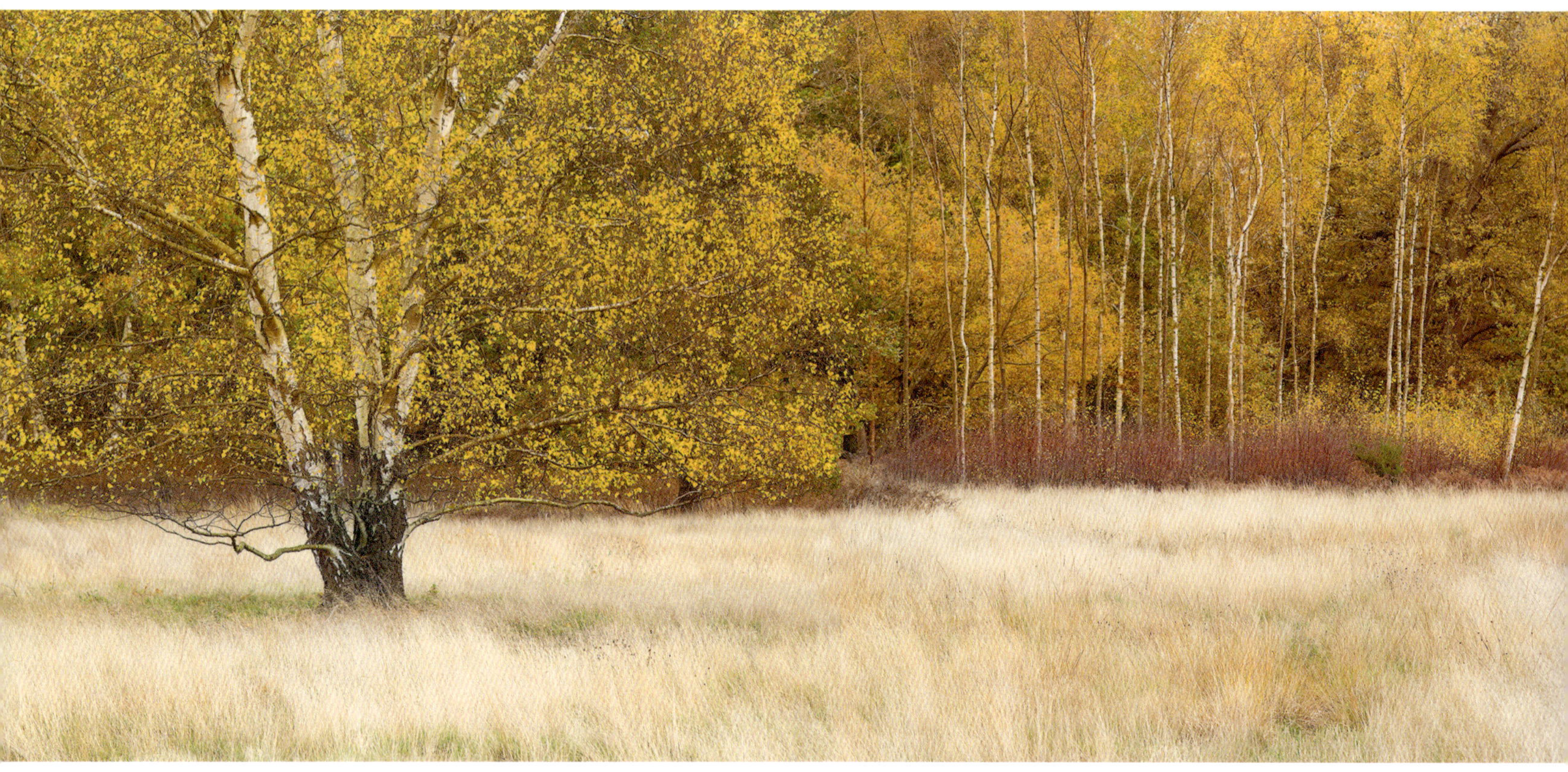

A grassy clearing near Cumberland Lodge

Windsor Great Park

The Great Park at Windsor is renowned for its majestic oaks and tree-lined avenues, but perhaps less so for its wilder habitats which include areas woodland and heath. One example of these is a beautiful grassy clearing which is partly surrounded by silver birch, located near Cumberland Lodge, a seventeenth-century house built shortly before the Long Walk was conceived.

I came across the area on a calm day in late November when the leaves were a rich shade of gold, but about to fall; below them the wispy grasses had faded to a pale yellow. I chose to capture the scene from a distance using a telephoto lens – this enabled me to isolate the best area of colour and exclude the overcast sky.

Virginia Water

The 2-mile long lake at Virginia Water was created in the eighteenth century from a much smaller one which previously existed on the site. It was developed as part of a royal pleasure ground complete with cascade, obelisk and ornamental bridges. However, it has not been a permanent feature – it was drained during the war to prevent it being used in enemy reconnaissance.

Today the lake straddles two counties – the border runs through the middle, with the western section lying in Berkshire and the east in Surrey. This autumnal view, captured at first light in November following a night of heavy rain, shows part of the five-arch bridge which was built in 1827.

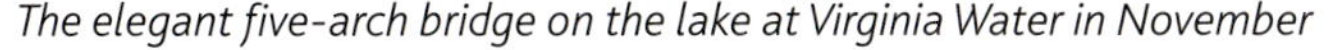

The elegant five-arch bridge on the lake at Virginia Water in November

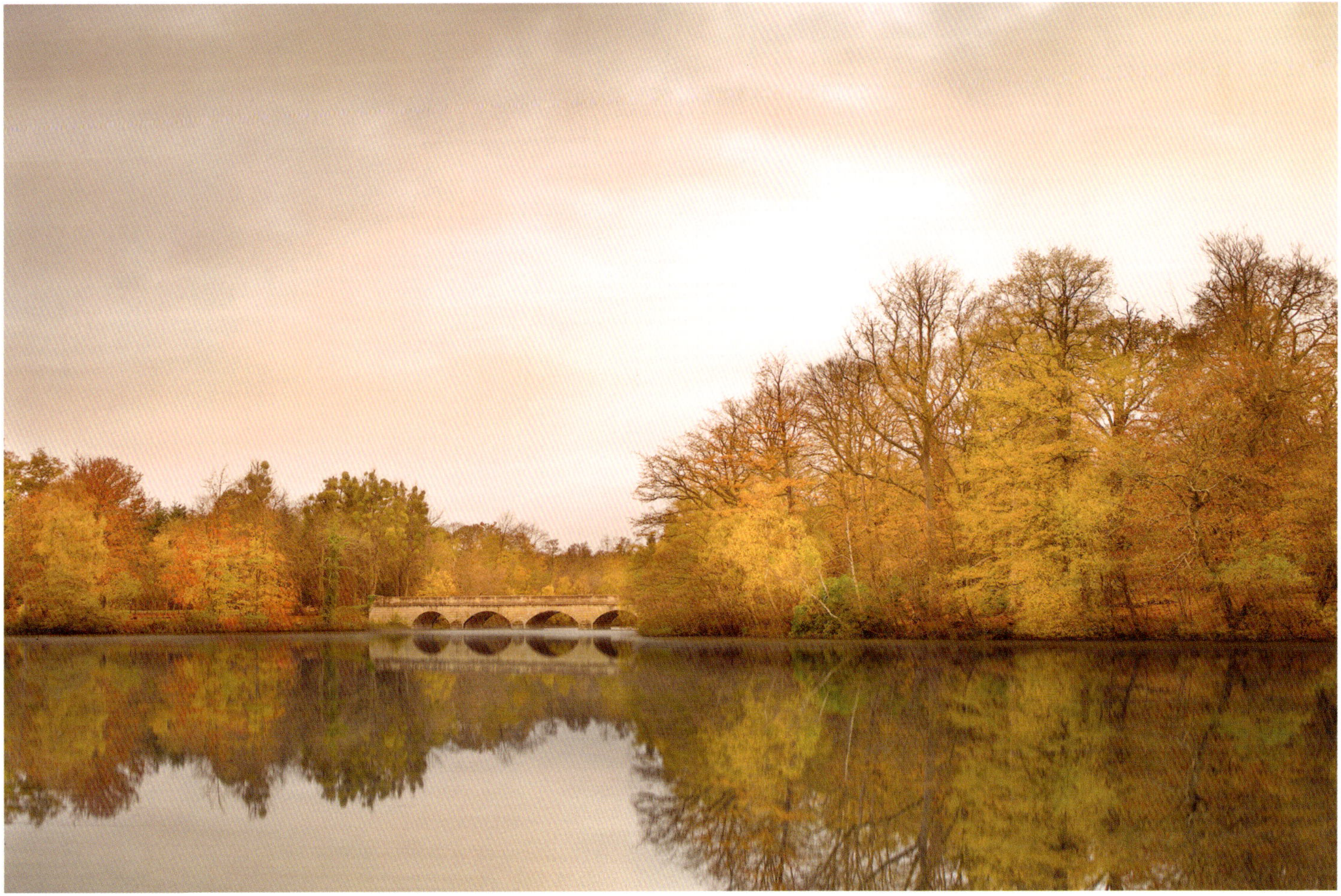

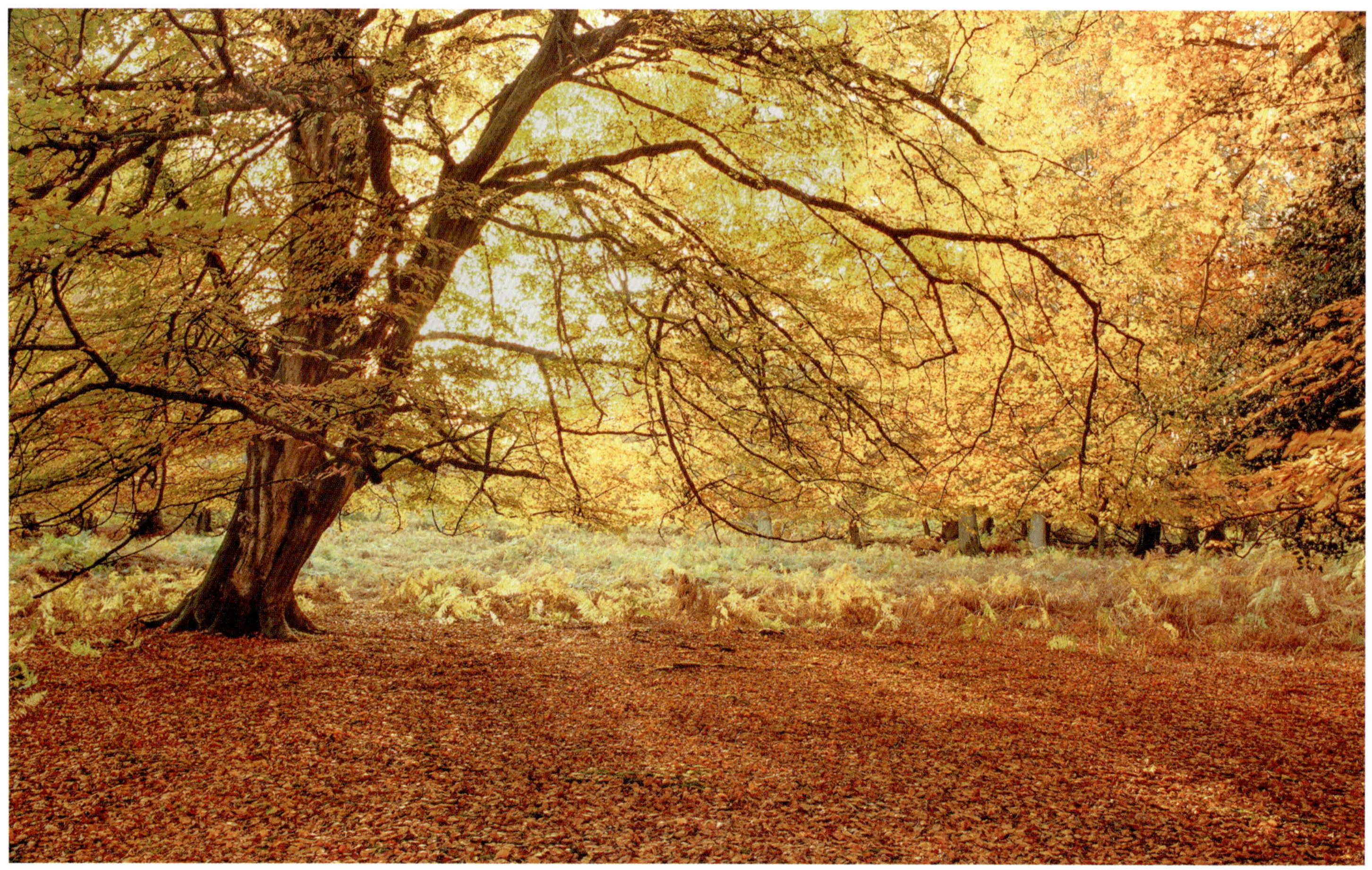

Autumn tints among the beech trees on Snelsmore Common

Snelsmore Common

Snelsmore Common Country Park is a varied landscape of woodland, heath and wetland, 2 miles north of Newbury. This small pocket of wilderness has managed to survive the pressures of development: its very existence was threatened when the A34 was re-routed in the 1990s, but the outcome was positive – although the road took away part of the land, an equivalent area of common was added to the west.

Impressions of the place depend greatly on the season. In the short days of winter the heaths are brown and soggy, scattered with leafless birch trees. In spring the woods are lit by the subtle green light which filters through the pale foliage, and in summer the open spaces come to life with flowering ling, bell heather and patches of cotton grass. But some of the best glimpses come on fine days in autumn, when the low sun sweeps into the margins of the wood and brings highlights to the golden foliage.

The Quiet Lane near Bucklebury

Perhaps one of the most peaceful routes in Berkshire is the small lane which winds its way through the beech woodland at Bucklebury. Entering this woody back-road is like stepping back in time, and it seems that this special quality has been officially recognised, because a number of discreet signs have been placed along the way marking it out as 'Bucklebury Quiet Lane'. A misty morning in early November seemed the ideal time to capture the spirit of the place.

Descending into the trees – the 'Quiet Lane' at Bucklebury

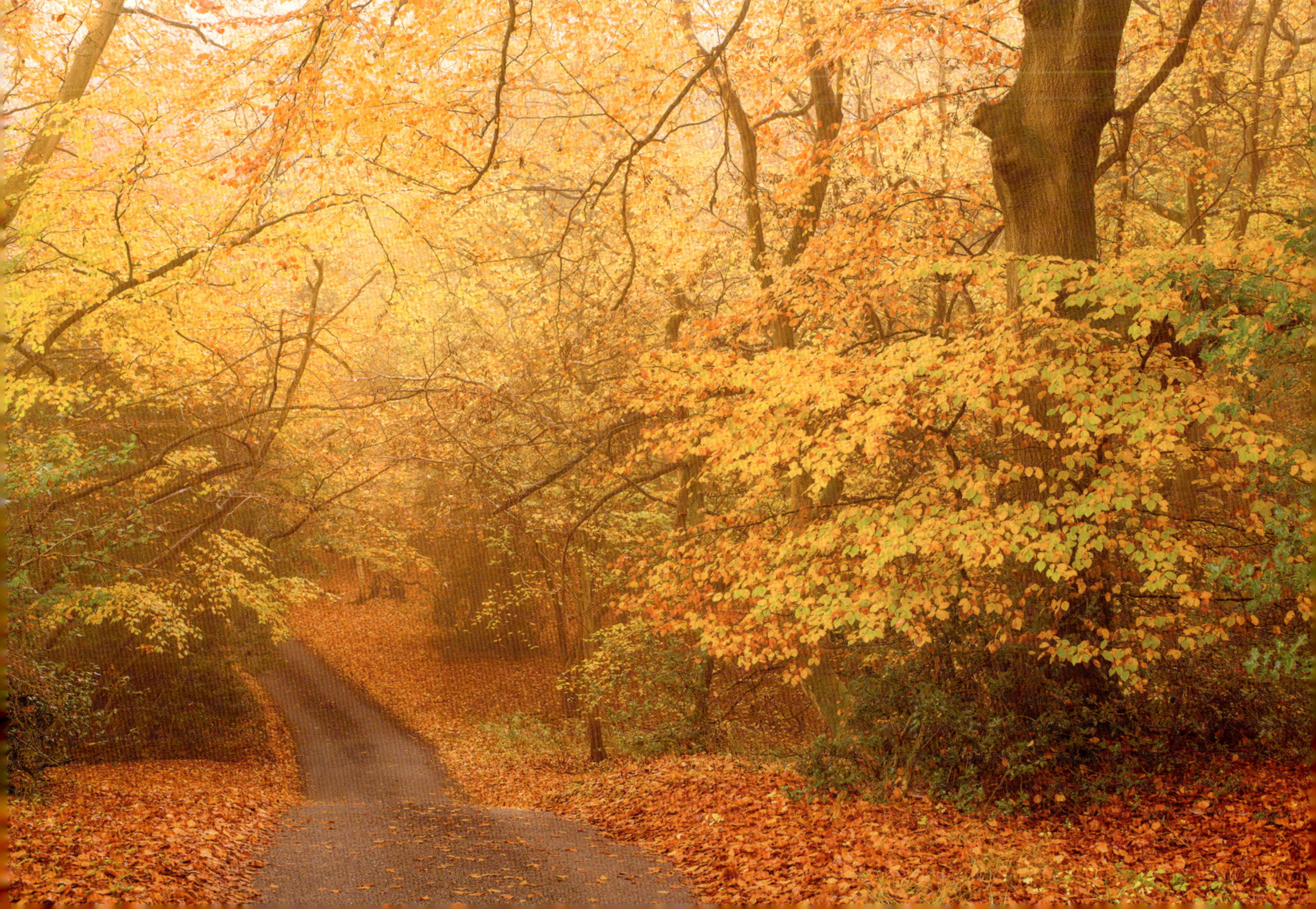

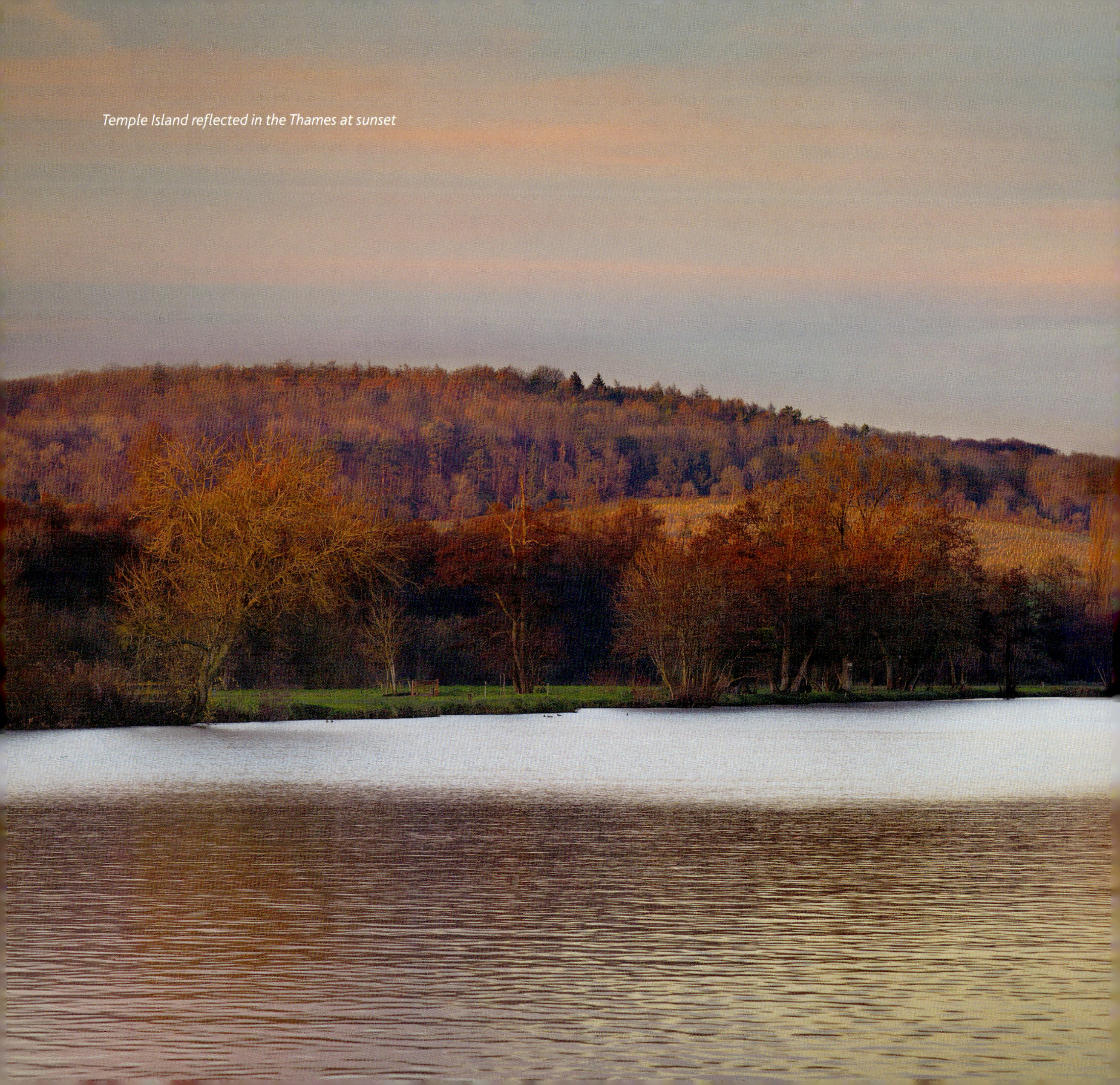

Temple Island reflected in the Thames at sunset

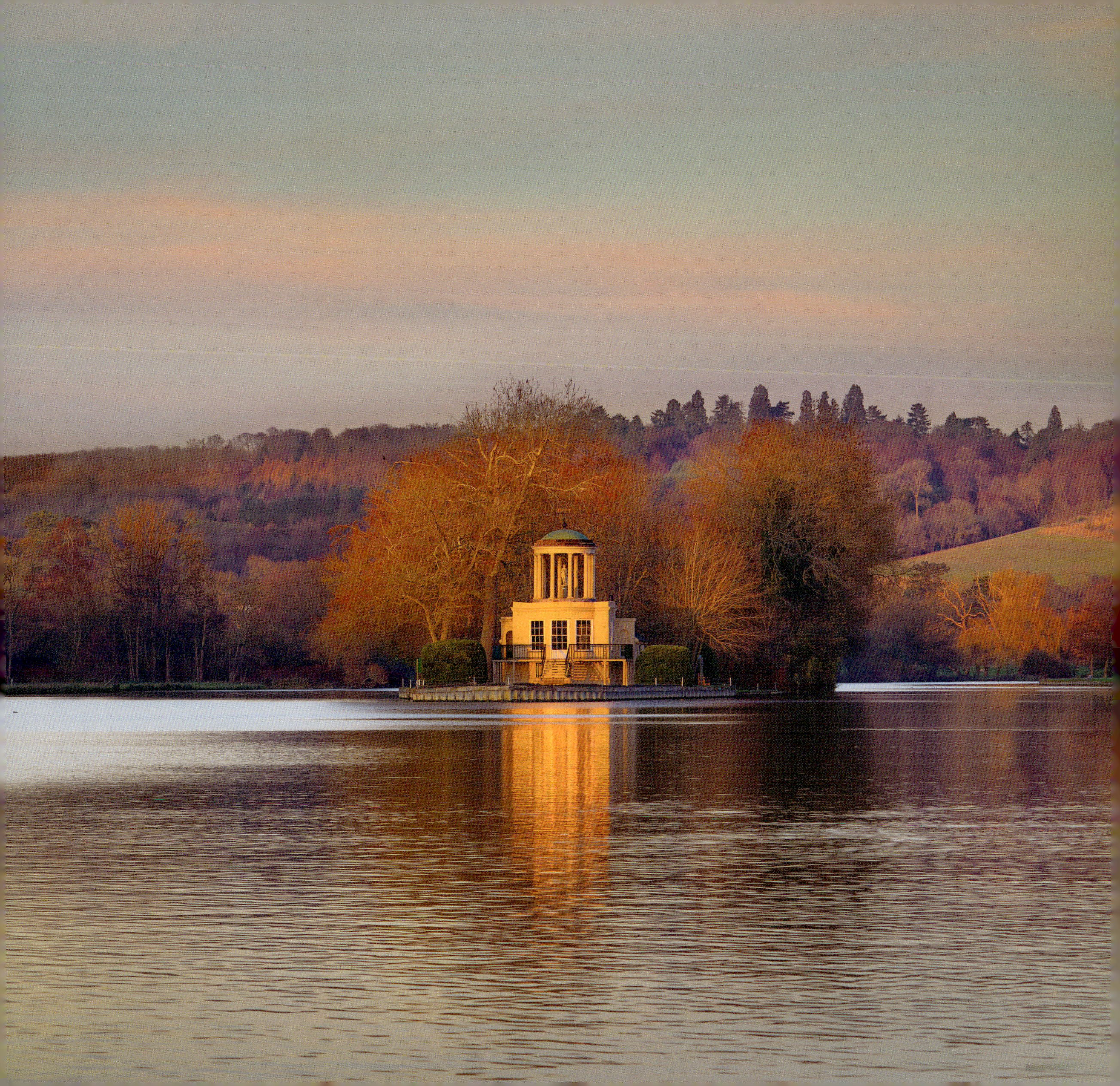

WINTER

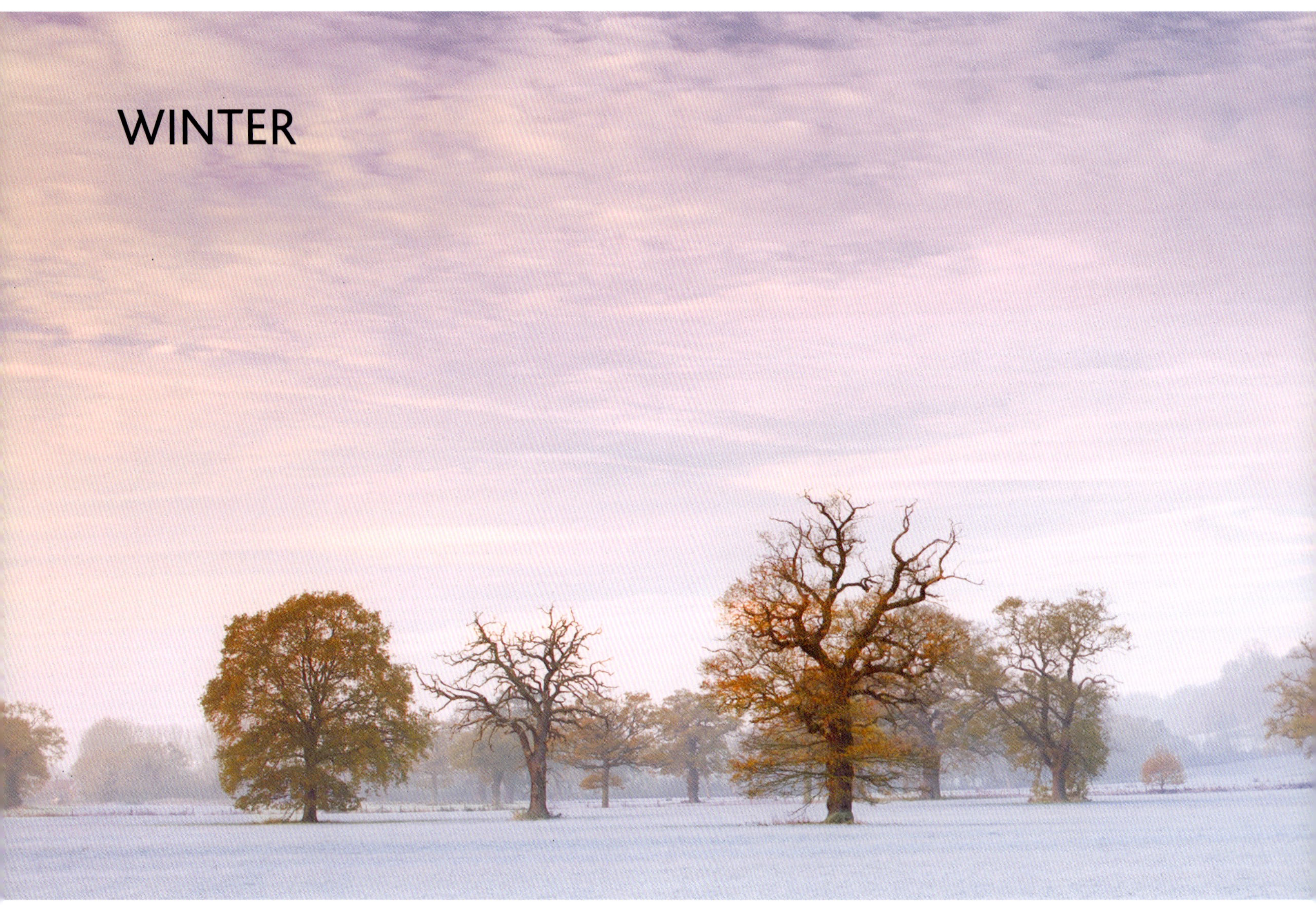

Landscape at Beenham

A scattering of grand oaks makes the field below Beenham House seem like a stretch of parkland. The trees are of various ages, some of them little more than woody relics which look out across the Kennet Valley. Although there are no footpaths, the view from the lane

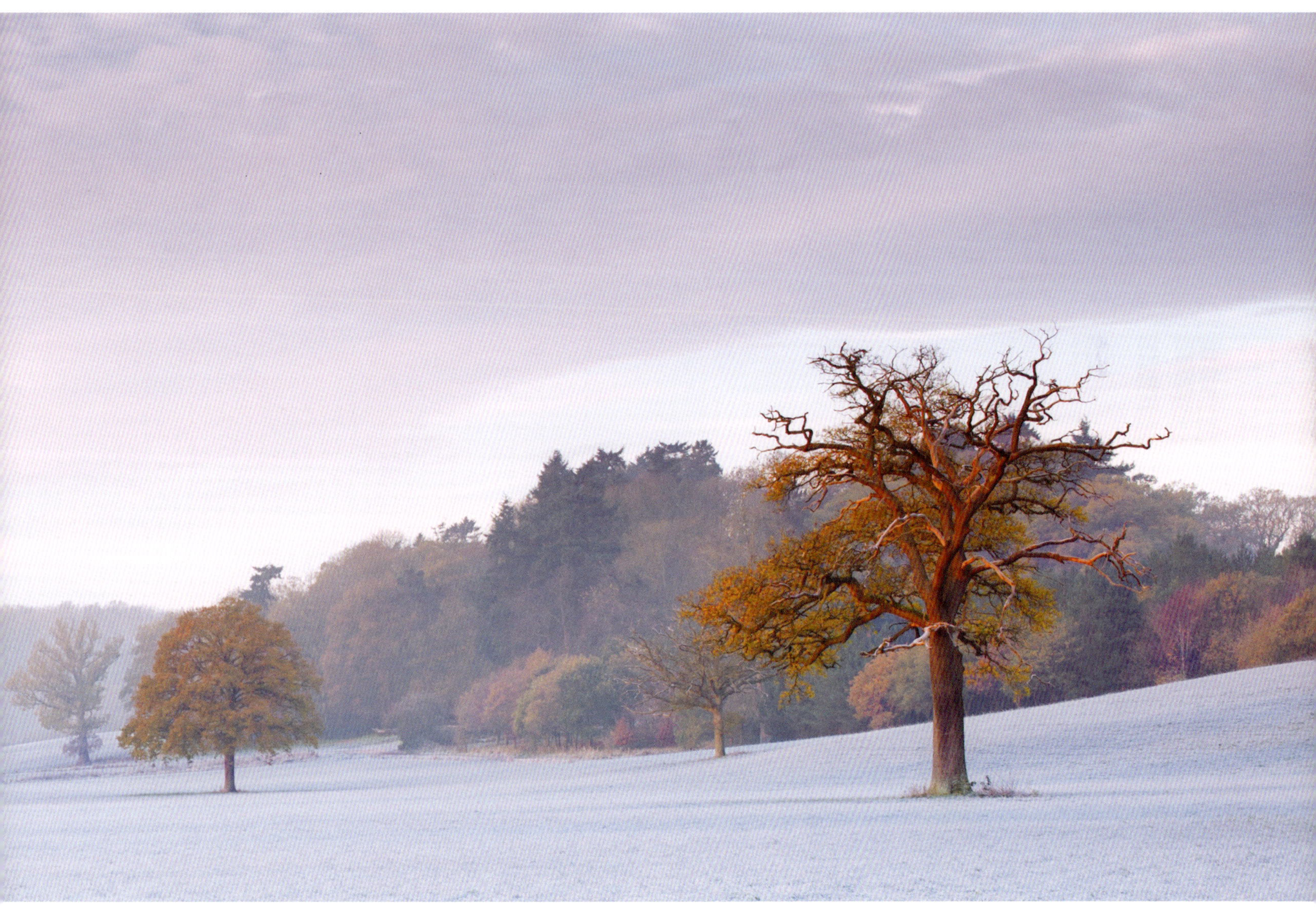

Oaks in frosted fields near Beenham

known as Lambden's Hill which lies to the east gives an inspiring glimpse of the scene, with the wooded slope of Mountsion Copse beyond. This photograph was taken in early December when the last leaves of autumn were dusted with frost.

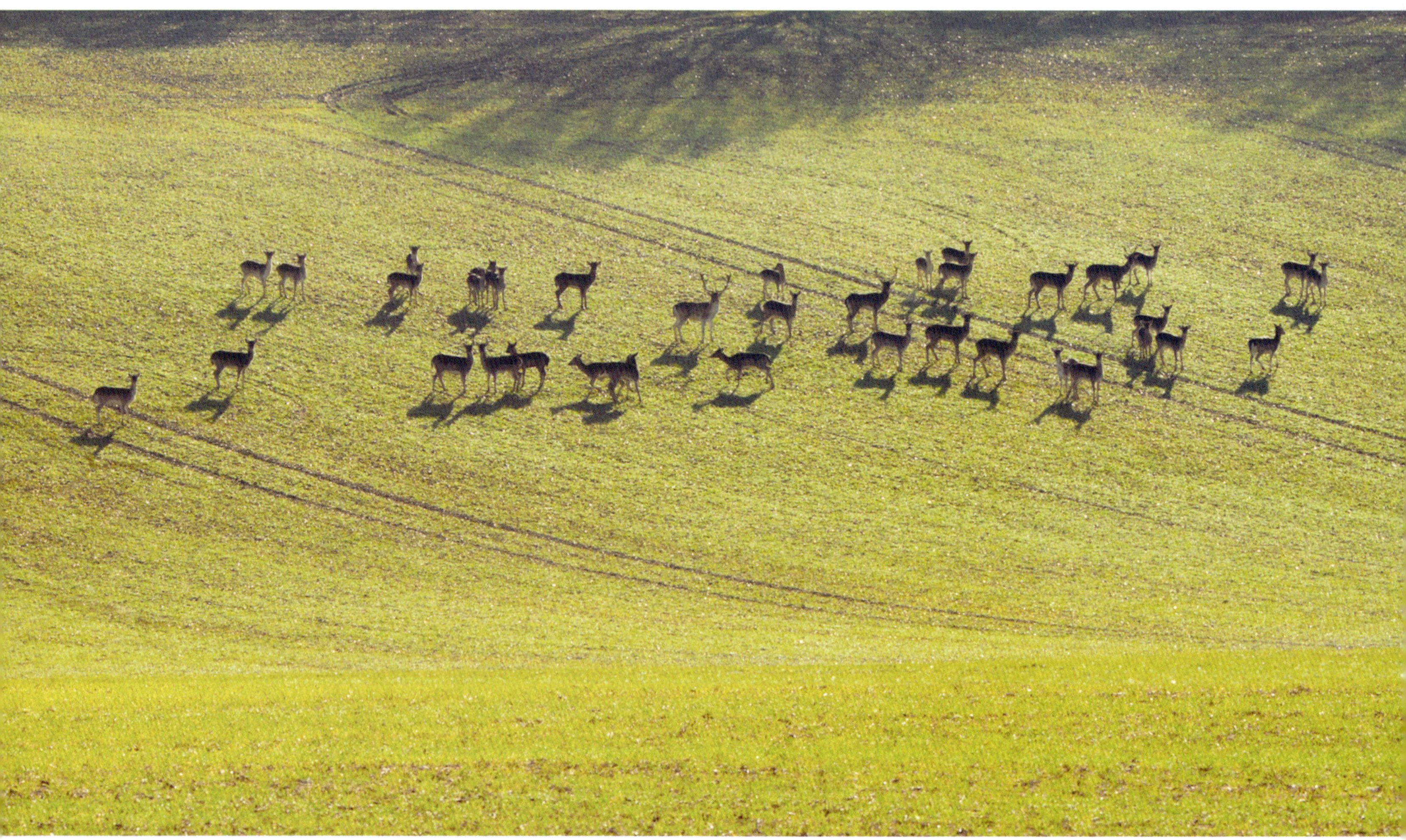

A large herd of fallow deer on winter barley

Deer near Peasemore

Encounters with deer are common in the West Berkshire landscape – I counted 37 in this fallow herd near Peasemore. Fortunately they were in an open setting, for had they been among trees they would not have looked so striking; equally important was the strong back-lighting which showed them in near-silhouette, with an interesting mix of shadows. They watched nervously for a minute or so, before dashing away to the south.

East Garston Down

The windy open space of East Garston Down is a walker's delight. It extends for 2 miles or more in a broad arc north of the village, and encompasses the ancient earthworks of Winterdown Bottom which are surrounded by gallops and chalk grassland.

The east side of the down is deeply cut by a long dry valley shown in the picture below. The valley is accessed by a small lane – a lovely quiet route which traces its way to a highpoint at Oakhedge Copse. The lane runs across the centre of this photograph, between the fields but hidden by grassy banks.

The down can be a bleak place in winter, but in the right conditions the low sun models the shape of the land, and on this occasion a scattering of clouds brought about a beautiful mix of light and shade.

Mottled sunlight on the downs

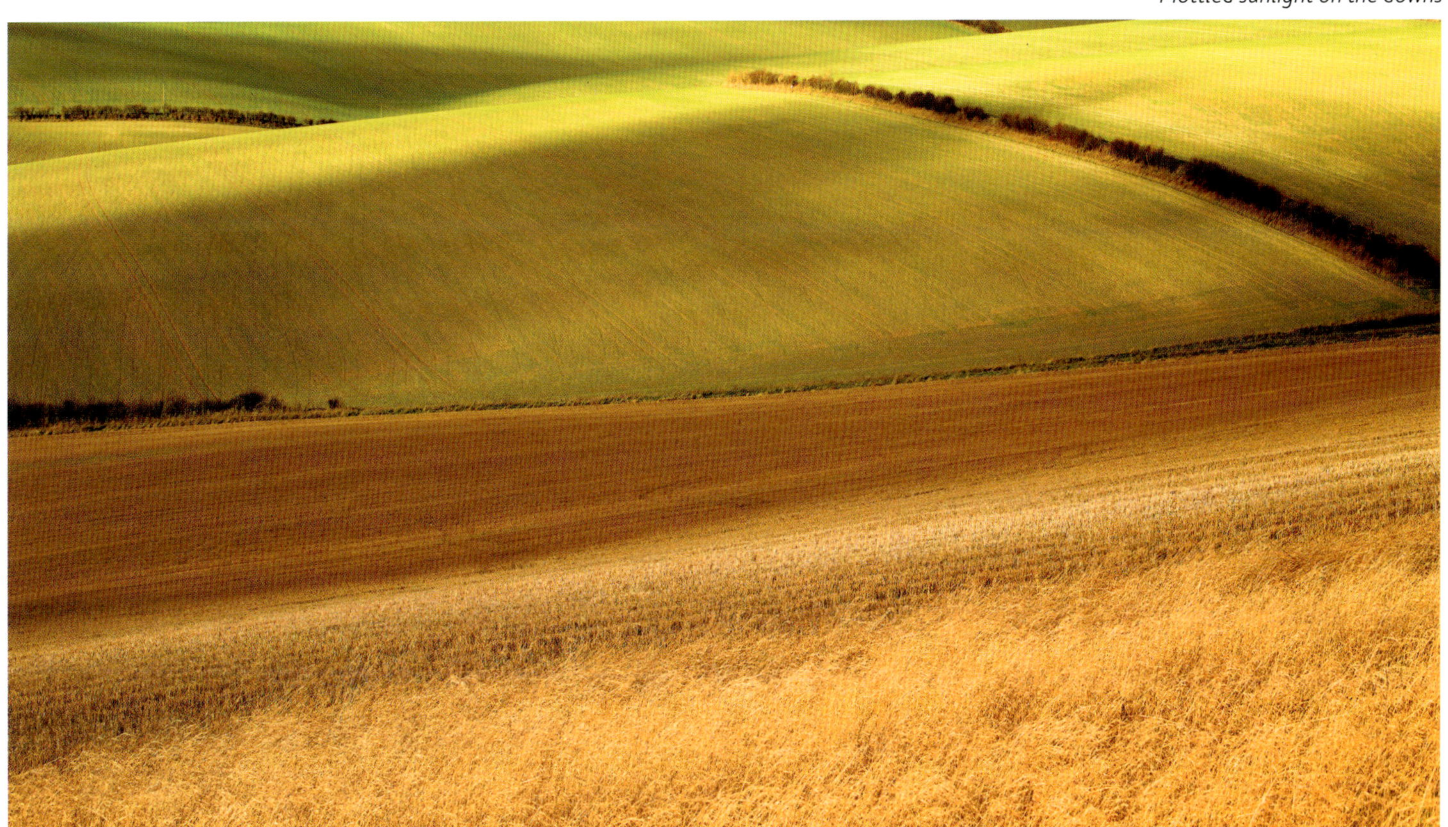

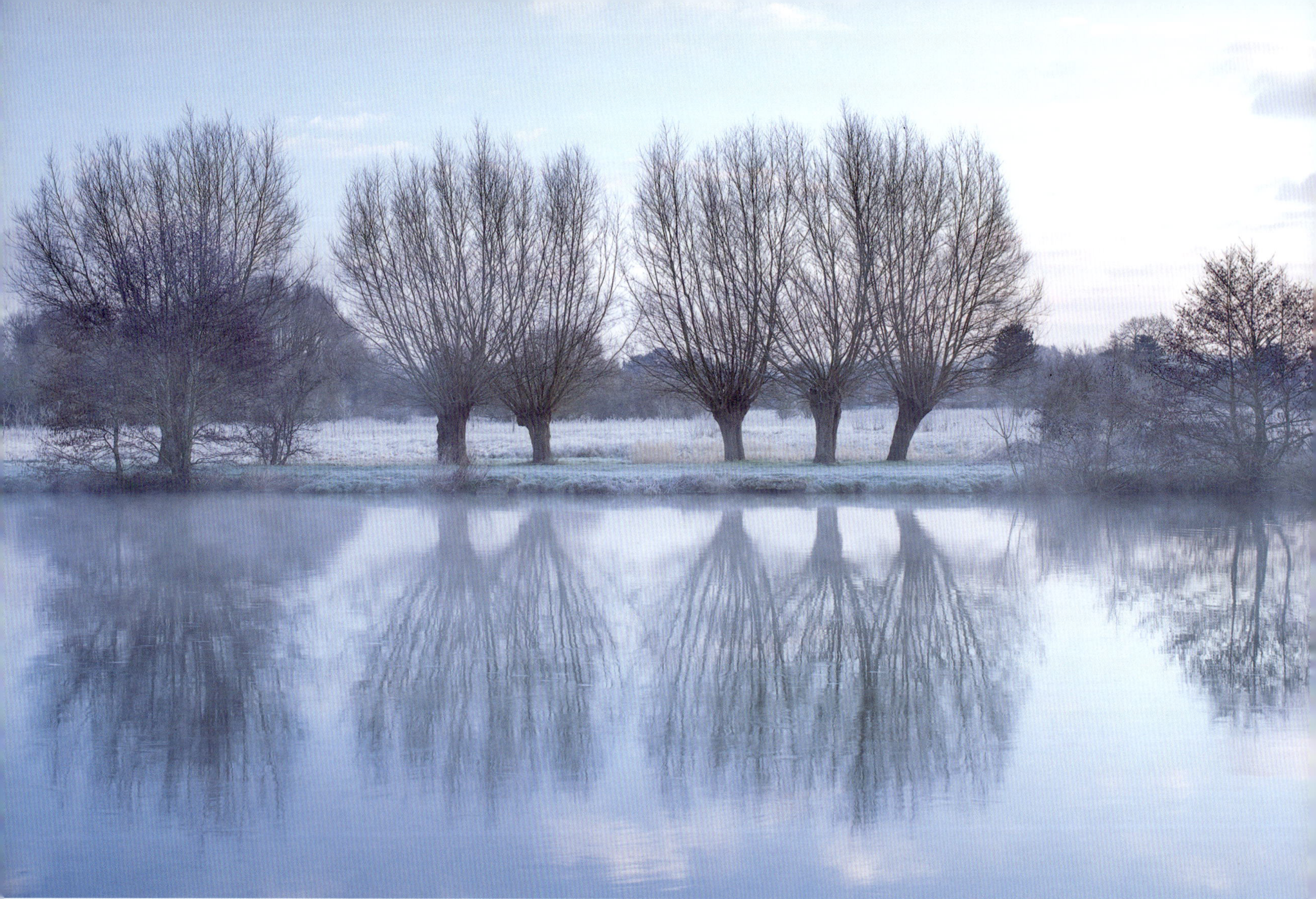

Shapely willows seen from the Thames Path near Streatley

Streatley to Moulsford

I first visited the place shown on this page in spring (page 23) when I captured a wide view of the river. My second visit was during the following winter – it was another frosty start, but on this occasion I decided to focus solely on the group of leafless willows on the far bank which stood out in bold outline against the pale blue surroundings. Their fan-shaped appearance made them a natural focal point which was emphasized by reflection.

The Kennet and Avon Canal at Ufton

The tow path which runs west from Ufton Lock looks across to a plantation of towering poplars – too tall for their reflections to be seen in the narrow canal. Beyond this the view opens out to the pastureland known as West Meadow and the path leads on to Towney Lock. This image shows the view from this part of the canal, looking south-west to a line of leafless willows; on this morning a sharp frost had penetrated the valley and smothered the reed beds which line the water.

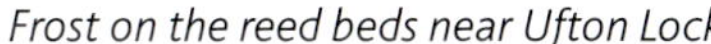

Frost on the reed beds near Ufton Lock

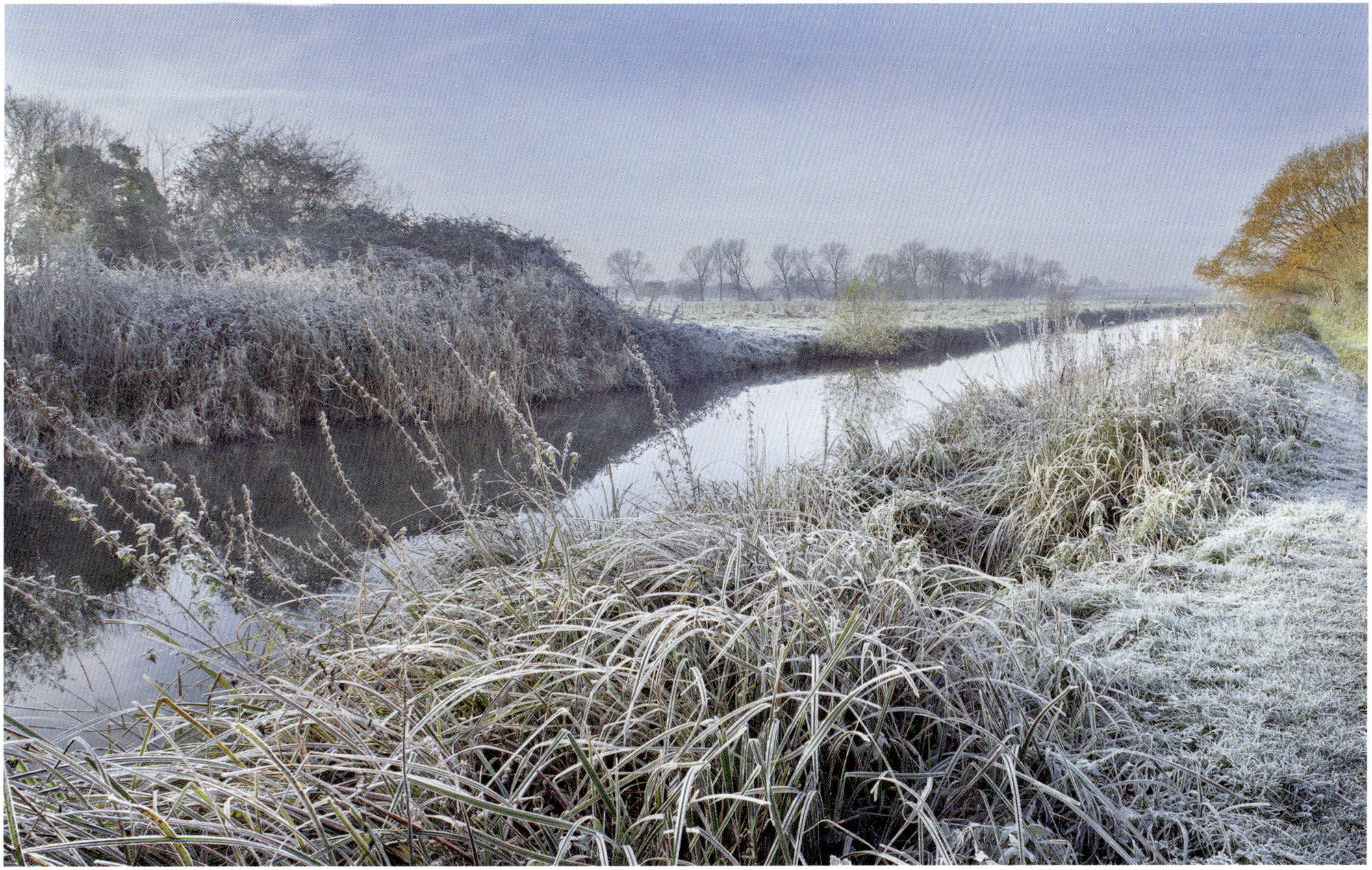

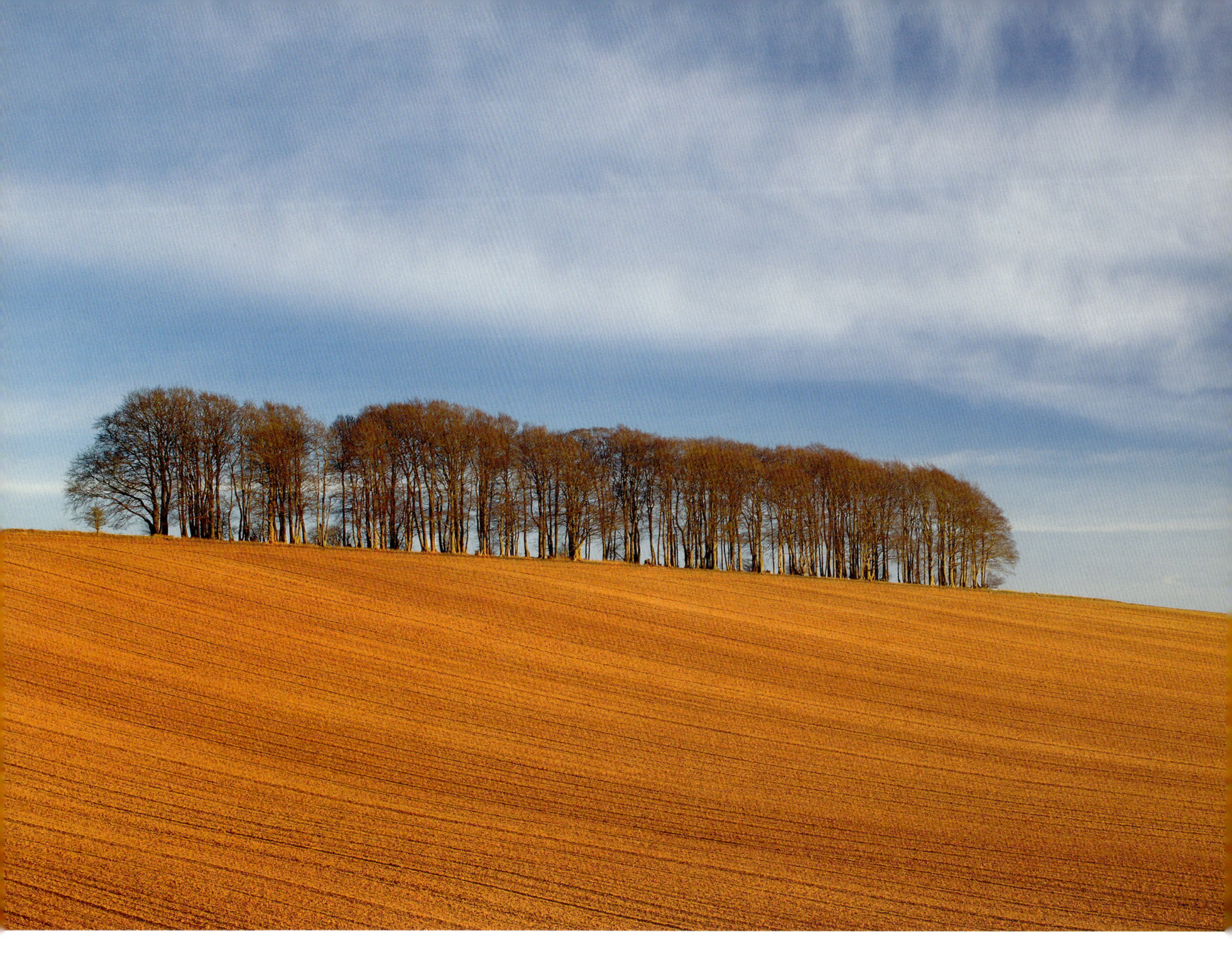

A stand of beech in winter sunlight on Sparsholt Down

Sparsholt Down

A mere stone's throw from Berkshire's north-west border is Sparsholt Down, a beech-topped hill which extends southwards from The Ridgeway.

The lane which runs along the west side of the down, from Lambourn to Kingston Lisle, is unfenced and without hedges, giving passers-by a sweeping view across the slopes and up to the tree-lined crest. In winter, late in the day, the low sun casts a warming sidelight across the scene, bringing out the earthy tones of the landscape and reflecting off the silvery trunks of the trees.

The Ridgeway at Ram's Hill

Although a popular route with walkers and ramblers, it's possible to be quite alone on The Ridgeway for many hours – something I experienced on Ram's Hill in early February. This is the most northerly point on the Goring-to-Avebury section of the ancient 87-mile route and, as if to mark this fact, a solitary sycamore can be seen to the north, with the Vale of the White Horse beyond.

A remote sycamore on Ram's Hill

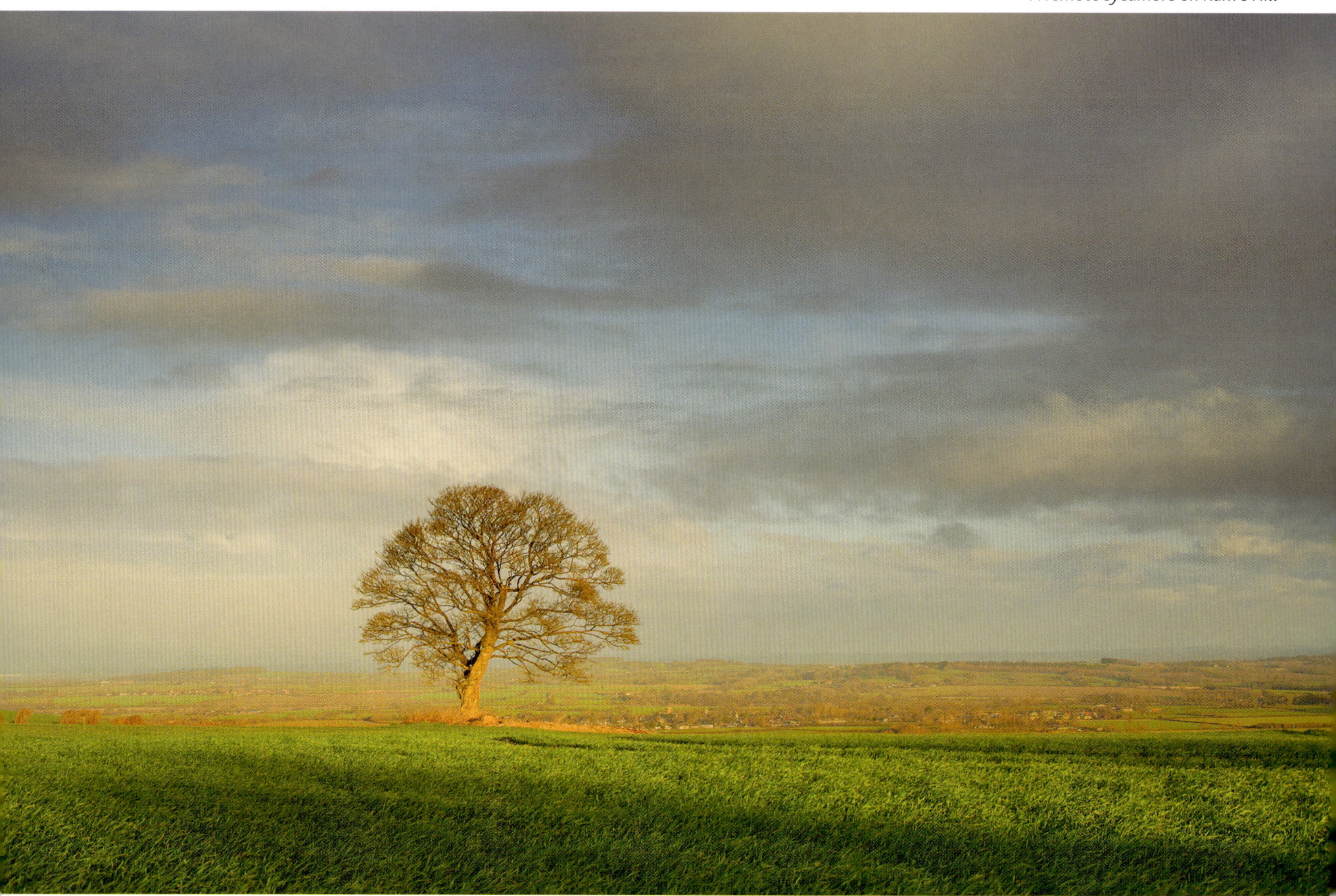

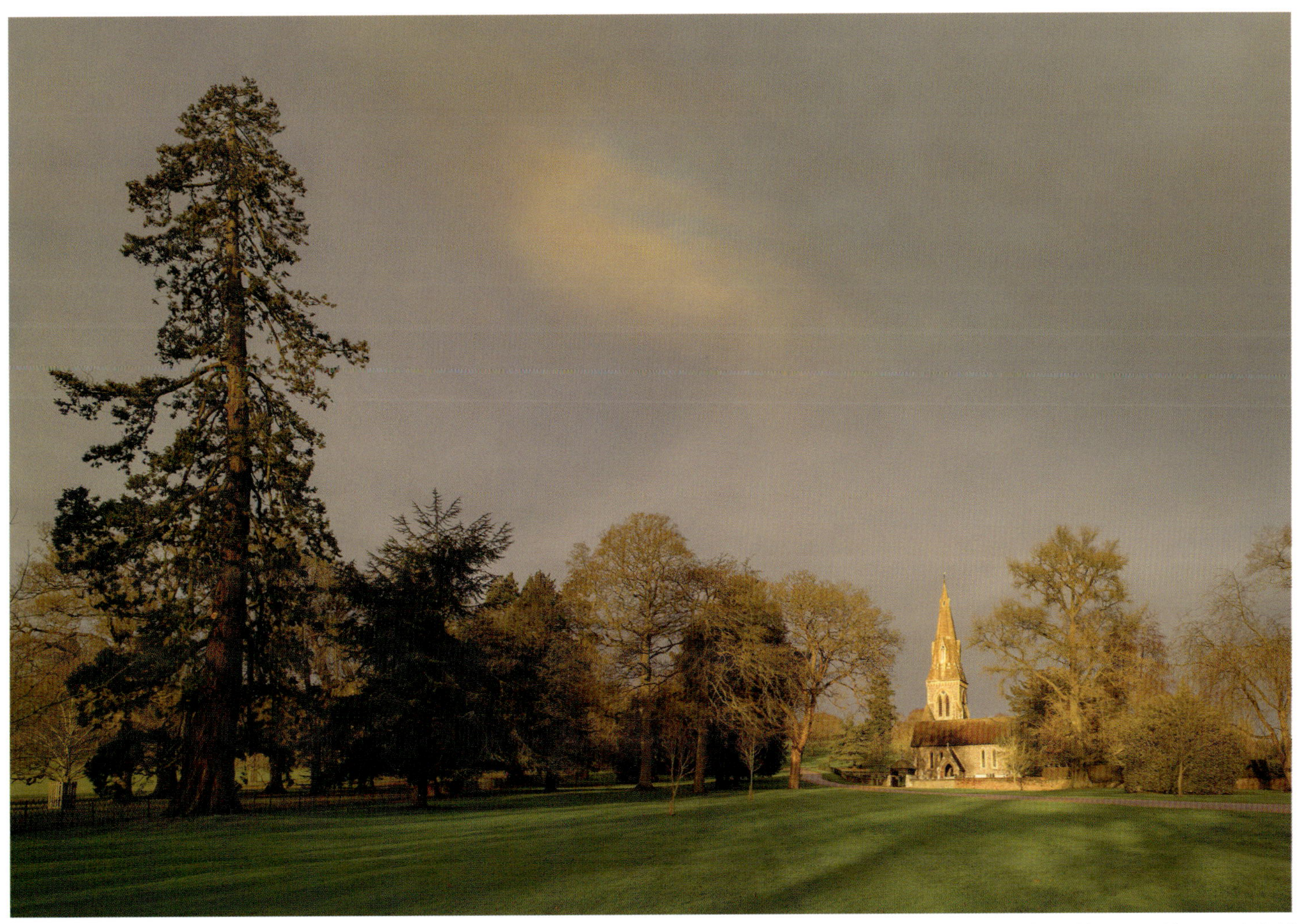

The towering redwood by St Mark's at Englefield

Englefield Church

Parts of Englefield church date back some 800 years, although the spire was not added until the nineteenth century. It lies at the end of a quiet lane within the grounds of the Englefield Estate, where it looks out across Cranemoor Lake and a deer park – an elegant landscape planted with cedars, oaks and other specimen trees.

This photograph shows the view from beneath the scarlet oak which was planted on the death of Sir Winston Churchill in 1965.

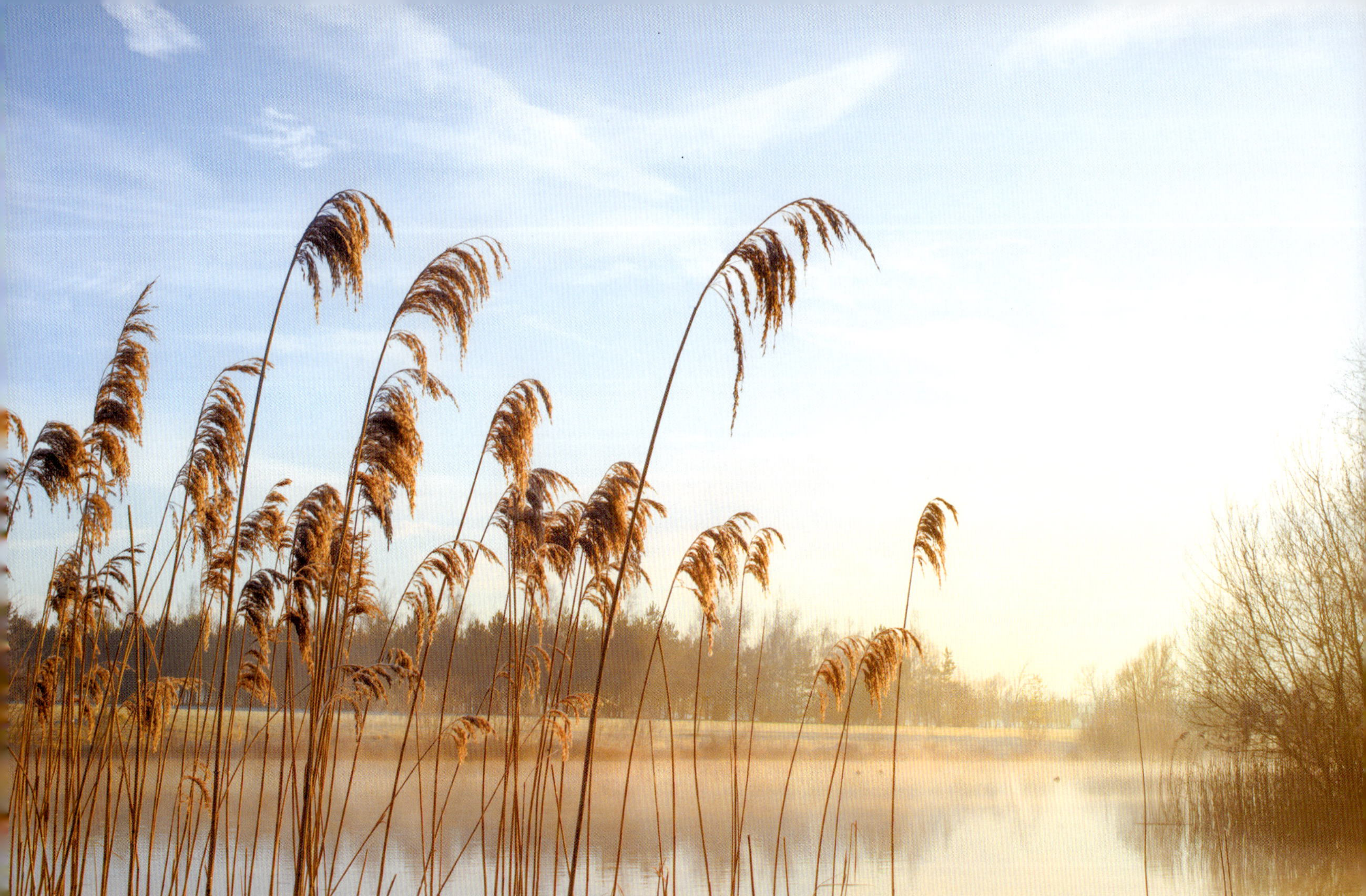

Sun-lit reeds by the lakes north of Burghfield

Burghfield Lakes

An Ordnance Survey map dating from the 1880s shows a wide swathe of farmland between Burghfield and the River Kennet, where today there is a large network of lakes. This dramatic change has come about as a result of gravel extraction which has taken place in the area over the last century. Most farms have disappeared altogether, but a notable exception is Searle's Farm which survives on a peninsula in the middle of the main lake.

A network of footpaths allows access to the area, which unfortunately is crossed by an elevated section of motorway. But while there's no peace and quiet among the tree-lined waters and islands, there are some stunning views to be found at first light in fine weather.

Farn Combe near Lambourn

Smoothly rounded hills are typical of chalk scenery, as are the dry valleys which often run between them. One such valley is Farn Combe which extends south-west from Lambourn, overlooked from the south by Coppington Down.

On a winter's afternoon I took the path which leads north from Woodlands Lodge and then skirts the edge of Coppington Down, reaching a small wooded embankment with a wide view across the valley. The clouds were broken, and as the sun sank low in the west its light revealed the graceful contours in the landscape around Thornslait Ridge.

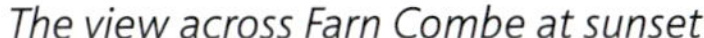

The view across Farn Combe at sunset

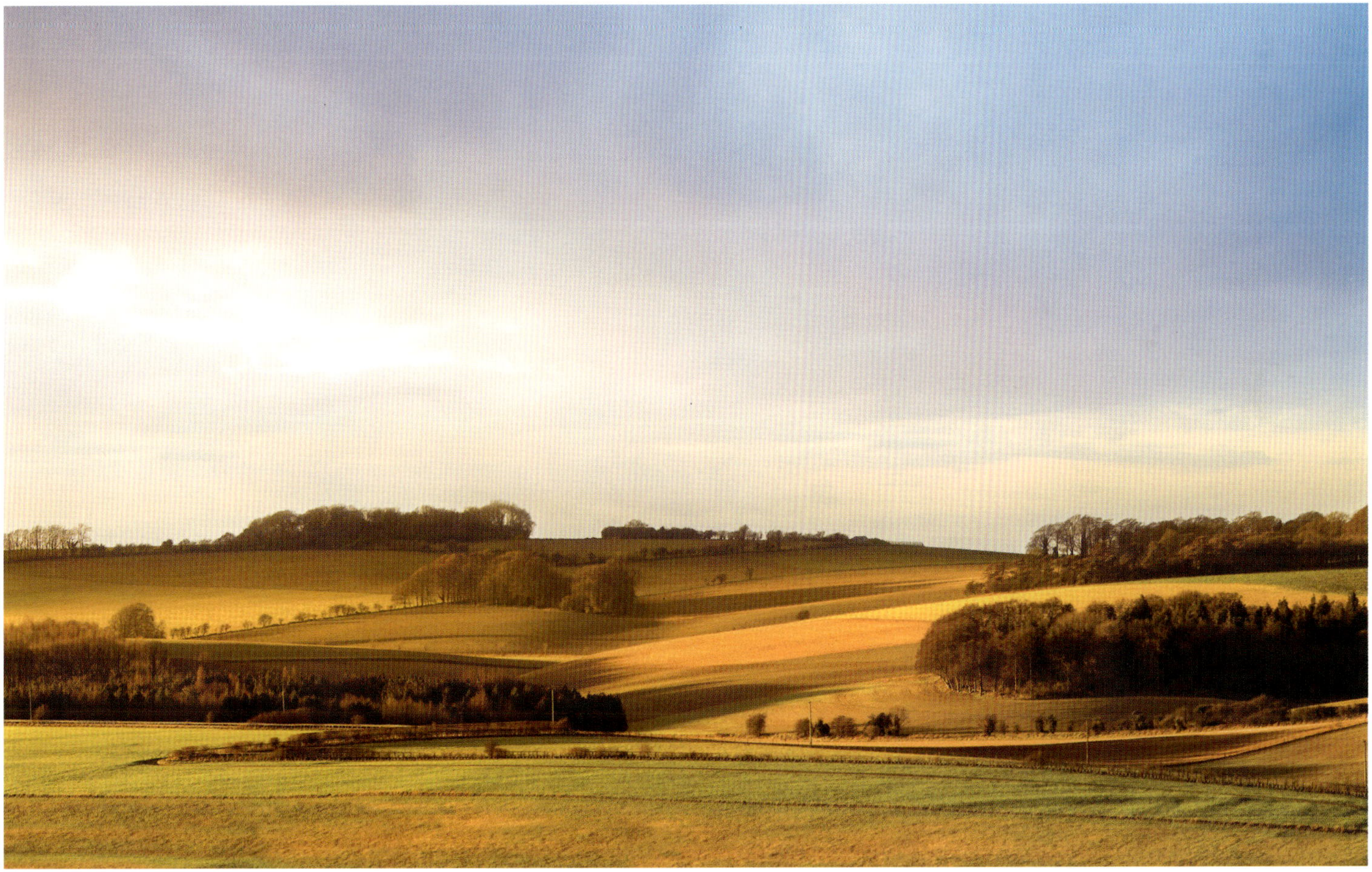

The Thames at Frogmill

The Thames Path National Trail was opened in 1996 and stretches for over 180 miles, beginning at the river's source at Thames Head in Gloucestershire, where a marker stone stands under an old ash tree. From there it follows the watercourse through several counties, passing landscapes which become gradually more lively as it travels towards the capital.

One of the most attractive sections of the path is between Henley and Hurley, where the river meanders lazily to the north. At this point it becomes a wide mature water, slow-flowing and fringed with the familiar alders and willows. The path follows the southern bank, giving plenty of stunning glimpses across the water to the Chilterns. This image shows the view near Frogmill where two canal boats (*Sagacity* and *Cornflower*) were moored on the northern bank.

Swans and canal boats on the Thames at Frogmill

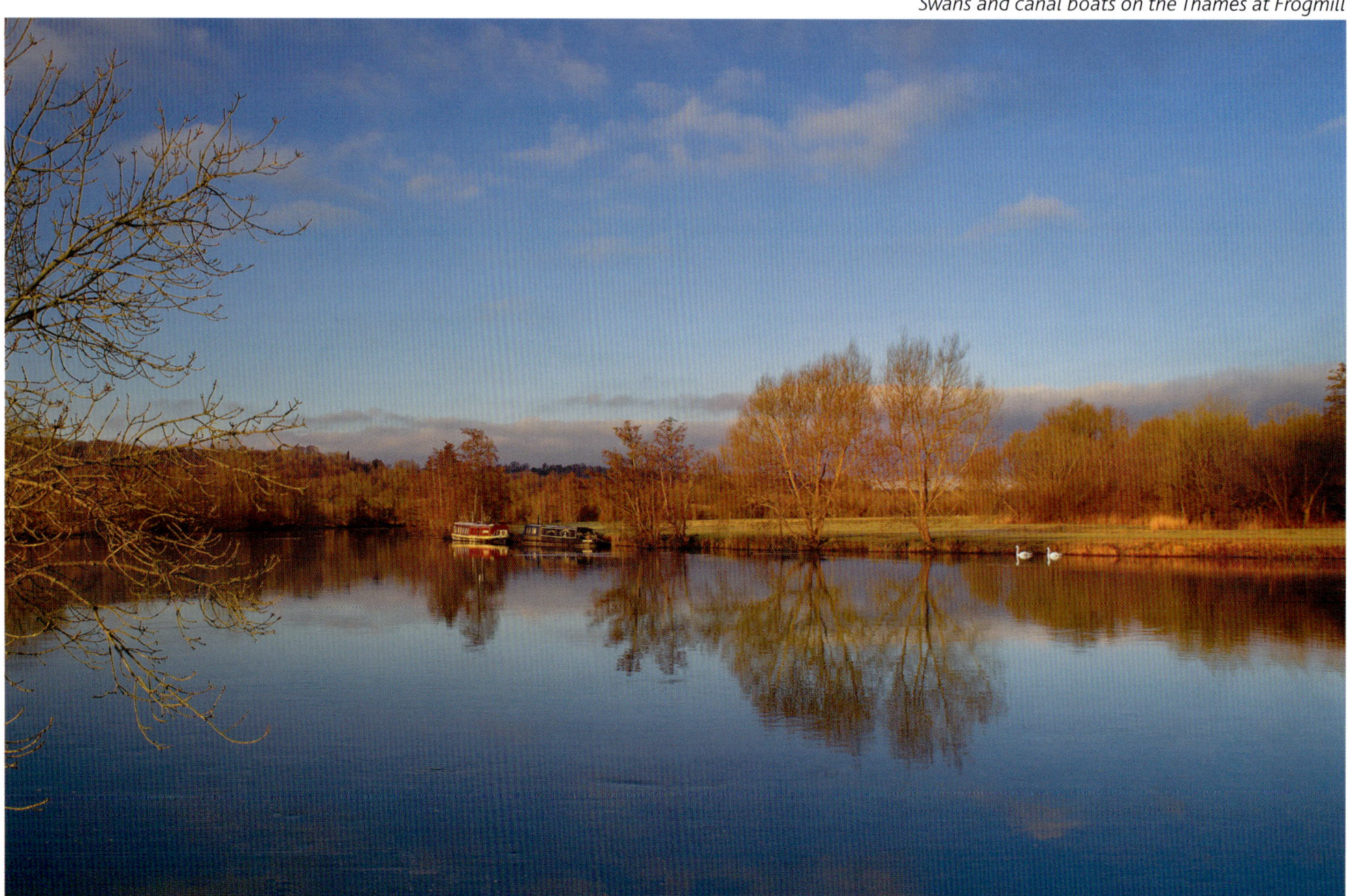

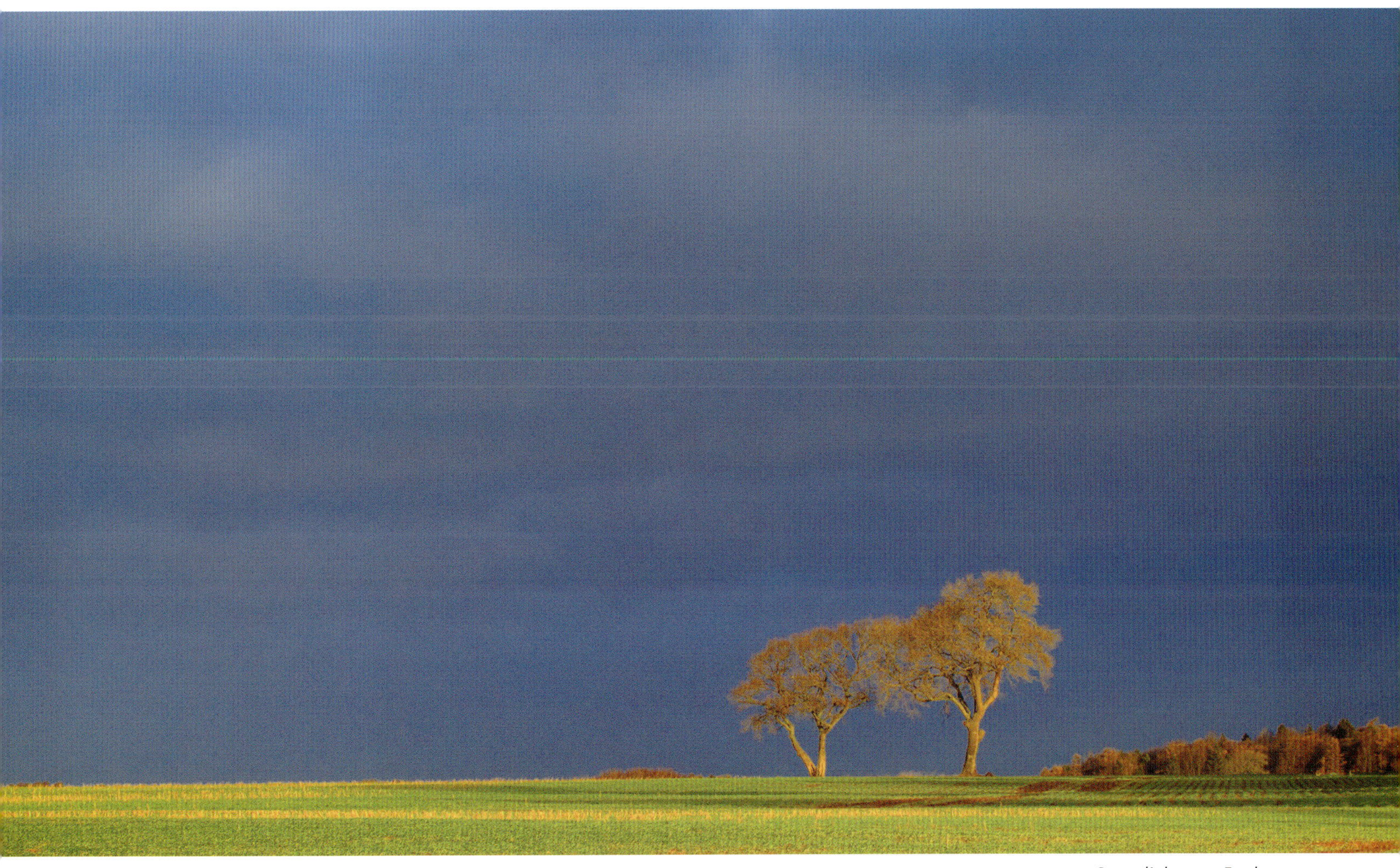

Stormlight near Fawley

Landscape near Fawley

A triangulation pillar to the west of Fawley marks a highpoint of 675 feet, and from this spot a vast field stretches away to Lang Down in the north-west. The view in this direction would be relatively featureless were it not for a pair of beech trees which stand exposed on the horizon to the west of Pit Plantation. This image shows the trees caught in a ray of sunshine on a stormy winter morning.

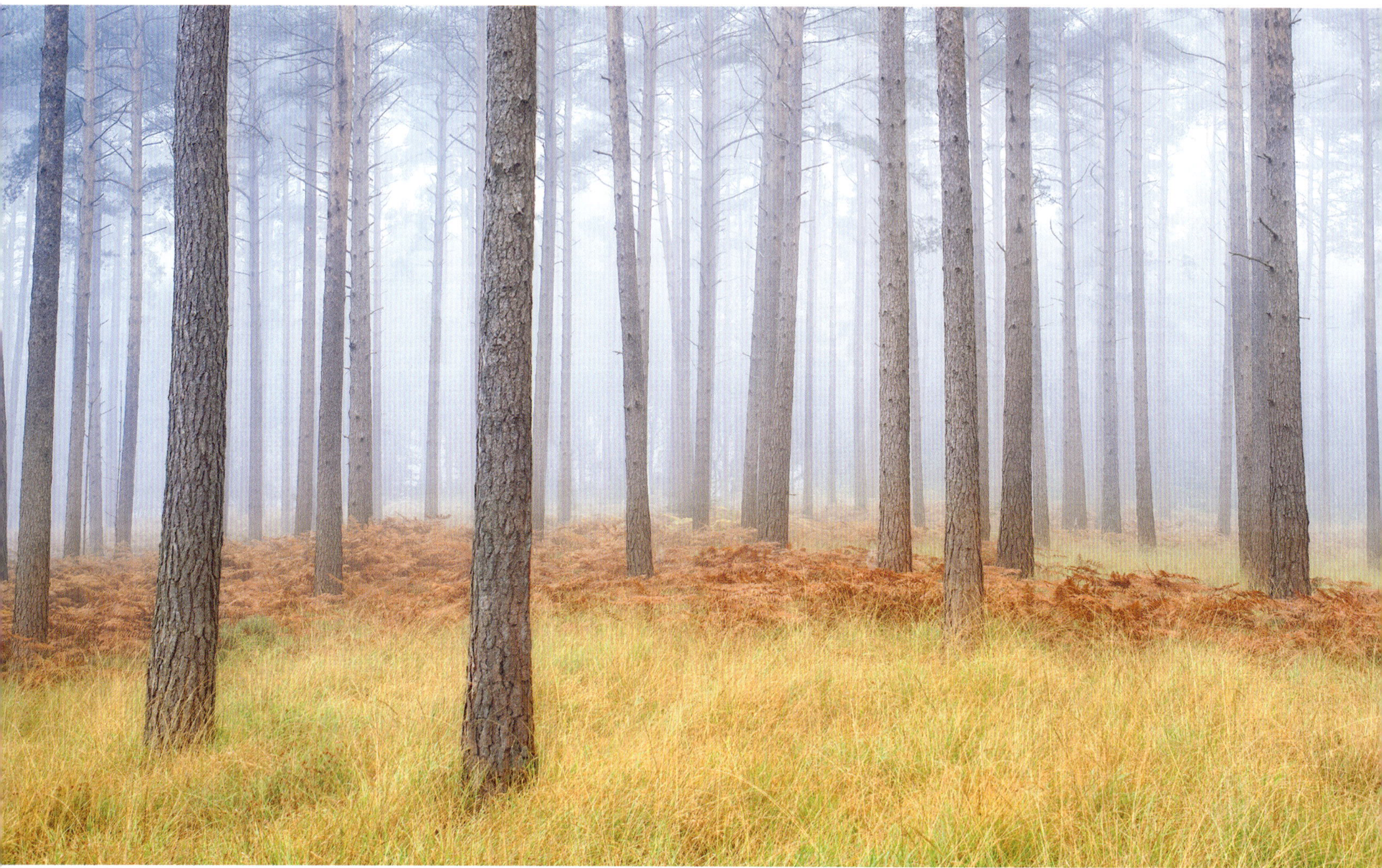

Swinley Forest
Some of the most attractive areas of Swinley are those where the forest floor is dominated by a type of fescue grass which grows in tufts and has long wispy stalks. Throughout the summer it's a pale shade of green, but in late autumn it turns amber-yellow and remains that colour until spring. It's often mixed with bracken and the two blend together well, giving a warmish glow to the under-storey.

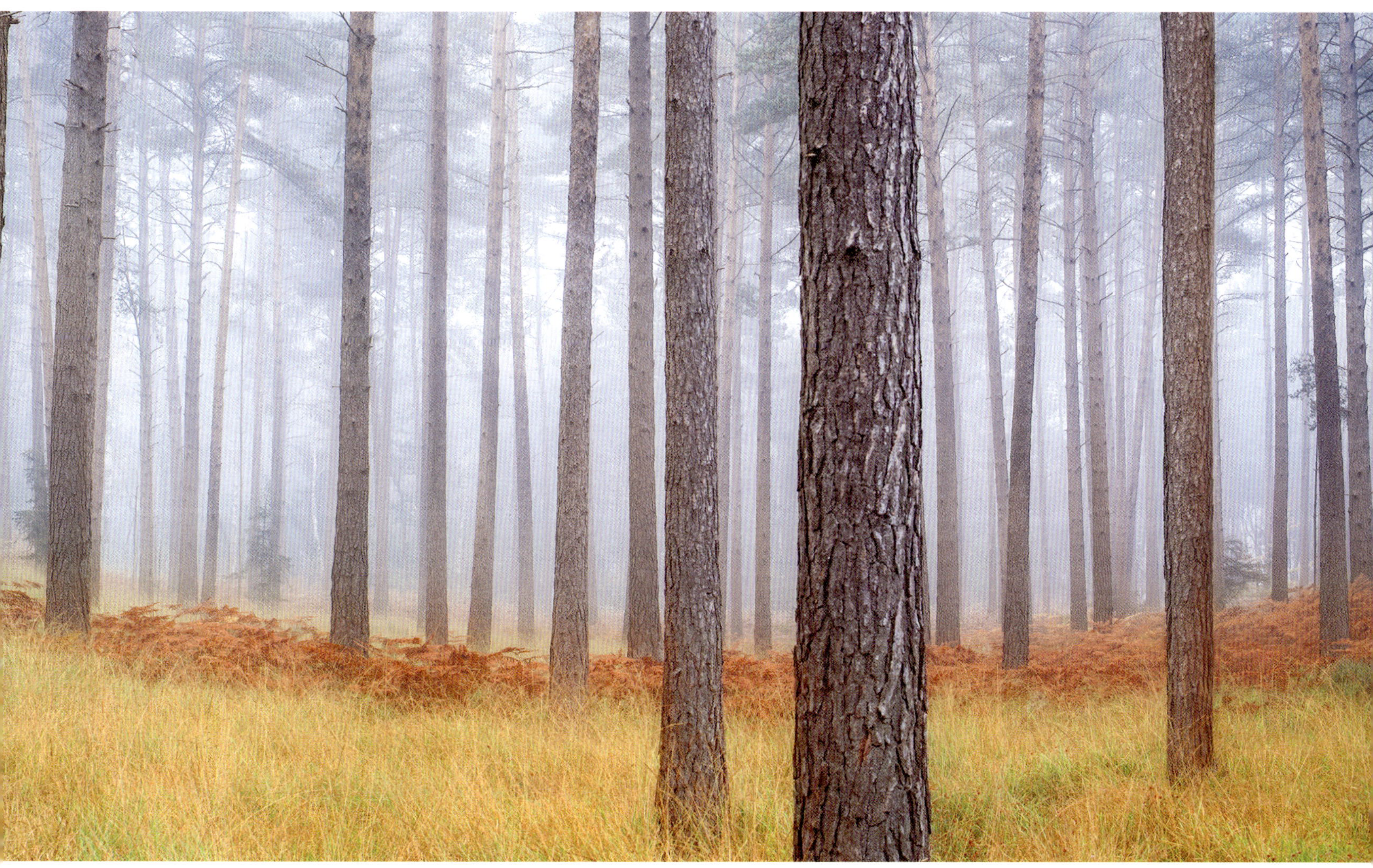

A colourful mix of grass and bracken on the forest floor

I chose to visit this location on a foggy morning; in these conditions woodlands have a great atmosphere and an exaggerated sense of depth. I was also keen to capture the beautiful but gentle contrast between the pale blue mist and the warmer mix of yellows and browns below.

Shottesbrooke Church

There can be few churches which match the elegance and beauty of St John's at Shottesbrooke. The building dates from the fourteenth century and it's said that the spire, which is visible from some distance away, was based on that of Salisbury Cathedral. Over the centuries it's survived damage by both fire and lightning, remaining as a perfect backdrop to the parkland.

Perhaps the best approach is from the footpath to the east; from this direction, on a winter's day, the leafless outlines of the surrounding trees form a natural frame around the lofty spire.

The handsome spire of St John's at Shottesbrooke

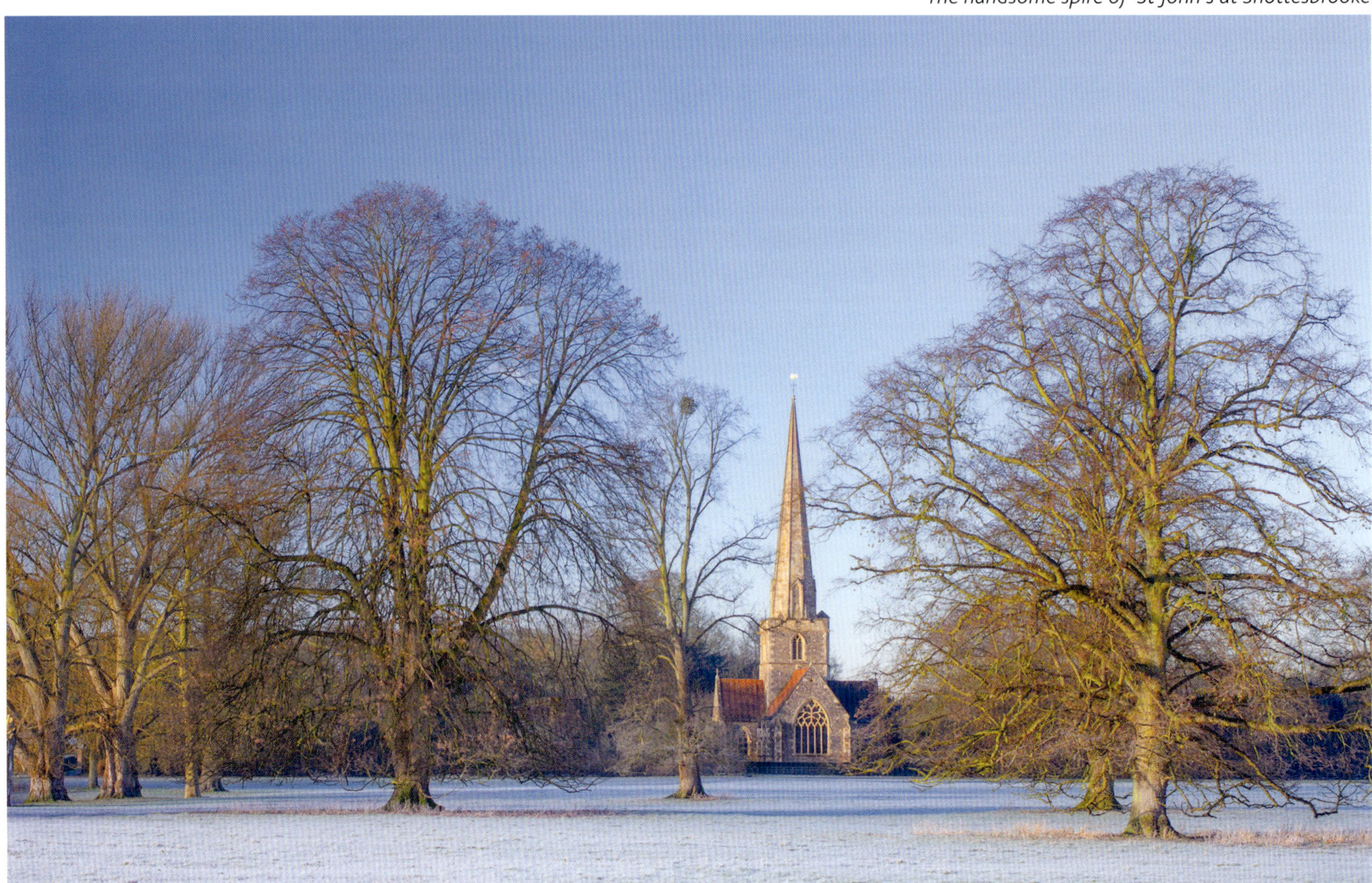

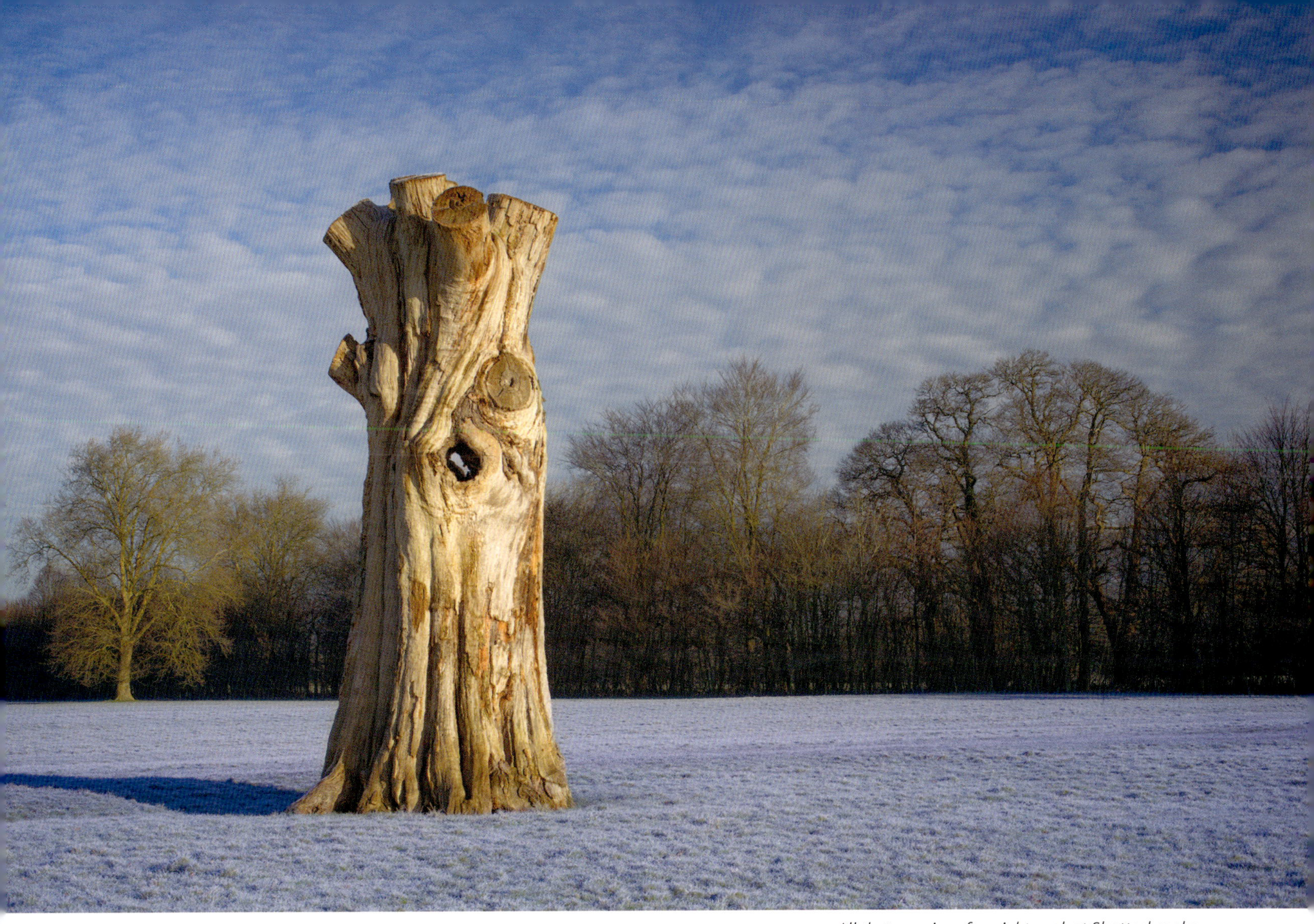

All that remains of a mighty oak at Shottesbrooke

Oak Tree Relic at Shottesbrooke Park

Among the statuesque trees in Shottesbrooke Park is an enormous stump – the remains of a grand oak which grew alongside the footpath to White Waltham. Without doubt the original tree was an impressive sight in its day, judging by the size of the truncated bole which stands at well over 20 feet and has become something of a feature in itself. An interesting detail is the shape of a human hand which has been artistically carved into a section of the wood.

No trace of bark remains, and as the image shows the structure is at least partly hollow. However, the root buttresses remain solid, and given the resilience of oak timber it seems likely that the trunk will stand for many years to come.

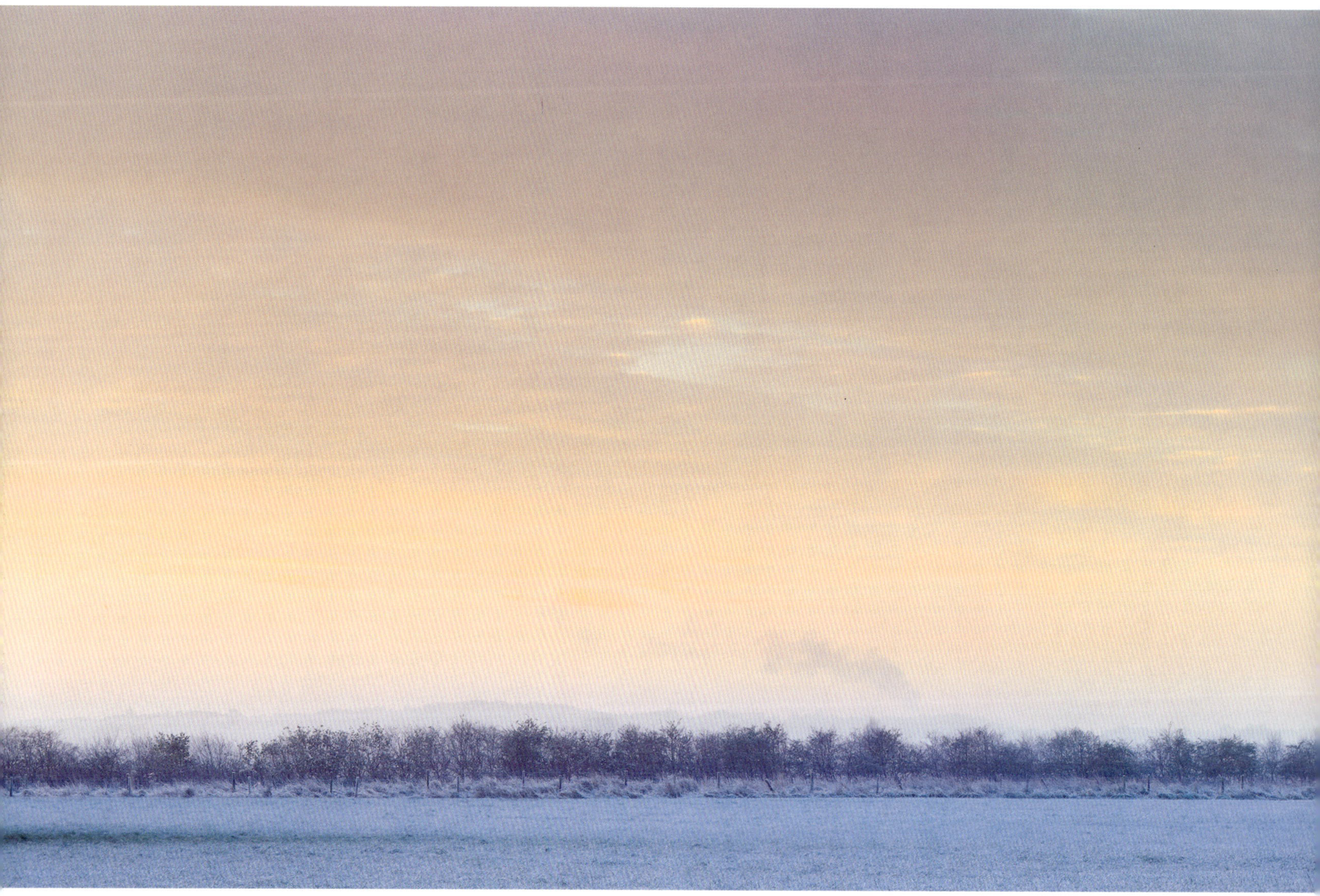

The Kennet Valley near Beenham
This pair of rounded oaks, framed by two smaller trees which lie beyond, can be seen from the lane at Lambden's Farm near Beenham. The surrounding land is as flat as a pancake, being an extension of the Kennet floodplain, and on this morning the fields were ice-blue with frost.

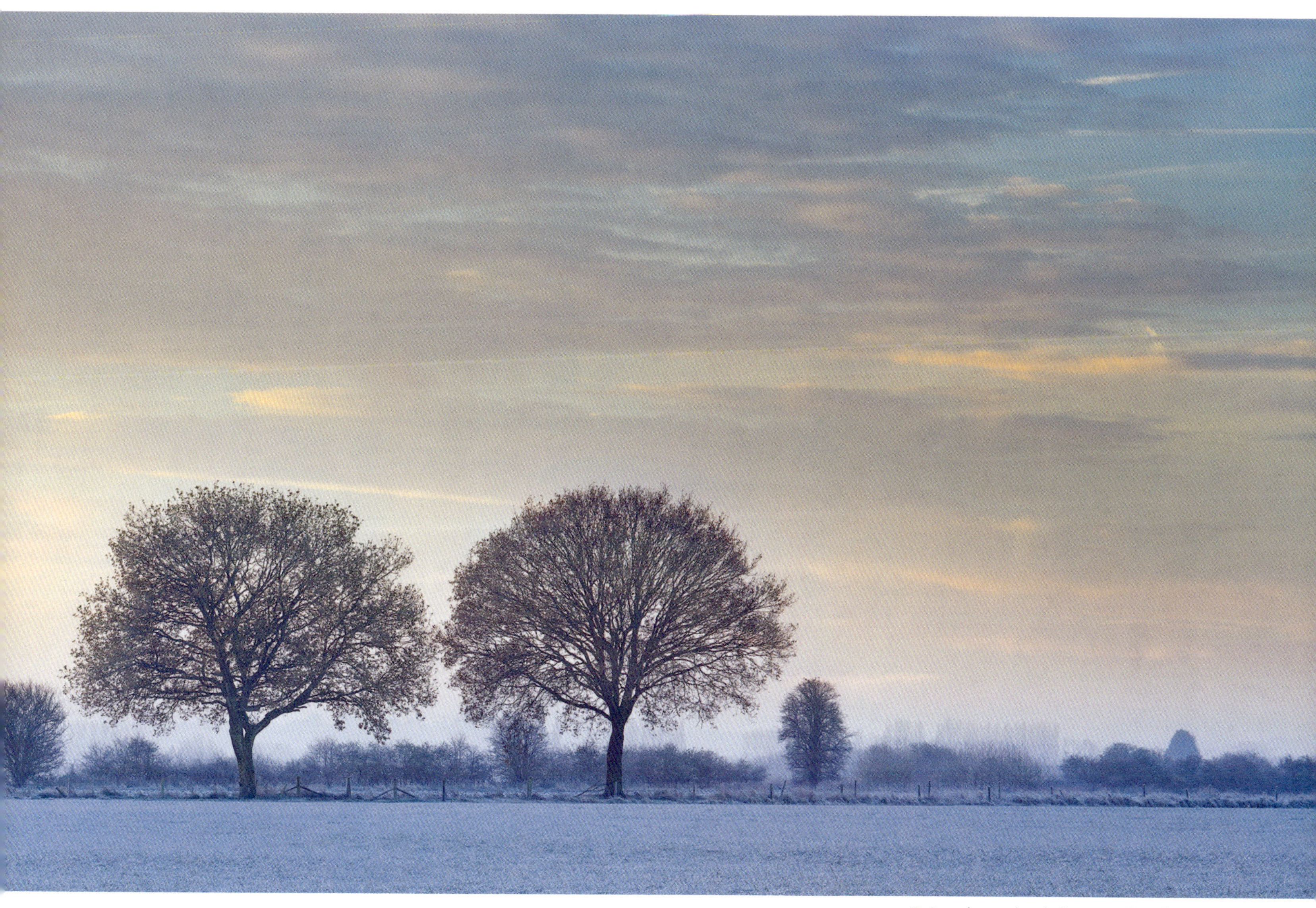

Twin oaks on the skyline near Beenham

The decorative light helps to give the scene a placid quality, but the setting is not as remote as it might seem – beyond the trees lies the busy route from Newbury to Reading, and just visible on the left of the picture is a piping industrial chimney. But at first light on a crisp winter morning these distractions can almost be forgotten.

Ashley Hill Forest near Maidenhead

An unusual feature of beech trees is their tendency to retain certain bands of leaves through the winter, especially around the lower section of the trunk. They hang in dense clusters, and are not shed until spring. The effect is most obvious in beech hedges, but also occurs in woodland where sprays of pale brown leaves break the monotony of bare trunks.

This photograph was taken on a misty winter's day in Ashley Hill Forest west of Maidenhead.

Mist-filled woods at Ashley Hill

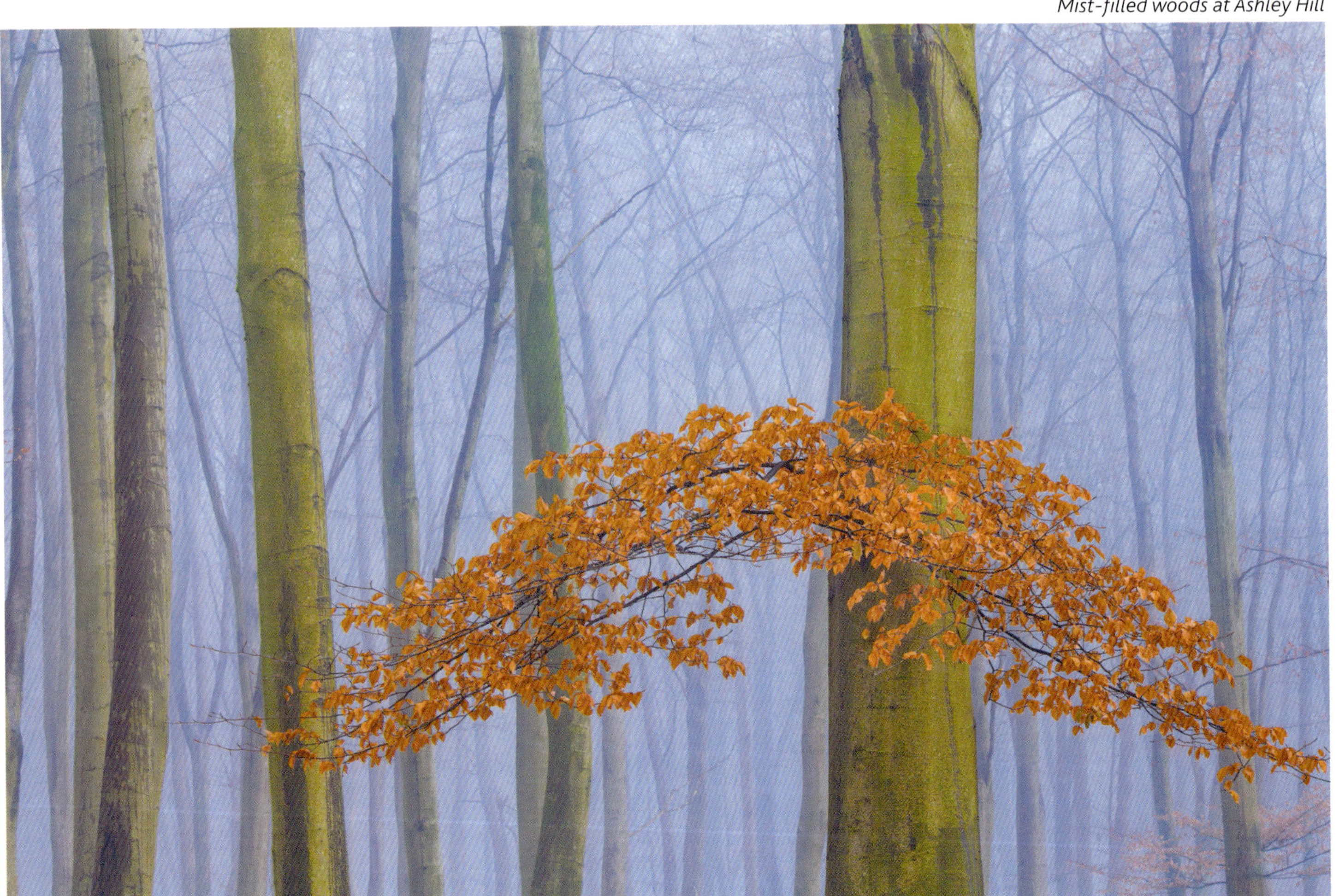

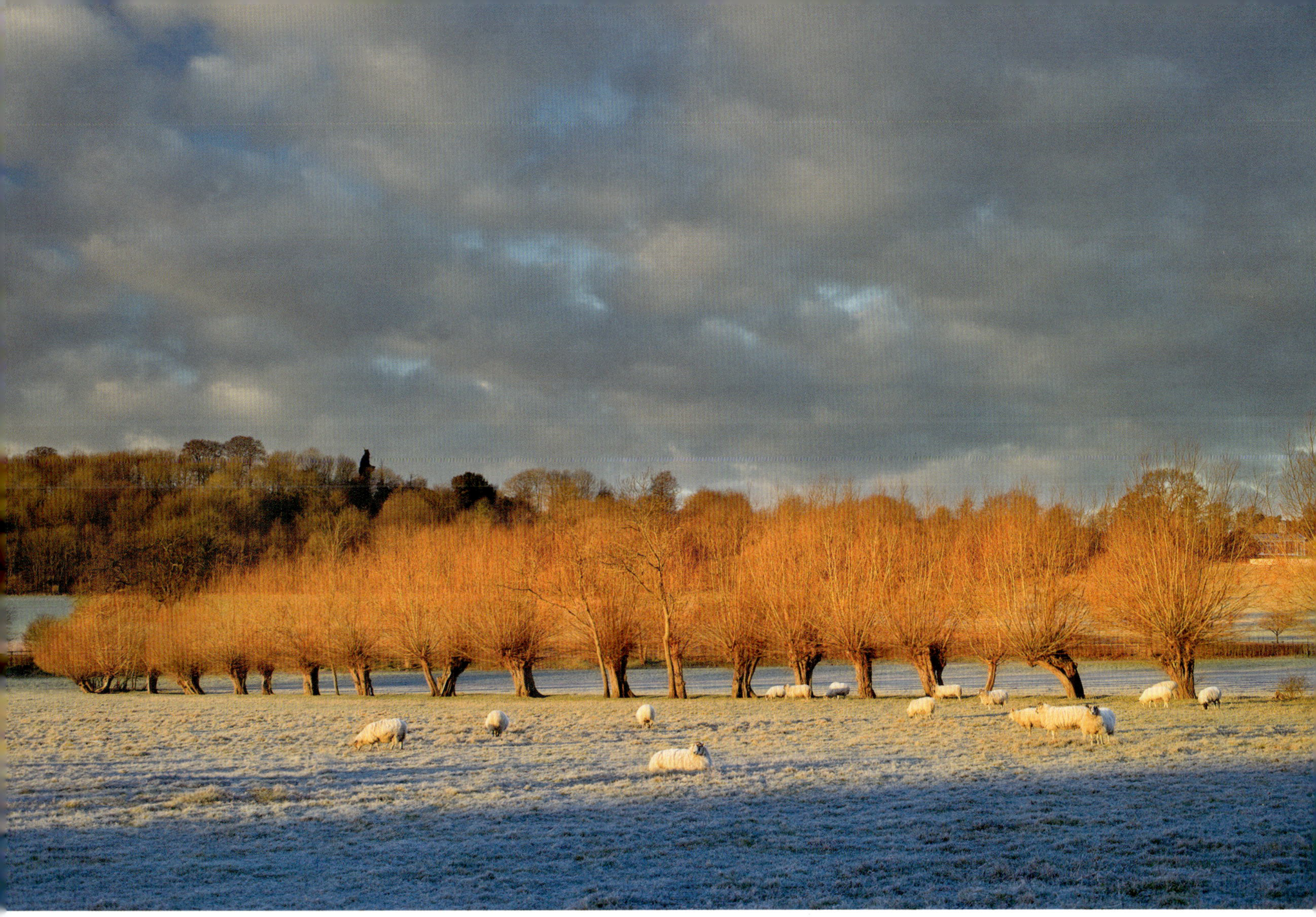

Sheep among the pollarded willows near Aston

Willows by the Thames near Aston

Going eastwards from the hamlet of Aston The Thames Path passes a line of willows which run along a small dyke. The trees are pollarded every few years – cut back to a short trunk which then sprouts an array of colourful young branches before being pruned once again. Here and elsewhere along the Thames they make a familiar feature of the riverside landscape, often leaning and twisting at all angles as they age.

It was the contrast which made this scene appealing – a cold frosty landscape, beneath warm sun-lit willows.

Pillbox near Hampstead Norreys
The RAF opened an airbase to the east of Hampstead Norreys in May 1940 – the site was bombed on two occasions but remained in use until the end of the war. Most of the land is now farmed as part of the Yattendon Estate, although a small private runway still exists on the site. In the surrounding area there are a number of wartime remnants including bunker-type buldings and at least nine pillboxes – the one shown here stands to the south-west of Haw Farm with a regimented line of beech trees beyond.

Just visible in this photograph is a thin vertical structure on top of the pillbox – this is part of a small weather station used by the farm.

Echoes of the past at Haw Farm

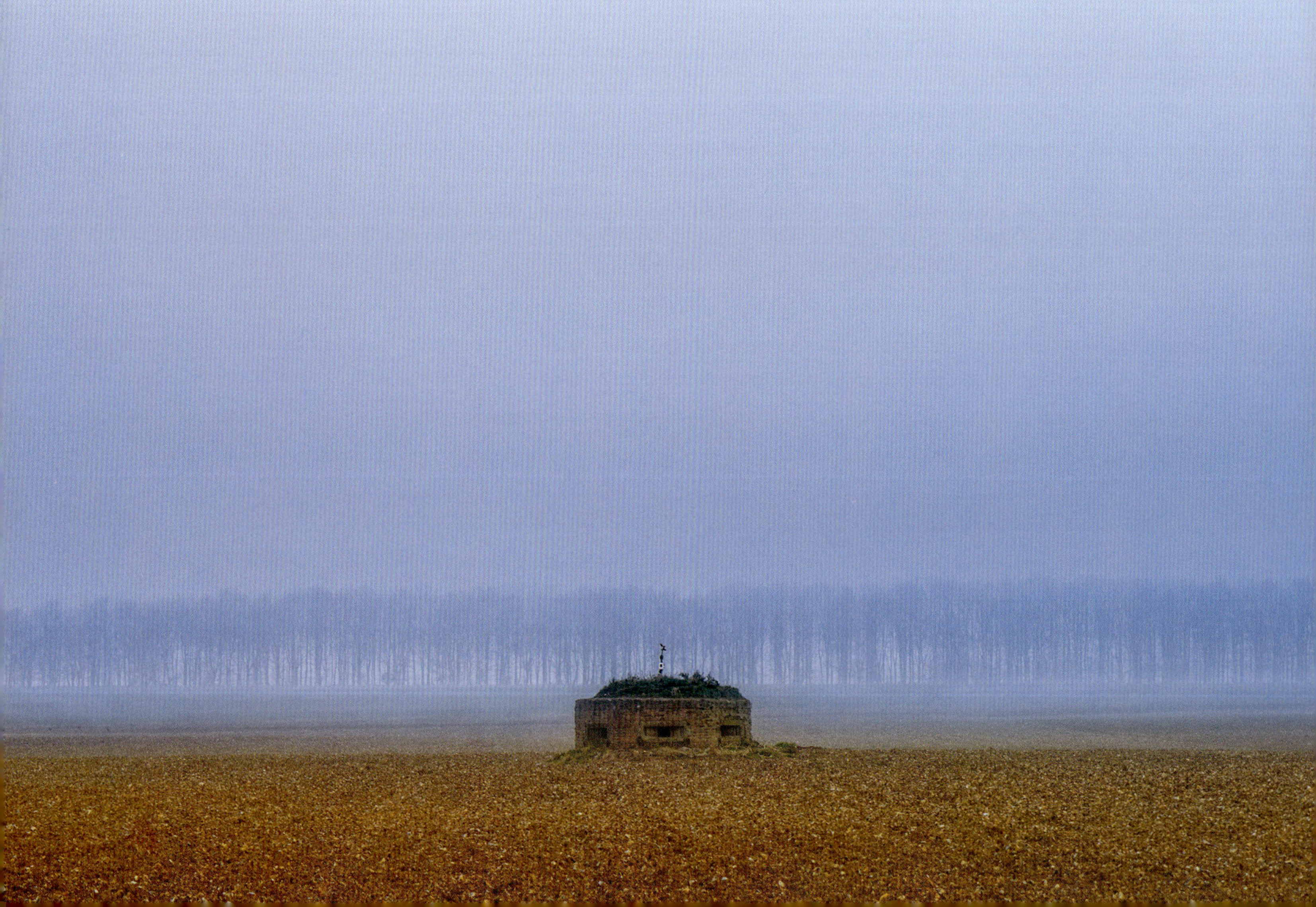

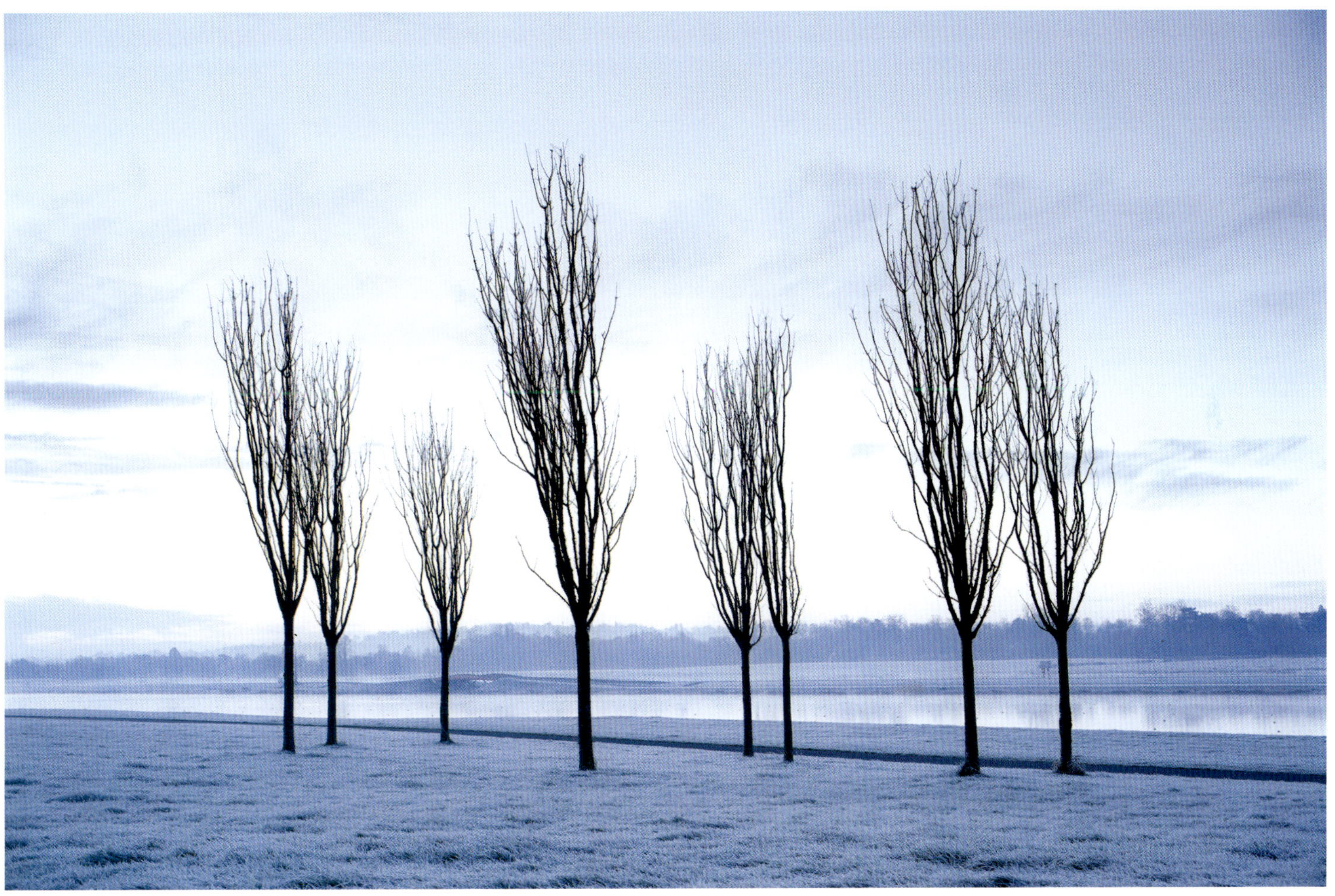

A graphic formation of trees overlooking the lake

Eton Dorney

The rowing lake and Olympic venue known as Eton Dorney lies just across the Thames from Berkshire, between Windsor and Bray. The site is owned by Eton College but there is public access – a wide stone pathway extends for nearly 3 miles around the lake. Lines of buoys divide the water into lanes which are in almost constant use, but there is room for nature too – the lake is lined with reeds and rushes which give shelter to the many water-birds which inhabit the area.

Much of the surrounding parkland is made up of well-kept lawns, but there are some fiery displays of dogwood together with plantings of ornamental trees. Some of these stand in tight symmetrical groups and were clearly planted this way for visual appeal; the effect is quite striking and is best seen in winter.

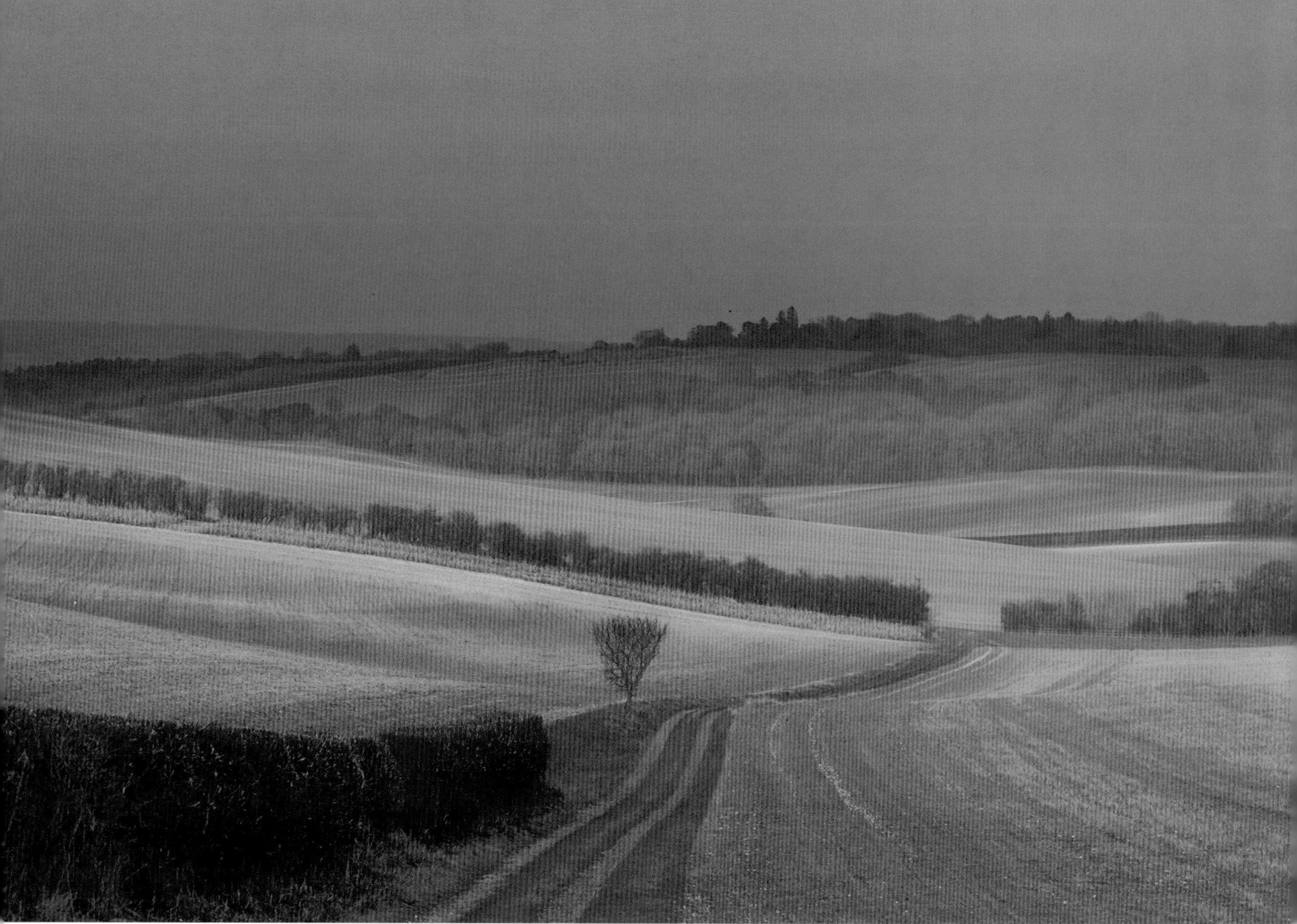

Downland at Westridge Green

Tucked away on the downs behind Westridge Green is one of Berkshire's most inspiring views. It can be found by strolling along the by-way which runs north-west from the village; the route is flat at first, but soon dips down to a gateway and reveals the viewpoint shown here.

This majestic sweep of countryside is completely unspoilt – no trace of modernity can be seen – and walkers are able to follow a footpath

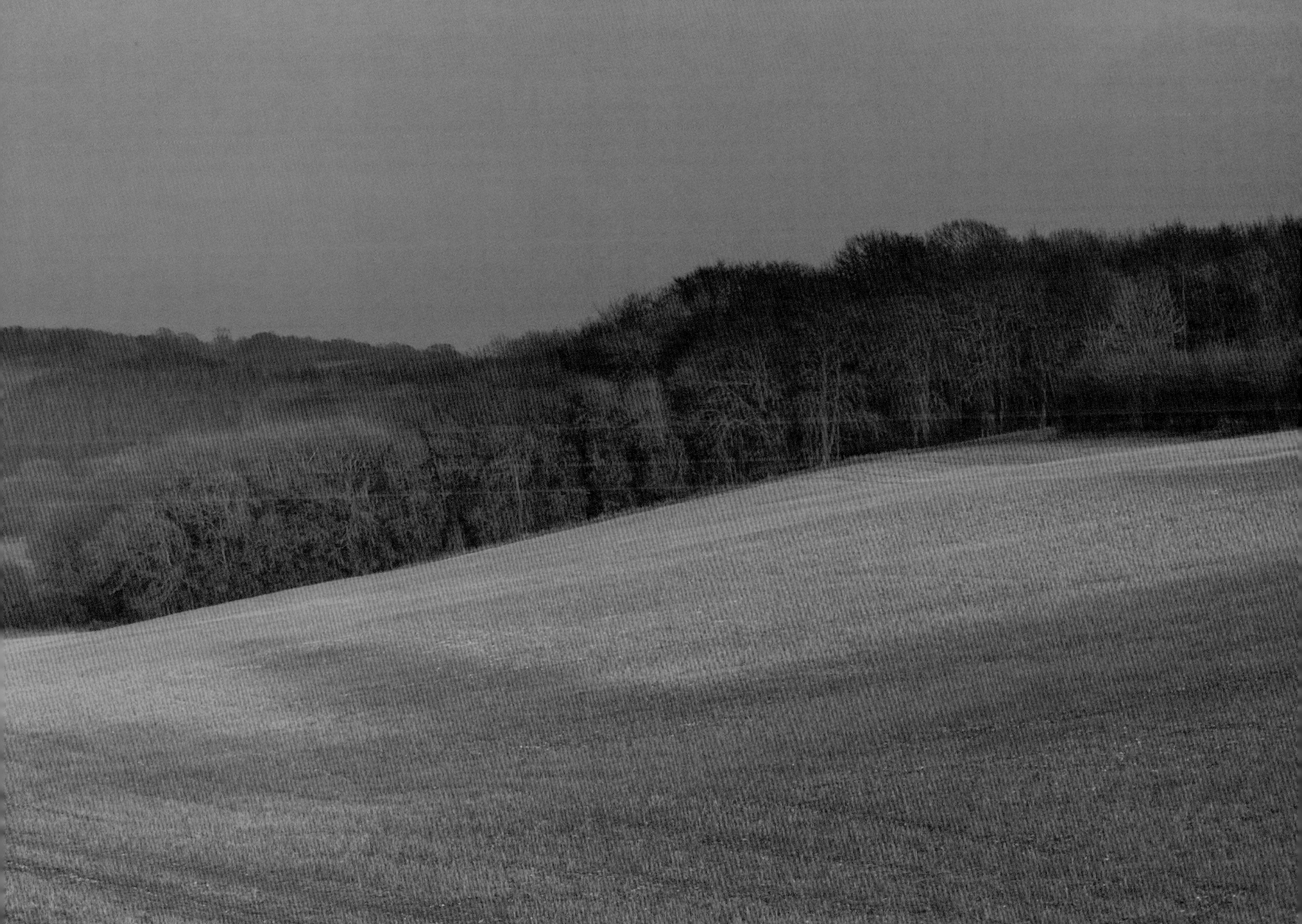

The golden hour – sunset over the downs in winter

(along the track on the left of the picture) which leads down into the centre of the landscape. The route then continues along the edge of Westridge Copse (seen on the right) and eventually meets The Ridgeway at Thurle Down.

This photograph was taken at the end of a fine day in mid-winter, with sunlight that was serene and golden.

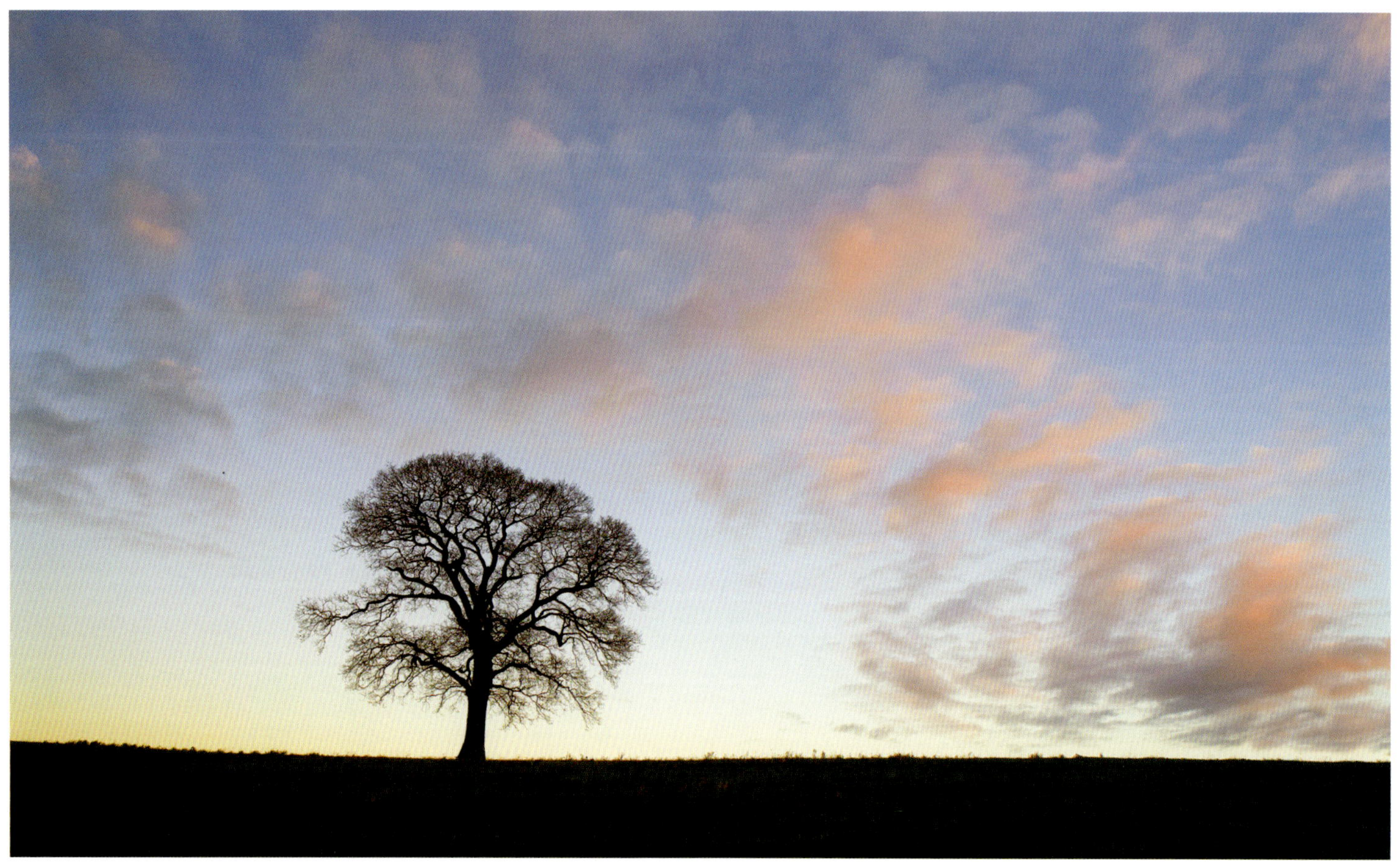

An oak in silhouette on Irish Hill near Kintbury

John's Tree near Kintbury

One-mile east of Kintbury a footpath weaves through a woody hedgerow, leading to a sloping field on the southern side of Irish Hill. The path then climbs the hillside, taking walkers to a towering oak which overlooks the surrounding area. The high chalk hills of Inkpen and Walbury can be seen across the landscape to the south.

The oak itself is a natural focal point, and though it is not the only tree on this part of the hill it is certainly the most impressive. At the base of the trunk, surrounded by a collection of flints, is a small plaque in memory of John Holmes who farmed the surrounding land for many years.

Oaks near Hamstead Marshall

Field oaks are a recurring feature in the countryside south of the Kennet, and there are many fine specimens which add to the fabric of the landscape. The one pictured below lies less than a mile from John's Tree, and is one of four which stand in a line by the curiously-named 'Illwills Border', north of Hamstead Marshall.

About half a mile to the east is the site of a seventeenth-century mansion, built for the first Earl of Craven but destroyed by fire in 1718. The building was surrounded by grand gardens, to which formal avenues of trees were added. It seems quite possible that the four oaks are the outlying remnants of one of those avenues.

One of four oaks which stand in a line near Hamstead Marshall

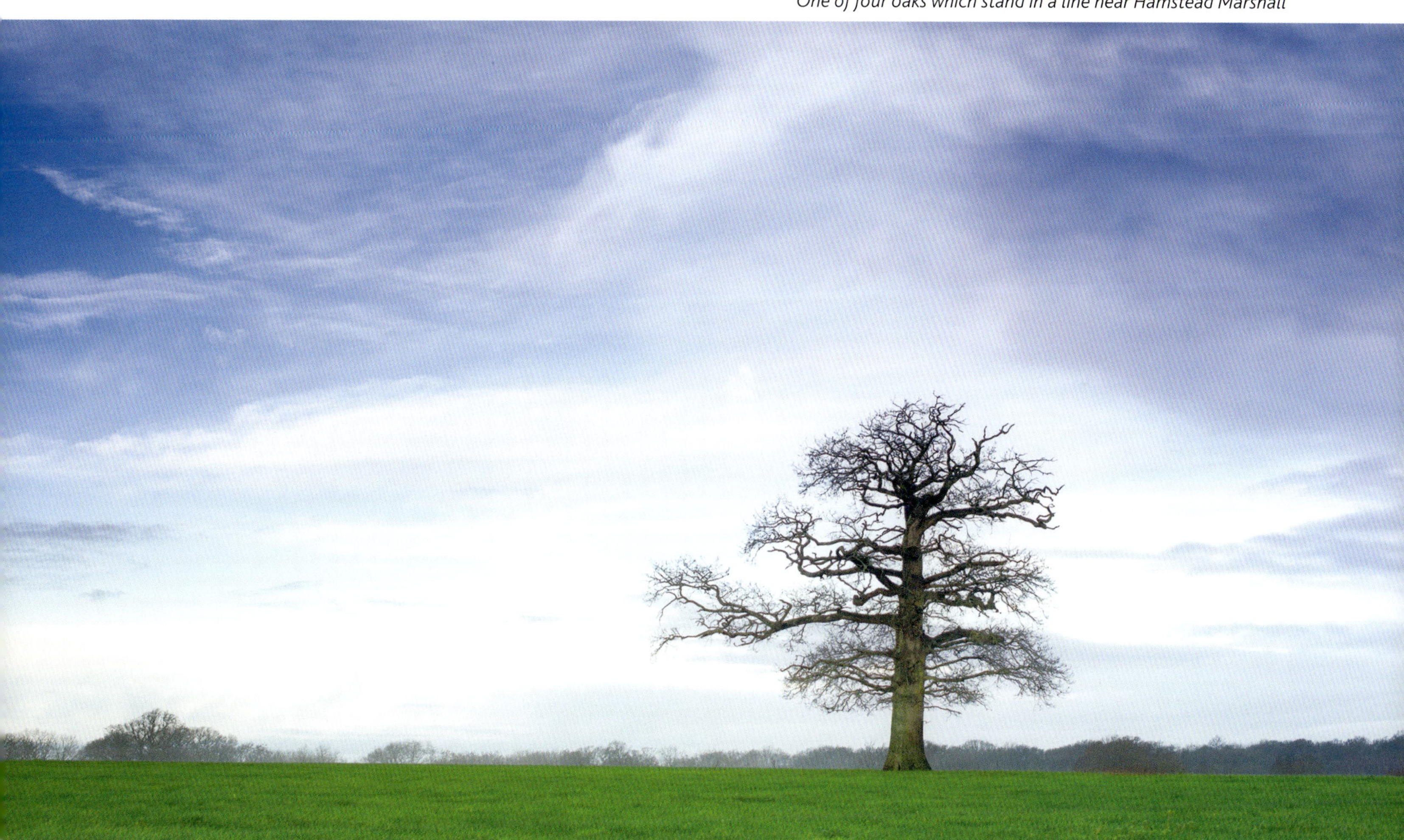

Old Down near West Ilsley

A hard frost on open downland transforms the landscape, and renders images which are akin to snow scenes. With strong colours muted subjects take on a monochromatic look, and the clear air and pure light associated with these conditions helps to emphasize shape and form.

This was the setting at Old Down – within a stone's throw of the Oxfordshire border – when I visited on a crisp morning in early January. Wandering along a by-way I noticed a flock of sheep were happily grazing the frosty grass, casting long shadows down the slope as the sun began to climb above the ridge. Shooting into the light is always challenging, but I was able to capture an image which shows the sheep in near-silhouette.

Within an hour the sun had warmed the landscape and the grass was green once again.

Sheep on the frosty landscape at Old Down

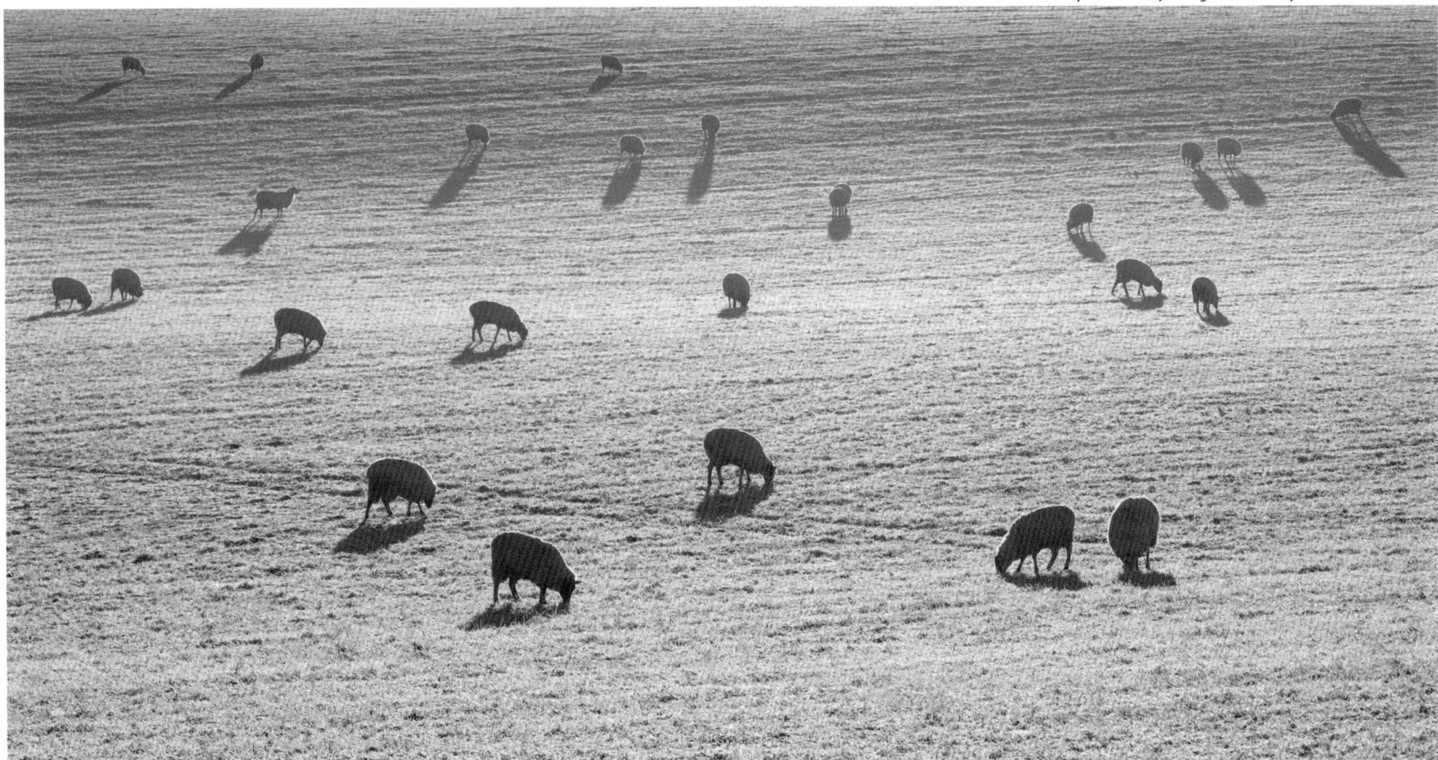

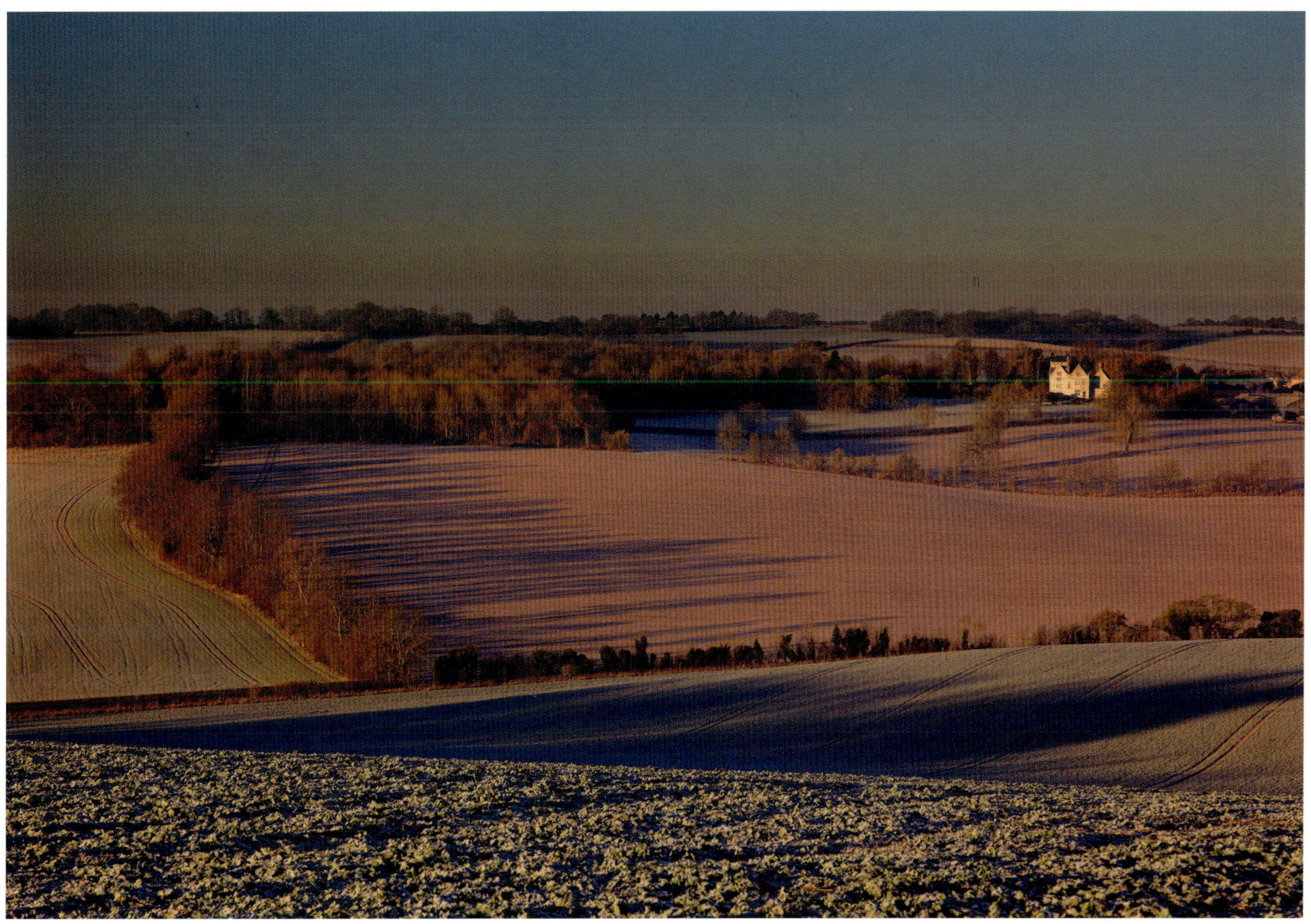

First light on Fawley Manor

Fawley Manor

Fawley Manor, a 400-year old Jacobean house, looks out across the West Berkshire landscape towards Woolley Down. The three-storey building was in a state of disrepair when it was bought in 1985; the new owner then set about renovating it almost single-handedly, creating Jacobean-style gardens to match.

The view shown here is from the lane which leads up to Woolley Farm, and was captured at first light on a frosty January morning, when the east-facing frontage was glinting in the low winter sun.

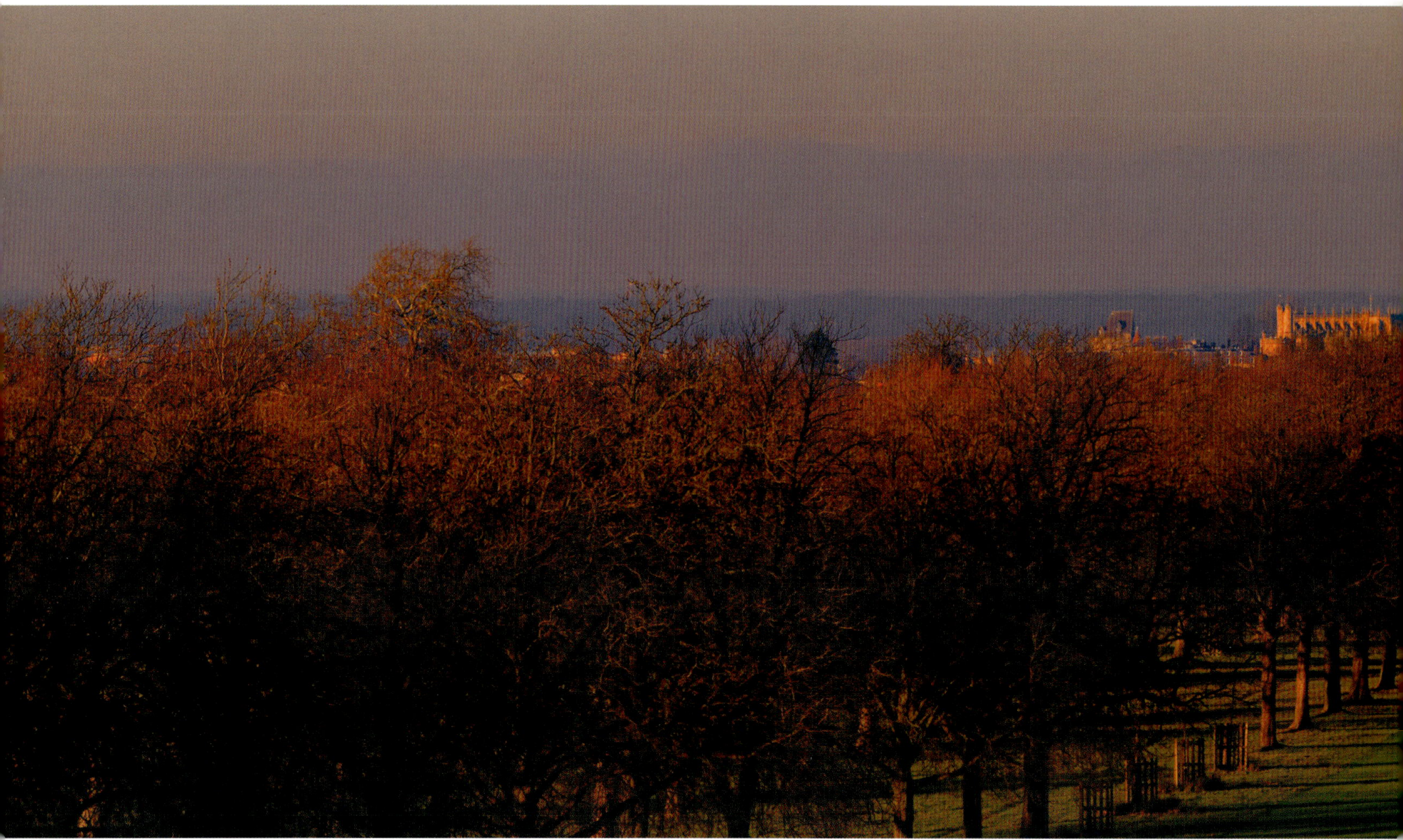

Windsor Castle
Windsor Castle, the oldest and largest inhabited castle in the world, is perfectly situated to catch the light from the setting sun in winter. Seen here from a viewpoint next to the Copper Horse statue, the entire south-facing frontage glows in the evening light, while in the foreground the sun's rays straggle through the trees which line the Long Walk.

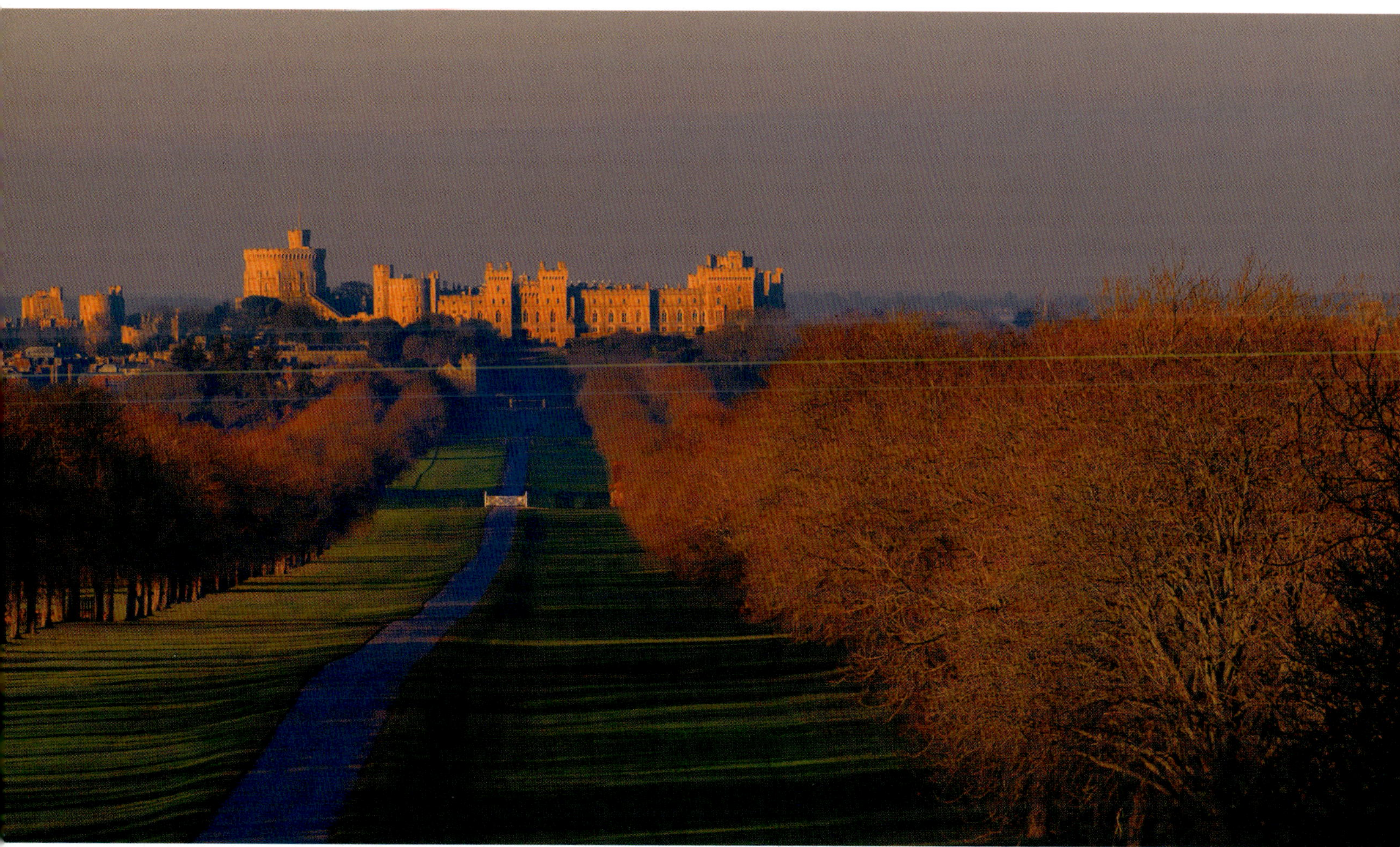

The south façade of Windsor Castle seen from the Great Park at sunset

Most prominent is the imposing Round Tower (the keep), the highest part of the castle which stands on a 50-foot high motte composed of chalk. The buildings which can be seen to the left of the tower make up the Lower Ward, where the gothic pinnacles of St George's Chapel can be seen just above the treetops. The Upper Ward lies to the right of the tower and includes the George IV Gateway which is aligned with the southern end of the Long Walk.

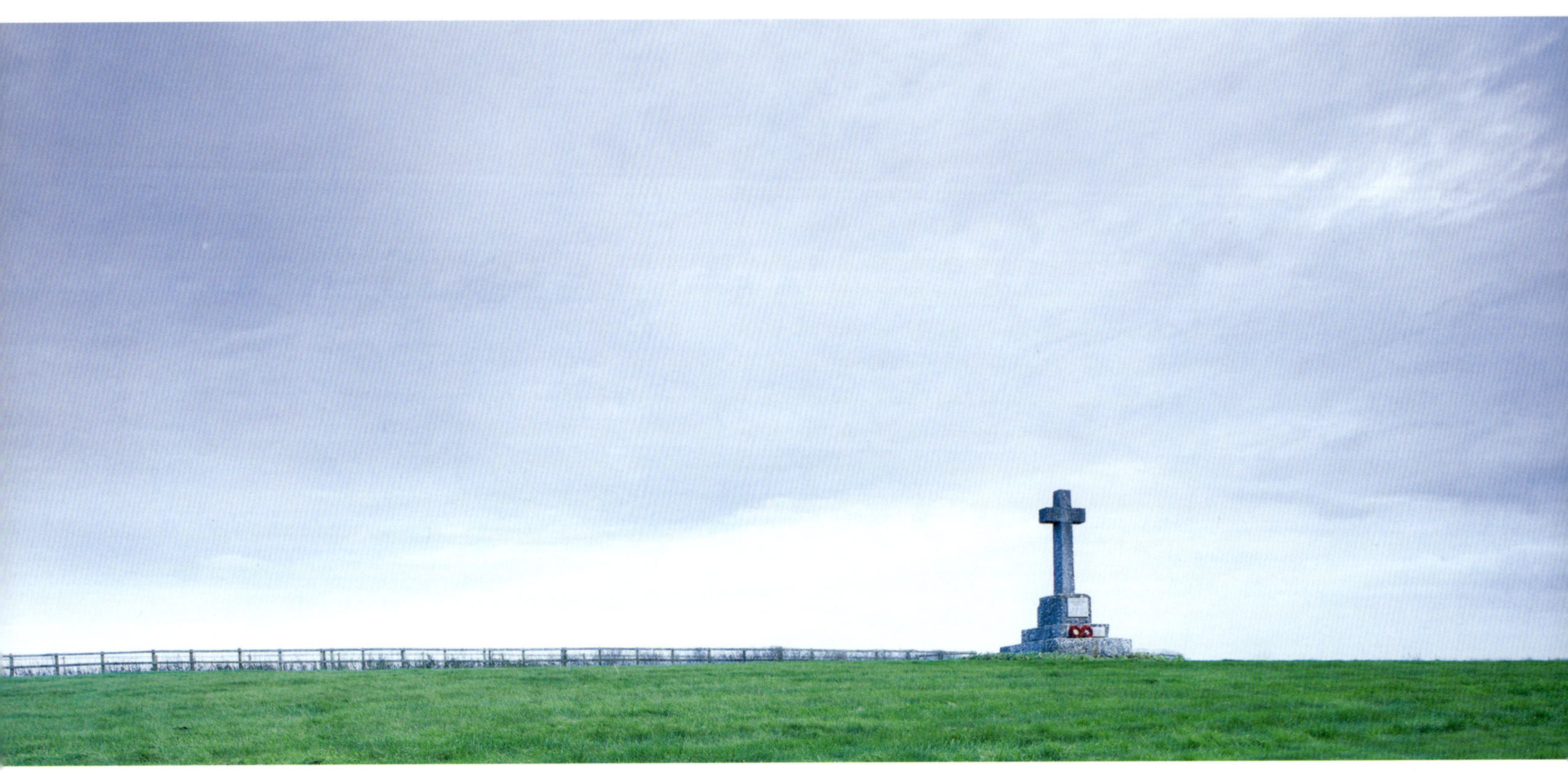

The stone cross on Woolley Down

Memorial on Woolley Down

On the edge of Woolley Down in West Berkshire is a large cross made of Portland stone. It was unveiled in 1925 as a war memorial in memory of Philip Musgrave Neeld Wroughton of Woolley Park, and of all those in the Berkshire Yeomanry who gave their lives for their country 1914 – 1918.